THE PUBLIC PRESIDENCY

THE PUBLIC PRESIDENCY

The Pursuit of Popular Support

GEORGE C. EDWARDS III

Texas A&M University

St. Martin's Press   New York

To Carmella
sine qua nihil

Library of Congress Catalog Card Number: 82-60470
Copyright © 1983 by St. Martin's Press, Inc.
All Rights Reserved.
Manufactured in the United States of America.
76543
fedcba
For information, write St. Martin's Press, Inc.,
175 Fifth Avenue, New York, N.Y. 10010

cover and book design: Levavi and Levavi
cover photograph: © 1979 Jan Lukas, Photo Researchers, Inc.

cloth ISBN: 0-312-65563-0
paper ISBN: 0-312-65564-9

CONTENTS

PREFACE

The Public Presidency is intended for use as a supplementary text for courses both in the Presidency and in Public Opinion. The idea for the book was the result of two discoveries. First, while writing a book on presidential influence in Congress, I came to realize how important a factor public support for the president is in explaining congressional support for the president's program. My second discovery was less specific but just as compelling. After nearly a decade of writing for journals and of participating in panels and other organizations focusing on the presidency, I found that when discussion turned to presidential leadership the bottom line was almost inevitably the president's relations with the public: his need for support and his efforts to achieve it.

Accordingly, I turned my attention to the subject of the public presidency. Others have considered this topic, of course, and made important contributions to our understanding of the complex relationship between the president and the public. Nevertheless, I felt that some areas of the public presidency (such as explanations of presidential approval ratings in the polls) needed a fresh perspective, while other areas (such as the president's ability to understand public opinion) had been generally overlooked. I also concluded that it was necessary to examine the various components of the public presidency together rather than in separate articles or books on, for example, presidential approval, presidential-press relations, or presidential leadership. Only a composite examination would, in my view, provide a satisfactory explanation of the interrelationships of these disparate elements that form the public presidency.

This book, which is the result, is therefore unique in its breadth of coverage. Most books on the public presidency focus on the relationship between the president and the press. Without neglecting this important area, I argue for a more comprehensive approach that includes discussion of the president's understanding and leadership of public opinion and the public's expectations and evaluation of presidents. The text also offers a good deal of original empirical analysis, using extensive data from public-opinion polls to develop interpretations of presidential politics that often depart from "conventional" wisdom.

A number of people have helped me at various stages of this project. Frank Kessler, Bert Rockman, and Lee Sigelman read the entire manuscript and Bob Bernstein, Tom Cronin, Jim Dyer, Michael Gant, David Hill, and John Kessel read parts of it. Each was generous with his time and each made valuable comments. They all have my sincere thanks. Carl Richard deserves a special mention for his aid with computer programming. Lisa Grubbs somehow managed to interpret my handwriting for the word processor, and Edna Lumpkin spent countless hours transcribing television tapes. As for my wife, Carmella, the dedication says it all.

George C. Edwards III

THE PUBLIC
PRESIDENCY

INTRODUCTION

"**P**ublic sentiment is everything. With public sentiment nothing can fail, without it nothing can succeed." These words, spoken by Abraham Lincoln, pose what is perhaps the greatest challenge to any president: to obtain and maintain the public's support. It is this ceaseless endeavor that is at the heart of the public presidency.

Why is the public presidency such a critical component of presidential politics? The answer is straightforward. As every student of the presidency quickly learns, the president is rarely in a position to command others to comply with his wishes. Instead, he must rely on persuasion.[1] The greatest source of influence for the president is public approval. In the words of Emmet John Hughes, a former presidential aide and authority on the White House, "Beyond all the tricks of history and all quirks of Presidents, there would appear to be one unchallengeable truth: the dependence of presidential authority on popular support."[2]

The importance of public support to the president is perhaps most obvious in his relations with Congress. Research has shown that the

1

higher the president's approval by the public, the more support he receives from representatives and senators.[3] According to a senior aide to President Carter, "Unquestionably, the success of the President's policies bear a tremendous relationship to his popularity in the polls."[4] When President Reagan was riding high in the polls in 1981, his economic reform program passed Congress largely intact. A year later his budget languished in inactivity in the same Congress. His standing in the polls had fallen.

Despite the importance of the president's relations with the mass public, we know relatively little about them, with the notable exception of presidential elections. How well does the president understand public opinion? Is he able to lead it? What role does the press play as it mediates the relationships between the White House and the public? Can the president influence it? What does the public expect of a president? According to what criteria does it evaluate him? We are limited in our ability to provide answers to these and related questions.

This book is designed to increase our understanding of the public presidency. In pursuing our central theme of the president's search for support, we focus on six fundamental relationships:

1. the president's understanding of public opinion
2. the president's leadership of public opinion
3. the president's influence of the press
4. the press's portrayal of the president
5. the public's expectations of the president
6. the public's evaluation of the president

The discussion below elaborates on each of these as we present an overview of each chapter.

OVERVIEW

In 1974 President Gerald Ford pardoned his predecessor, Richard Nixon. Ford's public support immediately plummeted and he spent the rest of his term unsuccessfully trying to regain the public's approval. Neither the president nor his advisors were prepared for the public's outrage at this action.[5] Even if Ford was determined to issue the pardon, he could have tried to prepare the country for it first. Instead, he plunged blindly ahead and bore the consequences. Whatever one may think of the pardon itself, this incident highlights the importance of the president's understanding of public opinion.

Presidents want to both please the public and avoid irritating it. They also want to lead public opinion. Accomplishing these goals is premised to a large degree on knowing what the public is thinking. In Chapter 1 we examine the president's ability to gauge public opinion, and we find him faced with a very difficult task. Citizens' opinions lack coherence and are often uncrystallized. The tools available to measure public opinion are far from perfect. Polls often do not provide the president with the information he needs concerning opinions on specific issues or the intensity of preferences. Moreover, they are subject to numerous flaws and idiosyncratic interpretations.

The results of elections for the presidency and Congress might provide a guide to public opinion. Certainly presidents do not hesitate to claim electoral mandates for their actions. Nevertheless, the nature of voters' political opinions, knowledge, and participation, the alternatives presented to them, and the vote as an instrument of expression on multiple issues make it difficult to infer public opinion on specific issues from election returns. Similarly, the great volume of mail that pours into the White House is not from a representative cross section of the population and generally does not focus on policy questions.

Presidents, of course, are not content to sit and passively read and follow public opinion. They are actively engaged in efforts to *lead* public opinion to support them and their policies. According to former presidential press secretary Jody Powell,

If a president has one indispensable function, it is to try to move and mold public opinion as that opinion affects public policy—to take us as a country a little beyond where we might otherwise want to go in one direction and to keep us from going as far as we might be inclined to go in another.[6]

Some of the attempts of presidents to influence public opinion are direct (such as addresses to the nation), and others are more subtle (as when presidents employ symbols and engage in public-relations activities). These are designed to bring the president's message to the public's attention, publicize his actions, and put him and his policies in a favorable light. There is also a dark side to presidential leadership of public opinion. The White House has engaged in efforts to control the information available to the public, sometimes even resorting to lying. It has at times deliberately tried to mislead the public and present a distorted picture of the president and his policies.

In Chapter 2 we focus on presidential leadership of public opinion. We examine the techniques of opinion leadership mentioned above and their likely effects, finding that attempts to lead the public often fail. Every president faces formidable obstacles to influencing the public, including an inattentive, skeptical, and individualistic audience, their own limited communications skills, the complexity of public policy, the context of their communications, and alternative sources of information, especially the press. We also discuss presidential manipulation of the economy to gain public favor, but find this severely limited by the nature of our economic system, economic policymaking, and our understanding of economics. Thus, presidents cannot depend upon leading the public any more than they can rely on understanding public opinion.

Most presidential efforts to lead public opinion are only the first step in a president's attempts to influence others more directly involved in governing. He must then use popular support to persuade others. But if the president can directly translate electoral support into seats for his congressional running mates, his programs will have an easier time passing Congress. Thus, presidential "coattails" are a special variant of presidential leadership of public opinion.

Coattails are often mentioned in political commentaries by scholars, journalists, and politicians, yet we actually know very little about them. The executive director of the Democratic Congressional Campaign Committee recently exclaimed that "only reporters and political scientists believe in coattails."[7] In Chapter 2 we also examine the question of just how many seats in the House are ultimately determined by presidential coattails. To do so we analyze the results of the last eight presidential elections, and we find that coattails are not very common and provide little help for presidents.

Although the president has a great stake in leading public opinion and makes substantial efforts to do so, most communications about an administration and its policies that reach the public come from the mass media. According to President Reagan's closest aide, Edwin Meese III: "The press acts as intermediary between the public and the government and as national interpreter of events. Its effect can't be overstated, since perception can be more important than reality."[8] Thus, in its attempts to lead public opinion and gain and maintain public support the White House must give press relations a high priority.

Since it is through the press that citizens learn most of what they know about the president and his policies, the White House is actively engaged in efforts to influence the coverage it receives in the media. These include coordinating the news, holding press conferences, and providing a range of services for the press including formal briefings, daily handouts, interviews, background sessions, photo opportunities, and travel accommodations. Sometimes the president and his aides trade the carrot for the stick and resort to punishments and harassments when they perceive media coverage to be unfair, unfavorable, or both.

In Chapter 3 we examine the context in which presidential relationships with the press occur, and we find it is often adversarial. We also discuss the structure of these relationships and the efforts of the White House to obtain favorable coverage in the mass media.

Presidents are almost never satisfied with press coverage of their administrations. Reflecting on the media's handling of policy issues, President Carter declared that "one of my biggest disappointments was the irresponsibility of the media."[9] After only two months in office Ronald Reagan complained to reporters that "maybe some of you were trying to make the news instead of reporting it."[10]

It is not uncommon for presidents to view the press as the major obstacle to their gaining and maintaining public support. If only the media did not emphasize such trivial matters, especially alleged presidential flaws and mistakes, and if only it was not so biased against the White House, the public would have a deeper appreciation for the president's performance in office and be more willing to give him their support—or so the argument goes.

In Chapter 4 we probe into several controversial issues in president-press relations, including leaks, biased reporting, trivialized coverage, and their effects. Analysis of transcripts of network television news coverage of President Carter's "crisis of confidence speech" and the subsequent shake-up in his cabinet provides an illuminating case study of news coverage. We find that coverage of the presidency is indeed superficial and often distorted, but that it is not systematically biased in favor of any person, party, or ideology, and that leaks are common and inevitable and frequently originate in the White House itself.

The president is in the limelight of American politics, and citizens come quite naturally to organize their political thinking and focus their hopes for the future around the White House. Although this attention provides the potential for presidential leadership of the public, it is purchased at a high cost. The public's expectations of the chief executive's policy performance, personal characteristics, and private behavior tend to be high. It is encouraged in this attitude by presidents and presidential candidates, our common political socialization, the president's prominence and our tendency to personalize politics, and our lack of understanding of the environment in which the president functions.

Not only are the public's expectations of the president high, they are also often contradictory with regard to both policy and leadership style. We want peace, prosperity, and substantial public services, without sacrifice. The promises of presidential candidates and the low level of understanding of public policy we see in Chapter 1 support such inconsistent expectations. We also want the president to display leadership and responsiveness, flexibility and firmness, statesmanship and political skill, openness and control, and empathy for the common man along with uncommon characteristics.

It is quite clear that no one can meet these expectations, yet they provide the context within which the president struggles to gain and maintain public support. His problems in meeting the public's expectations are aggravated by a number of features of American politics and policymaking that provide formidable obstacles to his achieving his goals, including Congress, the courts, our decentralized party system, the executive branch, and limits on rational decision making. In Chapter 5 we explore the nature of the public's expectations of the president and the conflict within them. We then examine the limits of the president's capacity to meet these expectations.

Probably the most visible political statistics in American life are the frequent measurements of the public's approval of the president. Political commentators duly note whether the president is doing better or worse than in the last poll (sort of a political batting average). But presidential approval, or "popularity" as it is sometimes misnamed, has significance beyond its entertainment value. It is, as we have noted, an important power resource for the president. The more support the president has in the public, the more likely he is to gain support from others in government, especially in Congress.

In Chapter 6 we rely on analysis of 450 Gallup polls and seven election surveys from the Center for Political Studies to examine potential influences on the public's approval of the president to explain what does or does not determine how the president rates in the polls. We begin by considering the influence of predispositions in the public, such as party affiliation, the positivity bias (a tendency to evaluate public figures and institutions positively), and the bandwagon effect, on its evaluations of the president. Together they provide an important component of the explanation of presidential approval.

Yet presidential approval changes more rapidly than do predispositions, and there are many other potential influences on the public's support for the president. The public does not evaluate the president on the basis of his personality or how policies affect them personally or even how successful policies seem to be at the moment. Rather it focuses on his job-related personal characteristics and his handling of, and stands on, the issues. Just how the public reaches its conclusions about the president and his performance on issues is a subject for another book, but the president's efforts to understand and lead public opinion and the press's portrayal of the president undoubtedly play an important role. Thus we end up where we began: with the president seeking the public's support.

In our exploration of the public presidency, we employ many types of analysis. In Chapters 2 and 6 we use statistics with which some readers may be unfamiliar. This should not be a cause of concern, however. The more arcane sections of the analysis are either in appendices or can simply be skipped by those more interested in the results than in how they were produced. There are no methodological prerequisites for following the arguments in each chapter.

NOTES

1. The classic work on this point is Richard E. Neustadt, *Presidential Power: The Politics of Leadership From FDR to Carter* (New York: Wiley, 1980).
2. Emmet John Hughes, *The Living Presidency* (Baltimore: Penguin, 1974), p. 68.
3. George C. Edwards III, *Presidential Influence in Congress* (San Francisco: W. H. Freeman, 1980), pp. 86–100.
4. Dom Bonafede, "The Strained Relationship," *National Journal*, May 19, 1979, p. 830.
5. Jerald F. terHorst, *Gerald Ford and the Future of the Presidency* (New York: The Third Press, 1974), pp. 232, 238.
6. "Meeting the Press," *Public Opinion*, December–January 1982, p. 11.
7. "Few Democrats Relying on Carter's Help," *Congressional Quarterly Weekly Report*, August 16, 1980, pp. 2367–68.
8. Dom Bonafede, "The Washington Press—An Interpreter or a Participant in Policy Making?" *National Journal*, April 24, 1982, p. 716.
9. "Every Four Years," Public Broadcasting Service Transcript, 1980, pp. 40–41.
10. Timothy Schellhardt and Gerald F. Seib, "Reagan Doesn't See a Bush–Haig Conflict, But Foreign Policy Concerns Are Raised," *Wall Street Journal*, March 26, 1981, p. 2.

UNDERSTANDING PUBLIC OPINION

Presidents need public support and understanding public opinion can be a considerable advantage to them in gaining and maintaining it. At the very least, presidents want to avoid needlessly antagonizing the public. Thus, presidents need reliable estimates of public reactions to the actions they are contemplating. It is equally useful for presidents to know what actions and policies, either symbolic or substantive, the public wants. No politician wants to overlook opportunities to please constituents and, perhaps even more significant, to avoid frustrating them. By knowing what the public desires, a president may use his discretion to gain its favor when he feels the relevant actions or policies are justified.

In addition, presidents often want to lead public opinion to support them and their policies. To do this they need to know the views of various segments of the public, whom they need to influence and on what issues, and how far people can be moved. Presidents usually do not want to use their limited resources on hopeless ventures. Nor do they want to be too far ahead of the public. Otherwise they risk losing their followers and alienating segments of the public.

Knowing how to avoid irritating the public, to respond to it, and to lead it are in large part contingent upon understanding public opinion. In this chapter we examine the question of the president's ability to gauge the American public's opinions on issues of importance to him. We begin by looking at the nature of public opinion and then move on to evaluate the means of learning about it that are available to the president, including public opinion polls, election results, and the mail.

AMERICANS' OPINIONS

Before a president can understand what opinions the public holds, citizens must have opinions. Although Americans are usually willing to express opinions on a wide variety of issues, we should not be misled into interpreting their responses as reflecting crystallized and coherent views. Some people respond to questions they know nothing about at all.[1] In a 1981 poll 70% of those surveyed said they knew little or nothing at all about the Clean Air Act, but 95% of the same sample also responded that experience indicated the act may need to be changed.[2]

Citizens' opinions are often rife with contradictions, because they fail to give their views much thought and do not consider the implications of their policy stands for other issues. In a national poll taken in August 1977, 58% of the people interviewed did not approve of government welfare in the abstract. They were then asked if they would support three specific welfare programs. One was to help poor people buy food at reduced prices, an implicit reference to the Food Stamp Program. A second was to provide financial aid for children in low-income, one-parent homes, an implicit reference to the Aid for Dependent Children program. The third welfare program on which responses were elicited was one to pay health costs for poor people, an implicit reference to the Medicaid program. The surprising results of these questions were that more than 80% of the respondents supported each of the specific welfare programs! Thus, the people opposed welfare but supported three of the most expensive and controversial federal welfare programs.[3] What can a president determine from this?

One poll can report that an overwhelming majority feel that most government regulations are "not practical and badly thought out." Yet another poll finds that a majority of citizens agree with the strong statement that "protecting the environment is so important that requirements and standards cannot be too high, and continuing improvements must be made, regardless of cost."[4]

A national poll in January 1981 showed that the American people placed a very high priority on balancing the budget. At the same time majorities favored maintaining or increasing spending on defense policy, social security cost-of-living increases, highways, mass transit, pollution control, unemployment, and student aid.[5] A poll in April of the same year found that, of those with an opinion, people overwhelmingly favored the president's budget-cutting proposals—in the abstract. When asked about specific policies, people favored maintaining or increasing expenditures for policies as diverse as aid to the arts, energy research, job programs, legal services for the poor, student loans, and defense (on which the president himself wanted to increase spending).[6]

Because public opinion is often not crystallized, it is subject to sharp fluctuations. One study found that about one-half of the U.S. adults changed their views on the war in Vietnam between November 1968 and March 1969. Moreover, voters may adapt their views on issues to conform to policy stands of candidates or officials whom they favor and to whom they are attracted for reasons of party affiliation or candidate image.[7] After watching the debates between President Ford and candidate Jimmy Carter in 1976, for example, voters did not change their candidate preferences if they disagreed with the candidate they had favored. Instead, they adopted the positions taken by their preferred candidate.[8]

Policymaking is a very complex enterprise, and most voters do not have the time, expertise, or inclination to think extensively about most issues, especially those as distant from their everyday experiences as federal regulations, nuclear strategy, and bureaucratic reorganizations. This may come as a surprise to those who work in the White House and who deal with politics and policy twelve to eighteen hours a day, but it is something that they must accept if they are to understand public opinion. In the words of former Vice President Hubert Humphrey,

> People do not pay as much attention to political commentary as the politicians themselves do. Particularly in Washington we read, analyze, and read again every story. Every nuance contains implications of cosmic importance, or so we think. Though national problems are of interest and concern, the average citizen is busy with other things. He has his mind on his job, his family, maybe his plans for a vacation, his favorite athletic teams and their success. His personal problems invariably take precedence over what seems so important to us. Mostly, he reads the headlines and possibly a few lead paragraphs.[9]

One of the most controversial issues before the American people in 1977–78 was the ratification of the Panama Canal treaties. Yet in late 1977, 26% of the people admitted to having not heard or read about the debate over the treaties. (We can only speculate as to how many others fell into that category but gave the more socially acceptable affirmative response.)

When asked the simple but crucial question of how often the biggest U.S. aircraft carriers and supertankers used the canal, only 14% correctly answered that they did not use it at all.[10]

In early 1979 a poll found that only 23% of the public knew the two countries engaged in the SALT II negotiations,[11] although the talks between the United States and the Soviet Union had been going on for seven years and the proposed treaty that resulted was one of the major issues of the day. A 1972 poll reported that, incredibly, only 63% of the people interviewed knew that mainland China had a communist government.[12]

Certainly the most important and most visible issues before the country in 1981 were President Reagan's budget and tax proposals. Yet in a national poll taken in late June, 53% of the people did not have an opinion on the president's budget proposals and 47% had no opinion on his proposed cuts in income taxes.[13]

There is further evidence of the lack of public knowledge and the absence of opinion on major issues with which the president must deal. A 1978 Gallup poll found that only half the population was aware that America had to import oil to satisfy its energy needs![14] Only 31% of the people correctly understood the meaning of "no fault" automobile insurance (although millions of people have it).[15] Finally, in 1969, only 41% of adults held opinions on the proposed antiballistic missile system (which was a defense against nuclear missiles) at the height of its controversy (it passed the Senate by one vote).[16]

In sum, anyone attempting to understand American public opinion operates under the handicap that many people do not have opinions on issues of significance to the president, and many of the opinions that the public expresses are neither crystallized nor coherent.

Nevertheless, sometimes opinions are widely held, such as on issues that touch the public directly like economic conditions and civil rights. Moreover, the president may desire to know the distribution of the opinions that do exist. Under these circumstances, what means can the president rely upon to measure public opinion?

PUBLIC OPINION POLLS

One common tool for measuring public attitudes is public opinion polls. Whether they are commissioned especially on behalf of the White House or on contract to various of the mass media, they allow the president to learn how a cross section of the population feels about a specific policy, conditions in their lives, or his performance in office. In this section we discuss the uses of public opinion polls by presidents and whether presidents use polls to lead or follow public opinion. But first we focus on the general limitations of polls and the reasons for their shortcomings as a means of informing the president about public opinion.

Limitations of Polls

An important limitation of polls is that questions usually do not attempt to measure the intensity with which opinions are held. This intensity might be of substantial salience to a president concerned about how opinions might translate into other political behavior, such as voting. People with intense views will probably be more likely to act on those views to reward or punish politicians than people who state a preference but for whom the issue is incidental and a matter of indifference to them.

A related problem with polls is that the questions asked of the public seldom mesh with the decisions that a president faces. He rarely considers issues in the "yes/no" terms presented by most polls. Evidence of widespread support for a program does not indicate how the public stands on most of the specific provisions under consideration. The president must make decisions that may determine a policy's success or failure in being passed by Congress or in meeting its goals. Yet such details do not lend themselves to mass polling because they require specialized knowledge that few Americans possess.

Another problem with polls is that responses may reflect the particular wording of the choices presented to citizens, especially for those people who lack crystallized opinions on issues. If questions are of the "agree/disagree" variety, there is a bias toward the "agree" alternative. As we shall see in the following chapter on presidential leadership of public opinion, if the "official" government position is indicated in a question, this often elicits a bias toward that position, especially on foreign policy issues. Before the U.S. invasion of Cambodia in 1970, only 7% of the public favored such a move, but the number rose to 50% after the president ordered the invasion; support for a bombing halt in Vietnam went from 40% before it was announced in 1968 to 64% afterwards; public attitudes toward China "softened considerably" after the president began making overtures toward establishing relations with the People's Republic. Cues in questions as to party or candidate stands may bias responses toward those of respondents' party and electoral choices.[17]

On policies that are very controversial, like intervention in the war in Vietnam, it may be impossible to ascertain public attitudes without some "contamination" by the use of "loaded" symbols in the questions.

> The specific words that go into a question asked by a pollster may be positive or negative symbols to an individual. If a question is asked in which negative symbols are associated with withdrawal from the war, people sound quite "hawkish" in their responses. Thus people reject "defeat,"

"Communist take-overs," and "the loss of American credibility." On the other hand, if negative symbols are associated with a pro-war position, the American public will sound "dovish." They reject "killings," "continuing the war," and "domestic costs." Turning the matter upside down we see the same thing. If positive symbols are associated with the war, the American public sounds "hawkish." They support "American prestige," "defense of democracy," and "support for our soldiers in Vietnam." On the other hand, if positive symbols are associated with "dovish" positions, the people sound "dovish." They come out in support of "peace," "worrying about our own problems before we worry about the problems of other people," and "saving American lives."[18]

Similarly, when people were asked in a 1981 poll whether federal "welfare" programs should be turned over to state and local government, 39% replied in the affirmative. In a survey the following month only 15% favored turning over federal programs for "aid to the needy."[19]

A final limitation of polls from the president's perspective is that, unless he pays for them, polls are not taken at his convenience. The questions asked and the timing of their being asked are determined by others. No questions will ever be asked on most issues. If opinion on an issue is measured, it is likely to be a one-time measurement, so the president will not be able to learn of changes in public opinion. Thus, the president cannot rely upon public polls to inform him of what the public is thinking on a given issue at a particular time.

Uses of Polls

In an attempt to understand public opinion on matters of special concern to them, recent presidents have commissioned their own polls. Franklin D. Roosevelt was the first president to pay much attention to polls, which were, of course, just being scientifically developed during his tenure in office. He retained Hadley Cantril of the Institute for Social Research to measure public opinion in the 1930s and 1940s on a variety of subjects including the economy, labor problems, World War II, international cooperation, postwar policy, peace negotiations, secrecy in national security affairs, agricultural programs, and his personal popularity.[20]

Presidents Kennedy, Johnson, Nixon, Ford, Carter, and Reagan all have retained private polling firms to measure public opinion for them. President Johnson assigned an aide to monitor polls for him.[21] President Carter relied on Patrick Caddell, head of Cambridge Survey Research, to provide him with soundings of American public opinion. Moreover, Caddell played a larger role as a high-level political advisor and shared a Georgetown home with two of the president's chief assistants.[22]

Richard Nixon was extremely interested in polls. One of his pollsters reports that

> Nixon had all kinds of polls all the time; he sometimes had a couple of pollsters doing the same kind of survey at the same time. He really studied them. He wanted to find the thing that would give him an advantage.

Polls were taken for the White House prior to the imposition of wage and price controls, after the mining of Haiphong harbor in North Vietnam, whenever the president appeared on television or went on a foreign trip, throughout the Watergate period, regularly on the economy, "on just about anything and everything."[23]

In 1971 the Nixon White House arranged a "truce" with Lou Harris, whom it felt had been rating Nixon too low in his presidential approval polls. In return for not trying to "get" Harris, the pollsters would provide the White House with Harris Survey results prior to their publication by subscribing newspapers and Harris would answer the president's queries about his poll results. (Similar services had been provided to Kennedy and Johnson.)[24] Nixon's aides developed relationships and picked the brains of many of the nation's other top pollsters as well.[25]

In contrast to his predecessor, Gerald Ford was not a devotee of public opinion polls. Although he was interested in their results, he did not spend much time studying them.[26] President Carter left the selection of poll questions to his aides, but he paid attention to the results of questions on a wide variety of issues including the Panama Canal treaties, the economy, the ERA, the SALT II talks, his energy proposals, and his image.[27] Ronald Reagan's White House appears to invest a substantial amount of time and money reviewing a wide range of poll results and has three polling organizations working for it.[28]

Since presidents do pay attention to public opinion polls and to some degree incorporate them into the store of information on which they rely in their decision making, it is important that the polls accurately reflect public opinion. In the fall of 1978 Patrick Caddell's Cambridge Research Corporation, which conducted polls for President Carter, asked a sample of approximately 1,500 people whether they agreed or disagreed with the statement that "People like me don't have any say about what the government does." 59% agreed and 31% disagreed. At about the same time a survey conducted by the Center for Political Studies of the Institute for Social Research at the University of Michigan asked a sample of approximately 2,300 persons the same question. 45% agreed and 53% disagreed, quite a different view from that presented by the president's pollster.[29] Although we cannot determine which poll was correct on the basis of this data, the results do indicate that a president must be cautious in relying upon one source of public opinion data.

In July of 1979 President Carter abruptly cancelled a nationally televised speech on energy. He retreated to Camp David, his hideaway in the Maryland mountains, for ten days of introspection and meetings with a stream of visitors. On July 15 the president addressed the nation, declaring that there was a "crisis of confidence" in America. He saw Americans worshipping self-indulgence and consumption and leading empty lives. According to the president there was also a growing sense of doubt about the meaning of our lives, a loss of a unity of purpose for our nation, and a loss of confidence in the future that threatened to destroy the social and political fabric of the country. Citizens were losing faith in government and in their ability to serve as the ultimate rulers of our democracy.

This was the most important speech of the Carter presidency, a speech in which he attempted to identify the causes of the nation's malaise and assert or reassert his leadership of the country to attempt to move it forward. The president's observations about the thinking of the American people were based in large part upon the polls of Patrick Caddell. The president's pollster found a convergence of pessimistic attitudes in the public on long-term national and personal expectations, short-term consumer confidence, and confidence in government and politics.[30]

The question of interest to us here is whether Caddell was correct in his assessment of public opinion. If he was not, then the president made a speech that was unlikely to strike a responsive chord with his listeners and was thus unlikely to provide him with sustained backing for his programs. As it turned out, Gallup polls taken in July and August showed no substantial increase in the president's standing in the public.

The day after Carter's speech, a CBS News/*The New York Times* poll asked the public whether there was "a moral and spiritual crisis, that is, a crisis of confidence, in this country today." Eighty-six percent of the respondents agreed. NBC/Associated Press and *Newsweek* polls reported similar results.[31]

On the other hand, in a survey of leading pollsters and public opinion experts, the *Christian Science Monitor* found unanimous disagreement with Caddell's conclusions. Although they agreed that the public was pessimistic, they argued that signs were mixed and that public opinion had been worse before.[32] Warren Miller of the University of Michigan's Survey Research Center concluded in a lengthy rebuttal to Caddell that confidence in government had actually increased among Democrats and had decreased among Republicans only because there was a Democrat in the White House.[33] The editors of *Public Opinion* magazine did not find a crisis in public attitudes about personal life or the nation and its institutions. Instead, they saw a response to poor performance in the economy and in the White House.[34]

It is impossible to apportion influence on the president's actions precisely among the innumerable advisors and ideas in his environment, of course, and it is unfair to assert that President Carter relied exclusively upon Patrick Caddell for his insights concerning the American people.[35] In response to a critical article in the *New York Times*, presidential press secretary Jody Powell provided a sample of writings that the president found relevant to his speech. These included sections of *Democracy in America* by Alexis de Tocqueville, *The Cultural Contradictions of Capitalism* by Daniel Bell, essays by Robert Bellah and Henry Ford II in the *St. Louis Post-Dispatch*, *The Culture of Narcissism* by Christopher Lasch, an essay by John Maynard Keynes, and magazine articles by John Herbers, Charles Peters, Albert Sommers, and James Q. Wilson.[36]

Nevertheless, it is reasonable to conclude that the speech the president delivered would have been substantially different and would not have stressed the "crisis of confidence" theme without the poll results from Caddell.[37] Once again, we find that presidents should guard against overreliance on a single source of public opinion data.

Leadership vs. Followership

Questions that inevitably arise when discussing presidents and polls include the following: How should presidents use public opinion data? Does use of this data constrain presidents rather than indicate where their persuasive efforts should be focused? Do presidents, in effect, substitute followership for leadership?

Of course, all modern presidents have relied heavily on polls during their election campaigns to clarify how the public feels about issues and perceives their candidacy. They are then most likely to moderate their stands or deemphasize certain issues if they conclude this will increase their popularity.[38] They also will be most concerned about anticipating public reactions to their actions during these periods. For example, in 1964 Lyndon Johnson checked with pollsters to see if his failure to respond to an attack on a U.S. Air Force base in South Vietnam would be taken as a sign of weakness on the part of the administration.[39] Nevertheless, most of the time a president is not running for reelection.

According to President Carter's chief media adviser, Gerald Rafshoon, "If we ever went into the president's office and said, 'We think you ought to do this or that to increase your standing in the polls,' he'd throw us out." Instead of using polls to determine his policies, Carter used them to measure how effective he was in getting his message across to the public and to determine the obstacles in his path. During the Carter administration pollster Patrick Caddell commented:

> This White House uses polls as a kind of a guidepost to determine the direction and distance the President has to go in terms of getting the public to move in favor of positions which he feels are necessary for the country.

They are a sounding board for that kind of movement. And they are obviously an indicator of political successes or problems that the President has.[40]

The issue of the ratification of the Panama Canal treaties under President Carter provides a good illustration of how presidents often use polls. Caddell's research revealed that many Americans did not understand certain provisions of the treaties. The polls also showed the sectors of the population that were susceptible to being persuaded to support the treaties. This information aided the White House in developing a strategy to win Senate approval of the treaties, but it did not deter it from seeking ratification in the face of public opposition.[41]

Franklin D. Roosevelt used polls similarly to help lead the country in the direction he felt was best. For example, he received a report from his pollsters on the public's lack of understanding that under the Lend-Lease policy toward Great Britain at the outbreak of World War II the United States received raw materials and foodstuffs from the British Commonwealth in return for its aid to the British war effort. Thus, the president went out of his way to clarify this point in a public message to Congress. A follow-up survey showed that he was successful in increasing the public's understanding of the program. According to his pollster, however, Roosevelt never altered his goals because public opinion was against him or uninformed.[42]

Neither John Kennedy nor Lyndon Johnson seemed to be a captive of public opinion polls either.[43] Johnson used polls to find out where he lacked support in the public so he could try to shore up that sector. He also used them as carrots and sticks to convince wavering and uncommitted policymakers and political leaders to support him. In the 1963–66 period, for example, he often greeted visitors to the White House with the latest indicators of his popularity.[44]

According to one close White House observer, "perhaps more than any other Administration, the Reagan White House uses polling, public opinion analyses and media and marketing research as contributory elements in the decision-making process and the selling of the presidency." Reagan's pollsters meet regularly with the president and his top aides. Their most important function is to determine when the nation's mood is amenable to the president's proposals. The White House wants the timing of the presidential agenda to be compatible with the political climate to maximize the probabilities of achieving the president's objectives.[45]

The biggest exception to the norm of presidents using polls to help them gain public support for their policies instead of for following public opinion is Richard Nixon, especially in domestic policy. During the Nixon administration Lou Harris wrote that "the gusts of new winds for change must be whipping upward before he [Nixon] will latch onto their swirl." In other words, Nixon at times waited for public opinion to coalesce before he took a stand. Harris and others have also argued that polls showing Nixon in trouble with the public for failing to control inflation and unemployment contributed heavily to the president's decision to act against his longstanding opposition to wage and price controls and impose them on the economy.[46]

PRESIDENTIAL ELECTION RESULTS

If presidents cannot always rely on polls to inform them about public opinion, theoretically they can gain valuable insights through interpretation of their own electoral support. In other words, perhaps they can learn what voters are thinking when they cast their ballots for president.

Before such an approach can be useful for a president seeking to understand public opinion, the following conditions must be met:

1. Voters must have opinions on policies.
2. Voters must know candidates' stands on the issues.
3. The candidates that voters support must offer them the alternatives they desire.
4. There must be a large turnout.
5. Voters must vote on the basis of issues.
6. The president must be able to correlate voter support with voters' policy views.

If voters do not have opinions on policies, then their votes are unlikely to be related to issues. We have already seen that this condition for understanding public opinion through the interpretation of election returns is often not met. Most people do not have crystallized opinions on a given policy issue.

Knowledge of Candidates' Stands

Voters must also know candidates' stands on the issues if their votes for a particular candidate are to be interpreted as support for that candidate's policy positions. The evidence on this condition is both limited and mixed. We do not have objective data on voters' knowledge of specific policy stands. Research does indicate, however, that the public generally grasped the ideological differences between Barry Goldwater and Lyndon Johnson in 1964, Richard Nixon and Hubert Humphrey in 1968, and Richard Nixon and George McGovern in 1972.[47] A complicating factor is that by election day many of the policy differences that voters thought existed between candidates had diminished as the candidates moderated and obscured their issue stands. Thus, even when voters have perceptions of candidates' stands, they may be inaccurate.[48]

The 1964 and 1972 elections were notable for the clear and well-publicized differences between the candidates on the issues, at least until late in the campaign. In the 1976 campaign people were generally unable to perceive the policy differences between Gerald Ford and Jimmy Carter, and there was substantial misperception of candidates' stands.[49] At the end of the campaign only one-third of the public could identify Jimmy Carter's position on a typical issue. Fifty-six percent of the people knew one-fourth or fewer of the presidential candidates' issue stands.[50]

An additional problem is that voters may selectively perceive candidates' issue stands. In other words, they may screen out information about policy positions of their favored candidate that are contrary to their own views. Similarly, they may project their own policy opinions onto candidates whom they favor for reasons of party affiliation or candidate image. Thus, supporters of a candidate tend to perceive that candidate as closer to themselves on the issues than the candidate is and to perceive the opposition candidate as more distant from themselves on the issue than he is.[51]

Alternatives Offered

Even if voters hold policy opinions and know candidates' issue stands, their votes cannot be interpreted as support for specific policies unless candidates offer them the policy alternatives they prefer. If alternatives are not offered or if they are vague, artificial, or hidden, votes for a candidate cannot sensibly be interpreted as support for particular policies.

Candidates for the presidency are often not very helpful in presenting specific alternatives to the voters. Instead, they tend to emphasize general goals and images in their presentations to the public. Since there is wide consensus on goals such as peace and prosperity, candidates stress their commitments to achieving these ends while remaining obscure on more specific issues. This strategy minimizes the possibility of alienating voters who might otherwise support them.[52]

After an extensive study of presidential campaign speeches, one author concluded:

> The average campaign speech . . . may include a reference to one of the handful of important proposals which candidates regularly repeat; it may include some pat phrases alluding to policy, or some minor proposals of an organizational or informational sort; but it does not present the candidate's

stands on many policies or in any great detail. The infrequency with which candidates discuss policy is a major factor preventing most Americans from learning what the stands are.[53]

The critical role alternatives play in interpreting election results is clearly illustrated in the 1968 presidential election. In that year many voters had strong opinions on the key issue of the war in Vietnam. Yet they were unable to differentiate between the positions of Richard Nixon and Hubert Humphrey. (Nixon claimed he had a plan to end the war, but he refused to reveal it.) When researchers studied the campaign statements of the two candidates on the war, they were also unable to differentiate their positions.[54] In sum, Nixon and Humphrey did not provide policy alternatives to the public on the most crucial issue of the day. Thus, Richard Nixon, the winner in the election, could not interpret the election outcome as support for a particular policy on the war.

One might assume that the policy stands of incumbent presidents running for reelection would be clear to the public. Yet their current policies are not always clear to voters or necessarily accurate guides to the future. Incumbent presidents are usually more vague than their challengers in issue stands, and they rarely present detailed plans for future policy on the campaign trail. In some instances, such as 1972 and 1976, they have not even campaigned very much.[55]

After the 1980 presidential campaign the chief pollsters for Jimmy Carter and Ronald Reagan were interviewed in *Public Opinion.* Patrick Caddell, Carter's pollster, commented that

we had to structure . . . a choice around a set of definitions that did not directly encompass all of the general feelings that people had either about issues or about the candidate—and specifically about his record.[56]

Reagan's pollster, Richard Wirthlin, agreed that the campaign from his side was based on emphasizing personality as much as issues or the president's record.[57]

Obscurity is not the only difficulty voters face in attempting to discern policy alternatives during election campaigns. In at least one instance in recent history it seems that presidential candidates actually agreed among themselves *not* to discuss certain issues. Senator Barry Goldwater reveals that in 1964 he met secretly with President Johnson, and they struck a deal not to criticize each other on the issues of civil rights and the war in Vietnam,[58] certainly two of the most important issues of the day.

Many issues are never discussed in any detail during a presidential election campaign. Moreover, because there are usually only two serious contenders for the presidency, voters' choices are limited to two sets of policy options. The odds of any candidate's set of issue positions matching those of a voter are very slim. As a result, the available candidates usually offer voters nothing more than approximations of their preferences.

Presidential platforms do contain fairly specific policy pledges.[59] This does not mean, however, that these pledges aid voters in comparing the parties' presidential candidates. As a leading student of platforms has written, "the parties do not stress the same issues in most elections, and direct comparison of their positions becomes difficult." Each party tends to emphasize its areas of strength and neglect the strong points of the opposition. If there is a clear consensus in the public on an issue area, the parties are more likely to be specific. They are also unlikely to disagree on such issues, there being little point in alienating a majority of voters. On issues on which there is no majority opinion, and thus on which the presentation of alternatives is most crucial for voters trying to vote for the candidate most likely to share their policy preferences, the platforms are most evasive. If they are specific on such issues, they may be making the same appeals to the same minorities. Thus, party platforms do not necessarily present voters with contrasting policy alternatives.[60]

The utility of platforms for offering alternatives is further reduced by the fact that, for many reasons, the fall campaign speeches of presidential candidates differ in both style and content from their platforms and acceptance speeches.[61] The candidates may disagree with certain statements in the platforms, and platforms and campaign speeches are aimed at different audiences. Despite the great amount of publicity surrounding the Republican party's decision to take no stand on the Equal Rights Amendment in its 1980 platform, a poll following the convention found that only 1% of registered voters knew what stand the GOP had taken.[62]

Presidential debates are not necessarily any more help than party platforms in clarifying alternatives for the voters. One study, for example, found that following the debate between Ronald Reagan and John Anderson during the 1980 presidential campaign, the public knew *less* than it had before about Reagan's issue priorities on domestic spending, the ERA, tax cuts, and military policy.[63]

Some differences between the policy stands of candidates for the presidency can be detected, and voters will usually perceive clear policy stands if candidates take them. But specific stands taken by candidates generally receive poor coverage in the mass media, which are the primary sources of political information for most voters. Once they have issued a public statement, candidates seldom repeat the details of their policy stands. Instead, they make statements lacking specificity as to the direction, timing, and magnitude of their policy intentions.[64]

At other times what seem to be alternatives may really be something much less. Richard Nixon ran on a strong law-and-order platform in

1968, emphasizing that he was the best candidate to reduce crime and public disorder. According to a campaign official who later became Nixon's counsel in the White House, the Nixon "program" was "bull——" and was nothing the current administration was not already doing.[65]

Voter Turnout

If a president is to interpret his electoral support as reflecting the public's policy views, a large portion of the public must vote. If there is only a small voter turnout, then the views of much of the public will not be expressed. Unfortunately, turnout in recent years has usually been low and appears to be declining. As Table 1.1 shows, only 53% of the adult population voted in the 1980 presidential election. In fact, more people did not vote than voted for any one candidate.

In this situation, winning candidates for president *never* receive support from a majority of the public. Only 27% of the adult public voted for Ronald Reagan in 1980, hardly a basis for a mandate. Moreover, in 1948, 1960, and 1968 the winning candidate did not even receive the votes of a majority of those who voted! Minor-party candidates drain support away from the Democratic and Republican nominees and further complicate the interpretation of election returns.

Of course, low turnout would not necessarily hinder a president in drawing inferences about public opinion if those who voted represented a cross section of the population. But they do not. People who are middle class, middle aged, white, and who affiliate themselves with a political party are more likely to vote than others. People with low incomes or limited educations, the young, the elderly, nonwhites, and Independents

TABLE 1.1   TURNOUT IN PRESIDENTIAL ELECTIONS

Year	Percentage of Voting-Age Persons Who Voted
1980	53
1976	54
1972	56
1968	61
1964	62
1960	63
1956	59
1952	62

SOURCE: Bureau of the Census, *Statistical Abstract of the United States 1981*, 102d ed. (Washington, D.C.: Government Printing Office, 1981), p. 496, Table 824.

are less likely to vote.[66] It is not too far-fetched to argue that if voter turnout had been considerably higher in recent very close elections, the winners would have been different.

Issue Voting

Even if voters study the issues carefully and turn out in large numbers to cast their ballots, their votes will provide little accurate policy guidance to the president if they do not vote on the basis of issues. Yet many voters base their candidate choices on party affiliation or candidates' images (their personalities and other personal characteristics). Sometimes they switch their views on issues to bring them in line with their favored candidate or party. Although issue voting seemed to be higher than normal in the 1964 and 1972 presidential elections, it dropped in 1976 and 1980. There does not appear to be a clear trend towards increasing issue voting. In general, issues have been less important than candidate image and party affiliation as influences on the vote for president.[67]

When citizens do make electoral decisions on the basis of issues, they vote on issues that are significant to them. These may not be the issues stressed in the campaign, making it difficult to infer support for these issues from vote totals. Sometimes the issues that influence votes may be phony. Raised advertently or inadvertently, they distract voter attention from real issues. In 1960, for example, John Kennedy decried the "missile gap" in which the United States supposedly lagged behind the Soviet Union in missile development. After taking office the gap "disappeared" without any shift in defense policy. Ronald Reagan campaigned in 1980 on cutting expenditures without reducing services—through eliminating waste, fraud, and abuse. When it came time to propose a budget, however, this waste, fraud, and abuse failed to appear.[68]

Some issues cannot be discussed during a campaign because they arise after an election is over. The 1973–74 Arab oil embargo, the taking of American hostages by Iranian militants in 1979, and the Polish crackdown in 1981 are just three examples of postelection events to which the president has had to respond.

Correlating Votes and Views

Because the five previous conditions for the public's signaling policy views through voting in presidential elections are rarely met, it is very difficult for the president to discern the relationship between voters' policy preferences and his victory at the polls. In addition, the president is faced with two complicating factors. First, there may be no majority opinion on an issue, even among those who have an opinion. Public opinion polls often force persons to choose one of a restricted number of possible answers. But we should not forget that opinion on any issue is probably quite fragmented, providing no majority opinion for the president to identify.

Second, voters may be concerned with several issues in an election, but they have only one vote with which to express their views. Citizens may support one candidate's positions on some issues yet vote for another candidate because of concern for other issues. Voters signal only their choice of candidate and not their choice of that candidate's policies when they cast their ballots. A president should be cautious in inferring support for specific policies from the results of this process.

Presidential Elections in Perspective

As a result of these problems of inferring public support for policies from election results, it is best to be suspicious of electoral "mandates." The electoral process provides a choice between people and parties whose differences are often unclear to the public. Electoral results provide a direction to government and perhaps a sense of relative priorities, but they usually do not mandate the adoption of specific programs.[69]

Let us summarize this section with the example of the 1980 presidential election. In it, Ronald Reagan defeated Jimmy Carter by 10 percentage points (51% to 41%). Yet polls showed that there was not a substantial shift to the right in the public's thinking on policy issues.[70] Polls also indicate that large percentages of Reagan's supporters voted for him because he was seen as the "lesser of evils," they were anti-Carter, or they felt it was time for a change. These vague and non-policy-oriented responses reveal that the election was more a rejection of Jimmy Carter than a vote of confidence in Ronald Reagan.[71]

Perhaps the most notable policy proposal Reagan made early in his term was for a substantial tax cut. Interestingly, before the election almost twice as many people were in favor of the smaller tax cut proposed by President Carter than the larger cut proposed by candidate Reagan.[72] Similarly, the public did not support decreased spending on domestic policy at election time.[73] Thus, inferring support for a specific policy from victory at the polls risks substantially misreading public opinion.

CONGRESSIONAL ELECTION RESULTS

Presidential elections occur only once every four years, so even if they did provide the president insights into public opinion, they might soon be dated. In the middle of each presidential term, however, congressional elections are held. We will focus in this section on whether the president can interpret the results of midterm congressional elections as referenda on specific policies or on his performance as president.

Midterm Elections as Referenda on Specific Policies

The conditions under which a president may infer public opinion about public policies through interpreting congressional election results are similar to those conditions necessary to interpret his own electoral support, and they are even less likely to be met. As we have seen above, crystallized opinions on issues do not typify the American voter.

Knowledge of candidates' stands is also unimpressive. In the 1978 House elections, 58% of adults could not say if they agreed with their representative's voting in Congress. Only 10% could remember a particular bill on which their representatives had voted, and only 20% could remember anything their representative had done in Congress for their district or for the people.[74]

When asked to identify their representative's position on five issues and on a general ideological scale, less than half of those in a national sample tried to do so. Only about 14% of the sample was willing to do so for the challenger for the House seat. Of those who felt they could identify their representative's positions, at least one-third were incorrect, even on issues they said they cared about.[75] Thus, citizens seem to be unaware of both the specific stands and more general ideological positions of their representatives.[76]

As one expert on congressional elections puts it, "mass public knowledge of congressional candidates declines precipitously once we move beyond simple recognition, generalized feelings, and incumbent job ratings." The public is largely unaware of candidates' policy stands, even on controversial issues.[77]

An evaluation of the extent to which policy alternatives are offered in congressional races must be mixed, as it was for presidential elections. One study shows that candidates for the House offered voters alternatives on civil rights, domestic welfare, and foreign policy issues.[78] On the other hand, we also know that in 1978 there was no real competition in 128 of the 435 congressional districts in the country.[79] We have also just seen that the issue positions of candidates for Congress, especially those of challengers to House incumbents, are not perceived by the typical voter. In addition, differences between candidates are usually not emphasized during campaigns. Candidates focus more attention on abstractions such as efficiency in government and on invoking symbols such as their party (if they are in the majority) and their experience. Most issues are not discussed at all, and the set of alternatives offered by a candidate is unlikely to match the set of policy preferences of any voter who holds opinions on several issues and who does not follow a candidate's lead in arriving at these opinions.

Turnout in midterm elections is low and has been declining over the last generation. As Table 1.2 shows, only 35% of voting age adults cast their ballots in the 1978 congressional elections. Thus, those who did not vote outnumbered those who did vote by about 2 to 1. This is hardly a base from which one can confidently draw inferences about public opinion. Moreover, as was the case for presidential elections, those who do vote are not a cross section of the population. Once again, those who vote are disproportionately middle and upper class, middle aged, white, and affiliated with a political party.

A related problem of sampling is that only one-third of the seats in the Senate are voted upon in any one election. These seats do not necessarily represent a cross section of the public since they represent only two-thirds of the states.

Issue voting in congressional elections is even less frequent than it is in presidential elections. Studies have found that, relative to other factors such as party and candidate image, issues play an unimportant role in congressional elections. In the 1978 House elections, for example, only 29% of the adult population could identify an issue in the campaign that was of at least some importance to them. Only 13% preferred a candidate because of an issue in the campaign. Members of Congress, especially those in the House, are evaluated more on the basis of party, personal characteristics, and constituent service than on their issue stands.[80]

As in the case of presidential elections, politicians may pose "issues" in midterm congressional elections that distort differences between parties or candidates or that are designed to distract voters from more significant problems. One high Republican official describes the White House's approach to the 1970 congressional elections as follows:

TABLE 1.2   TURNOUT IN MIDTERM ELECTIONS

Year	Percentage of Voting-Age People Who Voted
1978	35
1974	36
1970	44
1966	45
1962	45
1958	43
1954	42
1950	41

SOURCE: *Statistical Abstract of the United States*, p. 496, Table 824.

We were going to win this historic victory by hammering at the law and order issue. It was a totally negative approach, one that combined the national fear of increasing crime with undertones of racism. We would not emphasize our constructive achievements—new crime laws, more judges, more aid to police—rather we would damn our opponents as "radical liberals" who were soft on crime, who in effect were procrime. To a lesser extent, we appealed to patriotism on the war issue—the same radical liberals who were soft on crime at home were soft on Communism abroad. It was an approach that assumed little intelligence on the part of the voter, and assumed that cries of "law and order" could divert his attention from, among other things, the economic problems and inflation.[81]

Only a small percentage of all potential issues are raised in a congressional election campaign and few crises or issues that come into prominence later will be anticipated by the candidates. Moreover, the issues raised in elections will vary across the country. Water issues may be raised in the West, agricultural issues in the Midwest, and urban issues on the Eastern seaboard. This makes interpreting aggregate electoral results even more problematic.

In addition to the problems in relating voters' support for candidates with their policy views presented by the frequent absence of majority opinion on issues and the use of one vote to express preferences on several issues, a president faces a unique problem in interpreting House elections. The relationship between the percentage of votes a party's candidates receive nationwide and the percentage of seats the party wins in the House is neither necessarily close nor constant.[82] For example, in 1970 the Republicans won 45% of the nationwide vote for House seats and as a result won 180 seats (41%). In 1978, however, they again won 45% of the vote but this time won only 158 seats (36%).[83] The same distortion can occur in the Senate. In 1980, for example, Republicans won 65% of the seats up in that year with only 47% of the vote.[84]

Midterm Elections as Referenda on the President

If the president cannot interpret congressional election outcomes as referenda on specific policies, can he interpret them as general judgments of his performance in office? Scholars have found that the president's approval level correlates fairly strongly with the aggregate national vote received by candidates for the House of the president's party. Of course, these trends take place within the confines of party voting, so that it takes a substantial increase in presidential approval, for example, to increase by a small amount the aggregate vote percentage received by candidates for the House of the president's party.[85]

Studies have also found that voters who identify with the president's party but who disapprove of the president's performance are somewhat more likely to defect from their own party and support a congressional candidate of the other party than are those who approve of the president. The reverse is also true. Voters who identify with the opposition party but who approve of the president's performance in office are more likely to vote for a congressional candidate of his party than are those who do not approve. For example, in 1978, 26% of Democratic voters who disapproved of President Carter's performance as president voted for a Republican for the House while 22% of those who approved of the president voted for the Republican candidate. Similarly, 21% of the Republican voters who disapproved of the president voted for a Democrat for the House while 29% of those who approved of Carter voted Democratic.[86]

A different picture emerges, however, when we estimate the influence of presidential approval on voting in congressional elections in relation to other influences. In a recent study of the 1970, 1974, and 1978 midterm congressional elections (the only midterm elections for which we have appropriate data), the author found that evaluations of the president were less important in determining citizens' votes than the party identification, incumbency, and specific attributes of candidates for the House and Senate. In no case was the effect of evaluations of the president more than modest. Moreover, the impact of presidential evaluations seems to be declining over time.[87]

What we have, then, is a situation in which evaluations of the president are not a dominant cause of voters' decisions in congressional elections. They may be important enough, however, to affect the marginal change in the aggregate vote percentage for the candidates of the president's party in comparison with the most recent previous election.

These shifts seem to go regularly against the president. As Table 1.3 shows, a recurring feature in American politics is the decrease in representation of the president's party in Congress in midterm congressional elections. Under President Eisenhower, Republicans lost both houses of Congress in 1954 and met with near disaster in 1958, losing forty-seven seats in the House and thirteen in the Senate. Democrats under President Kennedy did better in 1962 when they actually gained four seats in the Senate while losing only four in the House. But in 1966 under President Johnson the Democrats lost forty-seven House and three Senate seats. In 1970 the Republicans held losses under President Nixon to twelve in the House and gained two seats in the Senate. In 1974, however, they lost forty-seven seats in the House and five in the Senate under President Ford. The Democrats had modest losses in 1978 of eleven in the House and three in the Senate under President Carter. Finally, in 1982 the Republicans lost 26 House and no Senate seats with Ronald Reagan in the White House.

TABLE 1.3 CHANGES IN CONGRESSIONAL REPRESENTATION OF THE PRESIDENT'S PARTY IN MIDTERM ELECTIONS

	House		Senate	
Year	Losses	Gains	Losses	Gains
1982	26	0	0	0
1978	11	0	3	0
1974	47	0	5	0
1970	12	0	0	2
1966	47	0	3	0
1962	4	0	0	4
1958	47	0	13	0
1954	18	0	1	0

But a president cannot interpret this vote shift as an accurate reflection of the public's evaluation of his performance. Samuel Kernell has carried the analysis further and suggested a reason why both Democrats and Republicans receive smaller percentages of the total congressional vote in midterm elections when the president is of their own party (even if the president is relatively popular, as he was in 1954, 1962, and 1970). He argues that negative opinions disproportionately influence political behavior and that the electorate votes *against* policies and incumbents more than it votes *for* new policies and candidates. The president is the only highly visible national actor and therefore is a prominent reference for choosing a candidate. Thus, a greater proportion of the voters who disapprove of the president are likely to vote than of those who approve, especially if the voters are Independents or of the opposition party. Moreover, disapproval of the president is a stronger source of party defection than approval, and defectors from party voting occur disproportionately within the president's party, primarily among his detractors. Because voting turnout is low in midterm elections, a relatively small amount of negative voting may have significant consequences. About the only thing a president can do to counteract this effect is to be popular so that few voters will have negative opinions about him.[88]

The seeming relationship between presidential approval and the vote for the president's party in midterm elections may also be influenced by another phenomenon. It is possible that national conditions, which also affect the president's public standing, influence the decisions of candidates to run for office, contributors to donate, and interest groups to become active in campaigns. If things are going well in the country and thus probably for the president, strong candidates should be representing his party, and they should be able to run effective campaigns. If things are going badly, the reverse should be true. In either case, it is national conditions influencing campaigns that affect the midterm elections rather than presidential approval.[89]

MAIL

The mail is another potential means for the president to learn about public opinion. Although estimates vary and record keeping is inconsistent, there can be no doubt that the White House receives a tremendous volume of communications from the public. President Carter received 30,000 letters weekly,[90] while President Ford received approximately 35,000 letters, telegrams, and mailgrams each week.[91] Another count put Richard Nixon's mail at 6 million pieces in 1969 and 1970.[92] In one week after a town meeting in Clinton, Massachusetts, President Carter received 87,000 letters and between 20,000 and 30,000 phone calls per day.[93] President Reagan received 100,000 letters and telegrams in the two weeks following the unveiling of his economic program in February 1981,[94] and typically receives between 12,000 and 20,000 pieces of mail daily.[95] Naturally, a president can read only a negligible percentage of this avalanche of messages. It is difficult for his staff even to summarize this much mail unless the public focuses on a specific issue over a short period of time.

The White House staff screens the mail, and much of it is forwarded to relevant agencies for action and response. Most of this mail comes from ordinary citizens and organizations seeking help with problems. Much of it is trivial from the president's perspective. Little of it deals with basic policy issues. There are also many requests from individuals and organizations for support and financial assistance. Almost all such requests are rejected by the president's staff.[96]

The president typically reads only a few items from a day's mail, and these are communications from personal friends, prominent and influential citizens, and interest group leaders. He may answer a few letters from ordinary citizens, primarily as a public relations gesture. President Reagan receives a weekly selection of the mail and the overall numbers, pro and con, on relevant issues.[97] Mail from important individuals and organizations the president wants to rebuff is usually answered by his top assistants.[98]

Even if the president could read the mail, this would not necessarily provide a useful guide to what the public is thinking about policy issues. As we have already noted, most of the mail does not focus on the issues with which the president must deal. In addition, those who communicate with the White House are not a cross section of the American people. They overrepresent the middle and upper classes and people who agree with the president. Thus, the president cannot rely on his mail to obtain an accurate perception of public opinion.[99]

CONCLUSION

We have seen that presidents find it difficult to understand public opinion. This is partially due to the state of Americans' attitudes and partially due to the mechanisms available for measuring them. This does not mean, of course, that presidents have no idea what the people are thinking. Politicians as talented as presidents usually have a basic understanding of the public.

What it does mean is that there is potential for slippage between what the public wants, what it is understood to want, and what it receives. One study found that members of President Nixon's Domestic Council had a reasonably accurate perception of public attitudes on policies. But the author also found that the lack of systematic cues on public opinion available to the White House also allowed the staffers to project their own attitudes onto those of the general public, producing a systematic bias towards, in this case, a conservative position.[100]

There is also the potential for the president to exceed the boundaries of what the public will find acceptable. There is no lack of examples of the White House being surprised by public reaction to events and presidential actions. These range from President Nixon's decision to invade Cambodia in 1970 to Ronald Reagan's efforts to halt increases in social security benefits in 1981.[101]

Even if presidents feel they understand public opinion on a particular issue, they do not necessarily follow it. A typical line in a presidential address to the nation on a specific issue goes something like, "Although the action I am taking may be unpopular, I am doing what I feel is in the best interests of the country." For example in a speech on the invasion of Cambodia in 1970 President Nixon stated:

> I would rather be a one-term president and do what I believe is right than to be a two-term president at the cost of seeing America become a second-rate power and to see this nation accept the first defeat in its proud 190-year history.[102]

Presidents often feel, with good reason, that they know more about policy than most members of the public and that they sometimes have to lead public opinion instead of merely following it. Gerald Ford expressed this view:

> I do not think a President should run the country on the basis of the polls. The public in so many cases does not have a full comprehension of a problem. A President ought to listen to the people, but he cannot make hard decisions just by reading the polls once a week. It just does not work, and what the President ought to do is make the hard decisions and then go out

and educate the people on why a decision that was necessarily unpopular was made.[103]

It is to the leadership of public opinion that we turn in the next chapter. We should keep in mind, however, that it is more difficult to alter the public's view if you do not know what it is thinking *before* you attempt to influence it.

NOTES

1. See George F. Bishop, Robert W. Oldendick, Alfred J. Tuchfarber, and Stephen E. Bennett, "Pseudo-Opinions on Public Affairs," *Public Opinion Quarterly* 44 (Summer 1980), pp. 198–209.
2. "The Clean Air Act," *Public Opinion*, February–March 1982, p. 36.
3. "Public Found Against Welfare Idea but in Favor of What Programs Do," *New York Times*, August 3, 1977, pp. A1, D15.
4. "Increasing Attention Focused on Regulatory Reform Plans," *Congressional Quarterly Weekly Report*, March 31, 1979, p. 561.
5. *CBS News/The New York Times Poll*, February 2, 1981, p. 4. See also Robert S. Erikson, Norman R. Luttbeg, and Kent L. Tedin, *American Public Opinion: Its Origins, Content, and Impact*, 2nd ed. (New York: Wiley, 1980), p. 31.
6. *CBS News/The New York Times Poll*, April 29, 1981, Part I, p. 3. See also Irving Crespi, "Does the Public Approve of Ronald Reagan?", *Public Opinion*, October–November 1981, pp. 20, 41.
7. See Erikson, Luttbeg, and Tedin, *American Public Opinion*, pp. 212, 214–15.
8. Alan I. Abramowitz, "The Impact of a Presidential Debate on Voter Rationality," *American Journal of Political Science* 22 (August 1978), pp. 680–90.
9. Hubert H. Humphrey, *The Education of a Public Man: My Life and Politics* (Garden City, N.Y.: Doubleday, 1976), p. 180.
10. "Different Attitudes on Treaty," *New Orleans Times-Picayune*, October 23, 1977, sec. 1, p. 8.
11. "Opinion Roundup," *Public Opinion*, March–May, 1979, p. 27.
12. Erikson, Luttbeg, and Tedin, *American Public Opinion*, p. 19.
13. *CBS News/The New York Times Poll*, June 30, 1981, pp. 7–8.
14. Kim Chatelain, "Pollster Says Americans Shaking Watergate Blues," *New Orleans Times-Picayune*, June 19, 1978, sec. 1, p. 8.
15. George Gallup, "Public Split on Merits of No-Fault," *New Orleans Times-Picayune*, September 15, 1977, sec. 3, p. 2.
16. Erikson, Luttbeg, and Tedin, *American Public Opinion*, 2nd ed, p. 20.
17. *Ibid.*, pp. 31–33, 45–46, 144.
18. Milton J. Rosenberg, Sidney Verba, and Philip E. Converse, *Vietnam and the Silent Majority* (New York: Harper and Row, 1970), pp. 24–25. See also John E. Mueller, "Trends in Popular Support for the Wars in Korea and Vietnam," *American Political Science Review* 65 (June 1971), p. 363.
19. Advisory Commission on Intergovernmental Relations, *Changing Public Attitudes on Governments and Taxes* (Washington, D.C.: Advisory Commission on

Intergovernmental Relations, 1981), pp. 1–4. See also Erikson, Luttbeg, and Tedin, *American Public Opinion*, 2nd ed., pp. 29–30, on federal aid to education.

20. Hadley Cantril, *The Human Dimension: Experience in Policy Research* (New Brunswick, N.J.: Rutgers University Press, 1967), chaps. 6–9, 11–12, 14.

21. Congressional Quarterly, *Congress and the Nation, Vol. II: 1965–1968* (Washington, D.C.: Congressional Quarterly, 1969), p. 626.

22. See Dom Bonafede, "Carter and the Polls—If You Live By Them, You May Die By Them," *National Journal*, August 19, 1978, pp. 1312–15; Dom Bonafede, "Rafshoon and Caddell—When the President Is the Client," *National Journal*, May 28, 1977, pp. 812–17.

23. Bonafede, "Carter and the Polls," p. 1314. See also Jeb Stuart Magruder, *An American Life: One Man's Road to Watergate* (New York: Pocket Books, 1975), p. 182.

24. Louis Harris, *The Anguish of Change* (New York: Norton, 1973), p. 72.

25. Michael Wheeler, *Lies, Damn Lies, and Statistics: The Manipulation of Public Opinion in America* (New York: Dell, 1976), chap. 1.

26. Bonafede, "Carter and the Polls," p. 1314.

27. *Ibid.*, pp. 1313, 1315; Bonafede, "Rafshoon and Caddell," p. 814.

28. Dom Bonafede, "As Pollster to the President, Wirthlin Is Where the Action Is," *National Journal*, December 12, 1981, pp. 2184–88; "Meeting the Press," *Public Opinion*, December 1981–January 1982, p. 11; Paul C. Light, *The President's Agenda: Domestic Policy Choice from Kennedy to Carter* (Baltimore: Johns Hopkins University Press, 1982), p. 93; "A Third Pollster for the White House," *Newsweek*, July 5, 1982, p. 17.

29. "Cambridge vs. Ann Arbor," *Public Opinion*, October–November 1979, p. 8.

30. Patrick H. Caddell, "Trapped in a Downward Spiral," *Public Opinion*, October–November 1979, pp. 2–7, 52–55, 58–60.

31. Everett C. Ladd, Jr., "A Nation's Trust," *Public Opinion*, October–November 1979, p. 27; David Gergen, "A Report from the Editors on the 'Crisis of Confidence,'" *Public Opinion*, August–September 1979, p. 4.

32. Richard J. Cattani, "U.S. 'Confidence Crisis' Overstated by Carter?", *The Christian Science Monitor*, July 24, 1979, pp. 1, 8.

33. Warren E. Miller, "Misreading the Public Pulse," *Public Opinion*, October–November 1979, pp. 9–15, 60.

34. Gergen, "A Report from the Editors," pp. 2–4, 54; Ladd, "A Nation's Trust," p. 27.

35. Caddell, "Trapped in a Downward Spiral," p. 2.

36. "The President's Reading," *New York Times Magazine*, August 19, 1979, p. 78.

37. See Sidney Blumenthal, *The Permanent Campaign: Inside the World of Elite Political Operatives* (Boston: Beacon Press, 1980), pp. 53–56, for a discussion of Caddell's role in the president's speech.

38. See, for example, Magruder, *An American Life*, p. 179.

39. Harris, *Anguish of Change*, p. 23.

40. Bonafede, "Carter and the Polls," pp. 1312–13. See also Bonafede, "Rafshoon and Caddell," p. 816.

41. Bonafede, "Carter and the Polls," pp. 1313, 1315; Bonafede, "As Pollster to the President," p. 2188.

42. Cantril, *The Human Dimension*, pp. 41–42, 71–73.

43. Harris, *Anguish of Change*, pp. 23, 26.
44. *Ibid.*, p. 23; Bonafede, "Carter and the Polls," p. 1314.
45. Bonafede, "As Pollster to the President," pp. 2184–88.
46. Harris, *Anguish of Change*, pp. 18, 33–34; Wheeler, *Lies*, p. 28. But see Nixon's comments in Richard M. Nixon, "Needed, Clarity of Purpose," *Time*, November 10, 1980, p. 32.
47. Robert D. McClure and Thomas E. Patterson, "Television News and Voter Behavior in the 1972 Presidential Election" (paper presented at the Annual Meeting of the American Political Science Association, New Orleans, September 1973), p. 8; Robert S. Erikson and Norman R. Luttbeg, *American Public Opinion* (New York: Wiley, 1973), pp. 230, 232; Benjamin I. Page, *Choices and Echoes in Presidential Elections: Rational Man and Electoral Democracy* (Chicago: University of Chicago Press, 1978), pp. 88–102.
48. See, for example, Page, *Choices and Echoes*, p. 95.
49. Erikson, Luttbeg, and Tedin, *American Public Opinion*, pp. 205–12; Doris A. Graber, *Mass Media and American Politics* (Washington, D.C.: Congressional Quarterly Press, 1980), pp. 139–40, 184–85.
50. Thomas E. Patterson, *The Mass Media Election: How Americans Choose Their Presidents* (New York: Praeger, 1980), pp. 155–56, 168–69.
51. See Notes 7 and 8 above.
52. Page, *Choices and Echoes*, p. 178; Edward G. Carmines and J. David Gopoian, "Issue Coalitions, Issueless Campaigns: The Paradox of Rationality in American Presidential Elections," *Journal of Politics*, 43 (November 1981), pp. 1170–89.
53. Page, *Choices and Echoes*, p. 160.
54. Benjamin I. Page and Richard A. Brody, "Policy Voting and the Electoral Process: The Vietnam War Issue," *American Political Science Review* 66 (September 1972), pp. 979–95.
55. Page, *Choices and Echoes*, pp. 168–69. See also Gerald M. Pomper with Susan S. Lederman, *Elections in America: Control and Influence in Democratic Politics*, 2nd ed. (New York: Longman, 1980), pp. 134–35.
56. "Face Off: A Conversation with the President's Pollsters Patrick Caddell and Richard Wirthlin," *Public Opinion*, December–January 1981, p. 2. See also p. 6.
57. *Ibid.*, p. 4.
58. Barry Goldwater, *With No Apologies* (New York: William Morrow, 1979), pp. 192–93.
59. See Jeff Fishel, "Presidential Elections and Presidential Agendas: The Carter Administration in Contemporary Historical Perspective" (paper presented at the Annual Meeting of the Western Political Science Association, San Francisco, March 1980); Pomper with Lederman, *Elections in America*, Chap. 7; Paul T. David, "Party Platforms as National Plans," *Public Administration Review* 31 (May–June 1971), pp. 303–15.
60. Pomper with Lederman, *Elections in America*, Chap. 7.
61. John H. Kessel, "The Seasons of Presidential Politics," *Social Science Quarterly* 58 (December 1977), pp. 418–35.
62. Michael J. Malbin, "The Conventions, Platforms, and Issue Activists," in *The American Elections of 1980*, ed. Austin Ranney (Washington, D.C.: American Enterprise Institute, 1981), p. 138, fn. 38.

63. Kathleen A. Frankovic, "The Public Opinion Trends," in Marlene Michels Pomper, ed., *The Election of 1980* (Chatham, N.J.: Chatham House, 1981), p.107.
64. Page, *Choices and Echoes*, chap. 4, pp. 161–65, 180–81, 184.
65. John W. Dean III, *Blind Ambition: The White House Years* (New York: Pocket Books, 1976), pp. 389–90.
66. See, for example, Raymond C. Wolfinger and Steven J. Rosenstone, *Who Votes?* (New Haven, Conn.: Yale University Press, 1980) and sources cited therein.
67. For an early analysis of the 1980 election see Arthur H. Miller and Martin P. Wattenberg, "Policy and Performance Voting in the 1980 Election" (paper delivered at the Annual Meeting of the American Political Science Association, New York, September 1981). See also Frankovic, "Public Opinion Trends," p. 103. For a good overview of the enormous literature on issue voting, see Erikson, Luttbeg, and Tedin, *American Public Opinion*, chap. 7; David B. Hill and Norman R. Luttbeg, *Trends in American Electoral Behavior* (Itasca, Illinois: Peacock, 1980), pp. 32–51.
68. William Greider, "The Education of David Stockman," *The Atlantic Monthly*, December 1981, pp. 32, 43.
69. On this see Humphrey, *The Education of a Public Man*, p. 241.
70. *CBS News/The New York Times Poll*, November 15, 1980, pp. 4–5. See also Frankovic, "Public Opinion Trends," pp. 103, 113–17; Gerald M. Pomper, "The Presidential Election," in *The Election of 1980*, p. 87.
71. *CBS News/The New York Times Poll*, November 15, 1980, Table 4. Frankovic, "Public Opinion Trends," pp. 97–99, 103; Miller and Wattenberg, "Policy and Performance Voting in the 1980 Elections"; William Schneider, "The November 4 Vote for President: What Did It Mean?", in *American Elections of 1980*, pp. 247–48; Everett Carll Ladd, "The Brittle Mandate: Electoral Dealignment and the 1980 Presidential Election," *Political Science Quarterly* 96 (Spring 1981), pp. 1–26.
72. *CBS News/The New York Times Poll*, September 27, 1980, p. 4, Tables 19, 23.
73. Miller and Wattenberg, "Political Performance Voting in the 1980 Election," p. 8.
74. Barbara Hinckley, "The American Voter in Congressional Elections," *American Political Science Review* 74 (September 1980), p. 644.
75. Patricia A. Hurley and Kim Quaile Hill, "The Prospects for Issue-Voting in Contemporary Congressional Elections: An Assessment of Citizen Awareness and Representation," *American Politics Quarterly* 8 (October 1980), pp. 425–48.
76. See also Erikson and Luttbeg, *American Public Opinion*, pp. 280–81; Barbara Hinckley, "Issues, Information Costs, and Congressional Elections," *American Politics Quarterly* 4 (April 1976), pp. 183–89; Donald R. Sanger, "Voter Knowledge of Congressional Issue Positions: A Reassessment," *Social Science Quarterly* 62 (September 1981), pp. 424–31.
77. Thomas E. Mann, *Unsafe at Any Margin: Interpreting Congressional Elections* (Washington, D.C.: American Enterprise Institute, 1978), p. 37. See also pp. 39, 46.
78. John L. Sullivan and Robert E. O'Connor, "Electoral Choice and Popular

Control of Public Policy: The Case of the 1966 House Elections," *American Political Science Review* 66 (December 1972), pp. 1256–68.

79. "Candidates' Campaign Costs for Congressional Contests Have Gone Up at a Fast Pace," *Congressional Quarterly Weekly Report*, September 29, 1979, p. 2157.

80. See Mann, *Unsafe at Any Margin*, pp. 38, 74; Hurley and Hill, "The Prospects for Issue Voting"; Hinckley, "The American Voter"; Barbara Hinckley, "House Re-elections and Senate Defeats: The Role of the Challenger," *British Journal of Political Science* 10 (October 1980), pp. 441–60; Hinckley, "Issues, Information Costs, and Congressional Elections"; Barbara Hinckley, Richard Hofstetter, and John Kessel, "Information and the Vote: A Comparative Election Study," *American Politics Quarterly* 2 (April 1974), pp. 131–58; Thomas E. Mann and Raymond E. Wolfinger, "Candidates and Parties in Congressional Elections," *American Political Science Review* 74 (September 1980), pp. 617–32; Alan I. Abramowitz, "A Comparison of Voting for U.S. Senator and Representative in 1978," *American Political Science Review* 74 (September 1980), pp. 633–40; Eric M. Uslaner, "Ain't Misbehavin': The Logic of Defensive Issue Voting Strategies in Congressional Elections," *American Politics Quarterly* 9 (January 1981), pp. 3–22; Alan I. Abramowitz, "Choices and Echoes in the 1978 U.S. Senate Elections: A Research Note," *American Journal of Political Science* 25 (February 1981), pp. 112–18; Glen R. Parker and Roger H. Davidson, "Why Do Americans Love Their Congressmen So Much More Than Their Congress," *Legislative Studies Quarterly* 4 (February 1979), pp. 53–61; Barbara Hinckley, *Congressional Elections* (Washington, D.C.: Congressional Quarterly Press, 1981), chaps. 3–6.

81. Magruder, *An American Life*, p. 144.

82. Edward R. Tufte, "Determinants of the Outcomes of Midterm Congressional Elections," *American Political Science Review* 68 (September 1975), pp. 822–24; Edward R. Tufte, "The Relationship Between Seats and Votes in Two-Party Systems," *American Political Science Review* 67 (June 1973), pp. 547–54. See also Walter Dean Burnham, "Insulation and Responsiveness in Congressional Elections," *Political Science Quarterly* 90 (Fall 1975), pp. 412–13.

83. " '78 House Vote Portends Difficulties for GOP," *Congressional Quarterly Weekly Report*, March 31, 1979, p. 572.

84. Miller and Wattenberg, "Policy and Performance Voting in the 1980 Election," p. 18.

85. Tufte, "Determinants of the Outcomes"; Edward R. Tufte, *Political Control of the Economy* (Princeton, N.J.: Princeton University Press, 1978), chap. 5; Samuel Kernell, "Presidential Popularity and Negative Voting: An Alternative Explanation of the Midterm Congressional Decline of the President's Party," *American Political Science Review* 71 (March 1977), pp. 44–66.

86. Mann and Wolfinger, "Candidates and Parties," p. 630. For data on other years see Kernell, "Presidential Popularity"; Robert B. Arsenau and Raymond E. Wolfinger, "Voting Behavior in Congressional Elections" (paper presented at the Annual Meeting of the American Political Science Association, New Orleans, September 1973); Candice J. Nelson, "The Effects of

Incumbency on Voting in Congressional Elections, 1964–1974," *Political Science Quarterly* 93 (Winter 1978–79), pp. 665–78.

87. Lyn Ragsdale, "The Fiction of Congressional Elections as Presidential Events," *American Politics Quarterly* 8 (October 1980), pp. 375–98. See also James E. Piereson, "Presidential Popularity and Midterm Voting at Different Electoral Levels," *American Journal of Political Science* 19 (November 1975), pp. 683–93. Piereson did find an impact on Independents, however. See also Hinckley, *Congressional Elections*, chap. 7.

88. Kernell, "Presidential Popularity." Hinckley raises questions about the statistical significance of these findings in *Congressional Elections*, pp. 118–21. She also suggests the need to control for strength of partisanship.

89. Gary C. Jacobson and Samuel Kernell, *Strategy and Choice in Congressional Elections* (New Haven, Conn.: Yale University Press, 1981).

90. Michael Baruch Grossman and Martha Joynt Kumar, *Portraying the President: The White House and the News Media*, (Baltimore: Johns Hopkins University Press, 1981), p. 126.

91. Merlin Gustafson, "The President's Mail (Is It Worthwhile to Write to the President?)," *Presidential Studies Quarterly* 8 (Winter 1978), p. 36.

92. James Keogh, *President Nixon and the Press* (New York: Funk and Wagnalls, 1972), p. 59.

93. Haynes Johnson, *In the Absence of Power: Governing America* (New York: Viking Press, 1980), p. 153.

94. "Slow Motion," *Wall Street Journal*, March 6, 1981, p. 1.

95. "White House Pen Pal," *Newsweek*, March 22, 1982, p. 31.

96. Gustafson, "The President's Mail," p. 39.

97. "White House Pen Pal," p. 31.

98. Gustafson, "The President's Mail," pp. 37–38.

99. We have better data on this regarding Congress than the presidency. See John W. Kingdon, *Congressmen's Voting Decisions*, 2nd ed. (New York: Harper and Row, 1981), pp. 57–58; U.S. Congress, Senate Subcommittee on Intergovernmental Relations, Committee on Government Operations, *Confidence and Concern: Citizens View American Government*, Committee Print, Part II (Washington, D.C.: Government Printing Office, 1973), pp. 332–33.

100. John H. Kessel, *The Domestic Presidency: Decision-Making in the White House* (North Scituate, Mass.: Duxbury, 1975), pp. 56–59.

101. See, for example, Saul Pett, "Interview Draws Rare Portrait of Carter," *New Orleans Times-Picayune*, October 23, 1977, sec. 1, p. 13; Richard M. Nixon, *RN: The Memoirs of Richard Nixon* (New York: Grosset and Dunlap, 1978), pp. 935, 945; Herbert G. Klein, *Making It Perfectly Clear* (Garden City, N.Y.: Doubleday, 1980), p. 341.

102. Richard M. Nixon, "Address to the Nation on the Situation in Southeast Asia," *Public Papers of the President of the United States: Richard Nixon, 1970* (Washington, D.C.: United States Government Printing Office, 1971), p. 410.

103. Gerald R. Ford, "Imperiled, Not Imperial," *Time*, November 10, 1980, p. 31.

CHAPTER TWO

PRESIDENTIAL LEADERSHIP OF PUBLIC OPINION

Presidents are not passive followers of public opinion. In the words of Franklin Roosevelt, "all our great Presidents were *leaders* of thought at times when certain historic ideas in the life of the nation had to be clarified." His cousin, Theodore Roosevelt, added that "people used to say of me that I . . . divined what the people were going to think. I did not 'divine'. . . . I simply made up my mind what they ought to think, and then did my best to get them to think it."[1] In 1982, polls showed that the public wanted to lower the federal deficit and did not want to cut social programs. They were willing to defer upcoming tax cuts and decrease planned military spending to accomplish these goals.[2] President Reagan refused to go along.

Presidents offer several rationales for not following public opinion. President Nixon claimed he was not really acting contrary to public opinion at all but rather he represented the "silent majority," who did not express its opinion in activist politics. Similarly, presidents may argue that their actions are on behalf of underrepresented groups such as the poor or an ethnic minority. The extreme case of this technique, of course, is for a president to say that he is representing a future (probably unborn) generation. This kind of rationale is used today on behalf of environmental and energy policies designed to save natural resources for the future population. Presidents have also wrapped themselves in the mantle of the courageous statesman following his principles and fighting the tides of public opinion.

Whatever the reasons given, presidents have generally not been content only to follow public opinion on issues or to let their popularity reach some "natural" level. Instead, they usually have engaged in substantial efforts to lead the public. Sometimes their goals have been to gain long-term support for themselves while at other times they have been more interested in obtaining support for a specific program. Often both goals will be present. In this chapter, we examine White House efforts to influence public opinion, including appealing directly to the public, manipulating the economy, employing symbols, controlling information, and engaging in public relations activities. We also analyze the electoral impact of presidential coattails. We do not assume, of course, that presidents are always successful in influencing the public. Thus, we are equally concerned with the utility of the various techniques of opinion leadership presidents use.

DIRECT OPINION LEADERSHIP

The most visible and obvious technique employed by presidents to lead public opinion is to seek the public's support directly. Presidents frequently attempt to influence public opinion with speeches over television or radio or to large groups. Not all presidents are effective speakers, however, and not all look good under the glare of hot lights and the unflattering gaze of television cameras. Moreover, the public is not always receptive to the president's message.

Quality of Presentation

The speeches of Harry Truman, the first president to be televised, were not impressive. He simply stood before a lectern and read from his text while staring into the cameras. His media advisor tried in vain to change the president's flat Missouri accent and rapid delivery.[3] Dwight Eisenhower's staff, sensing that more efforts would have to be made to exploit the potential of the new medium, hired actor Robert Montgomery as a consultant for the president's television appearances. The results were an improvement over his predecessor's style, but his speeches were rarely memorable occasions. John Kennedy, on the other hand, came across very well on television. His youthful attractiveness and vigor and his intelligence allowed him to project a favorable image to the country. Nevertheless, he was not able to arouse the country behind his legislative program.

Richard Nixon was better at speaking to a live audience than to a camera. He liked to get immediate reactions to his words and then respond to his listeners. Since he could not do this on television, he tended to freeze into a pose of what he thought appropriate.[4] Moreover, his general appearance and graceless mannerisms were distracting. Nixon even hired his own television producer as a special assistant to the president. One of the special assistant's contributions was to have the television camera aimed at the front of Nixon's face during press conferences instead of providing less flattering profile shots.[5]

President Johnson had similar problems speaking on television. He greatly feared making mistakes as he gave speeches before large audiences. Thus, he read stiffly from a formal text. According to one of his biographers, when he gave a public speech "he projected an image of feigned propriety, dullness, and dishonesty." The contrast between the earthy man reported in the press and the image of the pious preacher he projected was too great to accept.[6] He tried contact lenses, makeup, and a variety of electronic prompting devises to improve his television image, but nothing seemed to help.[7]

Gerald Ford's efforts were flat and uninspiring even though he hired a former television writer and stand-up comedian as a special consultant on the White House staff. He had the president dress less conservatively, shorten his speeches, and make them more humorous and less jargon-filled. Ford also practiced his speeches, as when he videotaped a rehearsal of a speech on his economic and energy proposals and then had his "kitchen cabinet" critique its content and delivery.[8]

Jimmy Carter's televised speeches suffered from his soft, soporific tone and an unusual cadence that caused him to "swallow" his best lines. Few people seemed to feel stirred by his words. Moreover, he made little effort to improve his presentation,[9] although he did consciously attempt to sound more authoritative in his "crisis of confidence" speech in 1979, raising his voice and pounding on his desk. The impact of these theatrics did not appear to be long-lasting, however.

President Reagan's experience as an actor may have won him few plaudits for his movie performances, but it has helped him to understand how he will appear on television and how his gestures and the use of his voice will affect his audience. His televised addresses to the nation in 1981 seem to have been quite effective in arousing support for his policies.

All presidents since Truman have had media advice from experts on lighting, makeup, stage settings, camera angles, clothing, pacing of delivery, and other facets of making speeches. Despite this aid and despite the experience that politicians inevitably have in speaking, presidential speeches aimed at directly leading public opinion have typically not been very impressive.

Public's Receptivity

No matter how effective a president might be as a speaker, he still must contend with the predisposition of his audience. In his memoirs Richard Nixon argues that the public cannot be aroused behind the president when they have high expectations and he must tell them that things are not so good.[10] Richard Neustadt adds that the president cannot depend upon an attentive audience. Most people are not very interested in politics, and the president has to wait until the issues he wants to discuss are on their minds for other reasons than his desire to discuss them if he wants to have their attention. This usually happens when an issue in question is pressing on their lives.[11]

The relative importance the typical person attaches to a president's address is illustrated by the attention President Carter gave to setting the date for his 1978 State of the Union message. He had to be careful to avoid preempting prime time on the night that offered the current season's most popular shows: "Laverne and Shirley," "Happy Days," and "Three's Company,"[12] and thus irritating the shows' loyal viewers.

The public's general lack of interest in politics constrains the president's leadership of public opinion in the long run as well as on a given day. Although he has unparalleled access to the American people, the president cannot make too much use of this situation. If he does, his speeches will become commonplace and will lose their drama and interest. That is why presidents do not make appeals to the public over television very often. Despite the fame and success of Franklin Roosevelt's "fireside chats," which were broadcast over the radio, he made no more than thirty of them in his twelve years in office.[13] He knew he had to maintain their uniqueness, and other presidents have followed the same principle. Presidents Nixon and Reagan turned to radio and midday addresses to reserve prime-time televised addresses for their most important speeches.[14]

As we will discuss in more detail in Chapter 4, television is a medium in which visual interest, action, and conflict are most effective. Presidential speeches are unlikely to contain these characteristics. Although some addresses to the nation, such as President Johnson's televised demands for a voting rights act before a joint session of Congress in 1965, occur at moments of high drama, this is not typical. Thus, style can sometimes give way to substance because of environmental circumstances, but usually it is an uphill battle.

Content

Presidents have to contend with not only the medium, but also their messages. Not all presidents are adept at producing speeches that will gain them support. Nixon speechwriter William Safire writes of the president making a "courageous" decision on the invasion of Cambodia and then wrapping "it in a pious and divisive speech" that "only Nixon could do."[15]

The most effective speeches seem to be those whose goals are general support and image-building rather than specific support. They focus on simple themes rather than complex details. This is how Calvin Coolidge used his successful radio speeches, and Franklin Roosevelt did the same with his famous "fireside chats." FDR was more concerned with long-run objectives than with specific policies. He tried to educate the public and build his image, placing events and policies in their broader context. (The only time he sought support for a specific policy in a fireside chat was for his "court packing" bill, and this was a notable failure.) His approach was light and subtle, not hard sell. All of this was aided by his personality and his natural flair for public speaking. He empathized with the people's problems, explained what was being done to alleviate them, and instilled in the populace renewed confidence.[16] The limitation of such an approach, of course, is that general support cannot always be translated into public backing for specific policies.

Success of Appeals

We should not be surprised, then, that direct appeals to the public often fail. Shortly after becoming president, Jimmy Carter made a televised appeal to the American people on the energy crisis, calling it the "moral equivalent of war." One year later the Gallup poll found exactly the same percentage of the public (41%) felt the energy situation was "very serious" as before Carter's speech.[17]

In perhaps the most famous presidential public appeal, Woodrow Wilson took his case on behalf of the League of Nations directly to the American people in a nationwide tour. His goal was to pressure the Senate into ratifying the Treaty of Versailles, which contained provisions for setting up the League. He failed in his goal, however, and permanently damaged his health when he suffered a severe stroke en route.

Despite all these limitations on presidents' ability to exercise direct opinion leadership over the public, they do not totally lack assets. They are aided in their attempts to lead public opinion by the willingness of Americans to *follow* their lead, especially on foreign policy. Foreign policy is more distant from the lives of most Americans than is domestic policy and is therefore seen as more complex and based on specialized knowledge. Thus people tend to defer more to the president on these issues than on domestic issues that they can directly relate to their own experience. Studies have shown public opinion undergoing changes in line with presidents' policies on testing nuclear weapons,[18] relations with the People's Republic of China,[19] and both escalating and de-escalating the war in Vietnam.[20]

Table 2.1 shows the results of Harris polls taken before and after televised presidential addresses by presidents Kennedy, Johnson, and Nixon. In each case the percentages of the population favoring the president's policy proposal or action increased, ranging from a negligible 4% for Kennedy's tax cut proposal to 43% for Nixon's invasion of Cambodia. Most of the changes are modest, however.

Before-and-after comparisons are inherently limited in evaluating the impact of presidential leadership on public opinion. Sampling errors of 3% are enough to make even 10-percentage-point differences insignificant. Or opinions might change as part of a long-range process or due to stimuli other than the president. Moreover, recorded opinions on issues are sometimes distorted by the wording of questions.[21]

Using a different technique, in a survey taken right after the United States' invasion of Cambodia in 1970, the Gallup Poll found dramatic evidence that the public sometimes takes its cues on public policy issues

TABLE 2.1   IMPACT OF TELEVISED PRESIDENTIAL SPEECHES

TV Appearance	% Favoring Policy	
	Before	After
JFK announces nuclear test ban treaty—July 26, 1963	73	81
JFK appeals for tax cuts— August 18, 1963	62	66
LBJ announces resumption of bombing of Vietnam—January 31, 1966	61	73
LBJ supports stronger gun control legislation—June 7, 1968	71	81
RMN announces phased withdrawal from Vietnam—May 14, 1969	49	67
RMN announces sending of U.S. troops to Cambodia—April 30, 1970	7	50

SOURCE: "Equal Time for Congress: Congressional Hearings, 1970," in Robert O. Blanchard, ed., *Congress and the News Media* (New York: Hastings House, 1974), pp. 106–113.

from the president. When asked if they "approved of President Nixon's decision," 51% of the respondents replied in the affirmative. However, when asked in the *same* poll if they approved of sending American troops into Cambodia, 58% disapproved and only 28% approved![22] When the sample of the public was asked about the same specific action without mentioning the president's name, many more disapproved. Another study described the Family Assistance Plan and asked a sample of citizens whether they favored it. Forty-eight percent did, 40% opposed it, and 12% were indecisive. When another sample were told that the plan was President Nixon's, support increased slightly to 50% and, more significantly, opposition decreased to 25% while 24% fell into the "indecisive" category.[23]

Such studies are rare and it is difficult to be sure that the public is really not aware of the president's actions and thus already influenced by them. In an effort to overcome this problem, Lee Sigelman directed a poll in Lexington, Kentucky, in December 1979. First he ascertained public opinion on six potential responses to the hostage crisis in Iran. Then he asked those who opposed each option if they would change their view "if President Carter considered this action necessary."[24] The policy options and the public's responses to them are shown in Table 2.2.

In each case a substantial percentage of the public changed its opinion in deference to the supposed opinion of the president. Between 40% and 63% of those originally opposed to each alternative altered their views in light of the hypothetical support of the president, and the greater the initial level of opposition, the more change that took place (there being a greater number of people who could potentially change their views).

Similarly, a poll of Utah residents found that two-thirds of them opposed basing MX missiles in Utah and Nevada. But an equal number said they would definitely or probably support President Reagan if he decided to go ahead and base the missiles in those states.[25]

TABLE 2.2 RECONSIDERING POLICY OPINIONS IN RESPONSE TO THE PRESIDENT

Policy	% Original Approval	% Approval after Reconsideration	% Change Due to President
Wait and see	58	83	25
Return Shah to Iran	21	53	32
Send Shah elsewhere	74	87	13
Naval blockade	62	85	23
Threaten to send troops	43	73	30
Send troops	29	62	33

SOURCE: Lee Sigelman, "Gauging the Public Response to Presidential Leadership," *Presidential Studies Quarterly* 10 (Summer 1980), p. 431.

Not all results are so positive, however. In one study different samples were asked whether they supported a domestic policy proposal dealing with welfare and a proposal dealing with foreign aid. One of the groups was told President Carter supported the proposals. The authors found that attaching the president's name to either proposal not only failed to increase support for them, but it actually had a negative effect because those who disapproved of Carter reacted very strongly against proposals they thought were his.[26]

A point to keep in mind as we discuss opinion change is that none of the studies we have discussed in this section control for the prestige of the president. Nor do they measure the firmness of any opinion changes that occur. As we learned in Chapter 1, the public generally does not have crystallized opinions on issues and is therefore often easy to sway in the short run. But this volatility also means that any opinion change is subject to slippage. As issues fade into the background or as issue positions confront the realities of daily life, opinions that were altered in response to presidential leadership may quickly be forgotten. This is especially likely to occur where the president's influence on public opinion seems to be greatest: foreign policy.[27]

Moreover, the public is not overly gullible, in spite of what some cynical observers believe. For example, in a conversation about the brewing Watergate scandal with his White House chief of staff on April 25, 1973, President Nixon commented:

> Bring it out and fight it out . . . we'll survive . . . Despite all the polls and the rest, I think there's still a hell of a lot of people out there, and from what I've seen they're—you know, they want to believe, that's the point, isn't it?[28]

Although the president remained in office for more than another year, the public's faith was limited.

Finally, although Americans might be attracted to strong leaders, and, indeed, those leaders whom we revere, such as Washington, Jefferson, Jackson, Lincoln, and both Roosevelts, were strong leaders, we do not seem to feel a corresponding obligation to follow that leadership. While each of the leaders mentioned above had a strong following during his presidency, each was also reviled by a significant percentage of the populace. Only upon their deaths did they attain near universal adulation.

Americans are basically individualistic and skeptical of authority, even though we might admire its exercise—over others. Thus, we do not like to sacrifice except in a period of obvious and sustained crisis like World War II. If inflation is raging, we want prices limited but not our incomes. If gasoline is scarce, we oppose higher taxes (which would limit purchases), limitations on driving (to conserve gasoline), or higher gasoline prices (to induce exploration). Content to blame others for our problems and determined to maintain our self-indulgent lifestyles, we do not readily adhere to our presidents' calls to act for the common good.

Summary

A balanced view of the president's ability to lead public opinion directly must take into consideration both the potential for and the obstacles to leadership. As in so many other presidential relationships, the direct leadership of public opinion provides opportunity, especially in foreign policy, but no guarantees of success. It is for this reason that presidents often rely on more subtle methods of opinion leadership.

MANIPULATION OF THE ECONOMY

Another way in which presidents may attempt to gain support, at least in the short run, is to manipulate the economy. It is something that touches the lives of all Americans and the president's handling of the economy, as we shall see later, is an important criterion for the public's evaluation of his performance in office. It is much easier to think about this manipulation, however, than to do it.

Evidence of Manipulation

The author of a highly original and influential book[29] has argued that presidents manipulate the economy to aid the election of members of their own party to Congress, their own reelection, or the election of a successor of their party. He concluded that between World War II and 1976 real disposable income tended to increase and unemployment tended to decrease at election time more than at other times. The economy is especially likely to be good, he found, when an incumbent president is up for reelection, the election in which the president would naturally have the greatest interest.

The most direct and immediate method of boosting the prosperity of citizens is to increase the transfer payments they receive. (Transfer payments include social security, veterans, and welfare benefits). The author presents some fascinating evidence to support his argument that these payments have been manipulated by incumbents. Most social security increases have come in election years and each, since 1954, has contained a notice with the name of the president on it. Veterans benefits tend to have their greatest quarterly increases in the fourth quarter of election years, and transfer payments tend to reach their yearly peak in October or November in election years but in December in non-election years.

Even if presidents can successfully manipulate the economy to their benefit, however, they can only do so for a short time. The research cited above is focused on election periods. If presidents could keep the economy consistently prosperous, they would certainly do so. The best evidence that they cannot do this is the fact that we have not had sustained prosperity. A burst of increased public spending is likely to be followed by inflation and perhaps high unemployment, too.

Most of the evidence of presidents manipulating the economy is circumstantial. In other words, no one has shown that decisions were made to rapidly increase real disposable income right before an election, for example. If there were no such decisions, then increases in transfer payments would have to be due to causes other than governmental elites manipulating the economy. Moreover, the government provides citizens with many other selective goods and stimulates the economy in other ways. So far no one has shown a relationship between these other factors and the electoral cycle.

Indeed, recent research has concluded that neither fiscal policy (taxes and expenditures) nor transfers policy, which should be the easiest aspects of the economy for the president to manipulate and have the shortest lag time in affecting the economy, are significantly related to the electoral cycle. The same is true for monetary policy. In addition, there is no systematic evidence that unpopular presidents try to stimulate the economy to boost their public support. Moreover, even large expenditures may bring only small increases in presidential approval.[30]

Furthermore, the evidence for even the specific manipulations cited earlier is inconsistent. The eight Eisenhower years generally deviate from the patterns the author found. Moreover, there were no social security increases at all in three of the six presidential elections he studied (1956, 1960, and 1964), two of which had incumbent presidents running for reelection, and the 1968 increase came in February, long before the presidential election. The record on unemployment is also mixed. In 1956, 1960, 1976, and 1980 there was *not* a clear trend toward lower unemployment at election time. Finally, real disposable income was actually *more* likely to increase in nonelection years than in election years. In 1980 real spendable earnings were considerably less than they were a year earlier in every month of the year.[31]

Limitations on Manipulation

There are many reasons why the president cannot manipulate the economy successfully. One is the state of the science of economics. We have not progressed far enough in our understanding of the workings of the economy to make it very responsive to our wishes. We are too ignorant of the consequences of alternative policies to choose the correct adjustments to make to assure prosperity. Many of these policies must be decided upon a year or even several years before they will have their full impact on the economy. The president's budget is prepared many months in advance of its enactment into law and at a time when it is unclear what the economy will be like when those impacts occur.

An additional restraint on presidential manipulation of the economy is our capitalist system. Since the private sector is much larger than the public sector, it dominates the economy. An increase in the price of steel or in the wages of auto workers, for example, can offset a host of presidential efforts to control inflation. Also, world events such as the 1973–74 Arab oil embargo and the subsequent large increase in the price of oil are largely beyond the president's control but may have profound effects on the domestic economy. Thus, government tinkering is inevitably at the margins of the economy.

The fact that the president cannot act alone on most economic policy is yet another constraint on him. Congress must approve expenditures and tax rates. Since Congress has often been controlled by the party that does not control the White House, we should not assume that there will be cooperation between the two branches. Why should a Democratic Congress help reelect a Republican president? Even if the president's party controls the Congress, its factions will not necessarily agree on policy. Special interests may have access to one or another faction of the party and effectively seek policies contrary to the desires of the president. And, as we shall see, the president can certainly not depend upon his own party to provide him cohesive support.

Turning to monetary policy, the president must contend with the Federal Reserve Board. It has the responsibility of controlling the supply of money in the economy and thereby regulating the rate at which individual firms and governments are likely to invest in new or expanded activities. The Federal Reserve Board establishes the reserve requirements of federally chartered banks (the amount of money they must keep in reserve and not lend), sets the "discount rates" at which banks may borrow from the central bank, and buys and sells government bonds. It also decides whether to borrow funds to cover the federal deficit or "monetarize" it, in effect, printing money to pay for it. The amount of money available, the interest rate that banks charge their borrowers, the inflation rate, and the availability of jobs flow directly or indirectly from the Federal Reserve Board's leverage on the money supply.

Since members of the Board serve fourteen-year terms (and therefore will not all be appointed by the president), and since they cannot be removed by the president except for cause (none ever have been removed), he cannot depend upon their cooperation. While he may attempt to persuade them to stimulate or deflate the economy, he is ultimately dependent upon their discretion.

Another limitation on the president's manipulation of the economy is the fact that about 75% of the federal budget (and more than 90% of nondefense programs) is "uncontrollable" in any given year. That is, the vast majority of federal spending is either mandated under existing law or required to liquidate previously contracted obligations. Moreover, most of the increase in the budget over the previous year also goes to uncontrollable expenditures. This reduces the president's flexibility since there are many expenditures he cannot easily reduce in order to lower the deficit or the percentage of the GNP spent by the public sector. Even the impressive budget cuts in 1981 were only at the margins of entitlement programs, and, because they were accompanied by tax cuts, did little to decrease the federal deficit.

A major component of uncontrollable expenditures is payments to individuals: social security, Medicare, Medicaid, civilian and military pensions, public assistance, veterans compensation, and unemployment insurance. Each of these policies (and others like them) entitle individuals to benefits by law as long as they meet stated eligibility requirements. These entitlements are independent of specific appropriations by Congress. (In 1974 Congress decided to peg social security benefits to the Consumer Price Index, forsaking decision making even on the levels of benefits. Naturally, the president is not in a position to manipulate the increase in these payments.) Congress has obligated itself to provide whatever funds are required to serve those who qualify. In recent years the entitlement programs have grown more rapidly than other federal civilian commitments and have made nondefense spending increasingly uncontrollable. Congress has frequently cut the "controllable" portion of budget requests and then increased the costs of entitlement programs by relaxing eligibility requirements and raising benefits.

Other major uncontrollable annual expenditures are outlays from prior contracts and obligations (which the government is committed to pay), interest on the national debt, general revenue sharing (a state and community entitlement program), payments for farm price supports (the government formally reimburses the Commodity Credit Corporation for losses), and deficits in the operation of the United States Postal Service.

Even those expenditures that can be cut without a change in the statutes are not as controllable as they seem. The largest such items are personnel and day-to-day operating costs. The costs of policies like national defense and the National Park Service, which require direct federal administration and large expenses for personnel, are potentially the most controllable. Salaries and fringe benefits for federal employees are obligated for only a few weeks at a time, and appropriations for them undergo yearly review. However, civil service seniority rules constrain decision makers from eliminating employees. Because those with the least seniority must go first, cutbacks could mean retention of the least-needed personnel. Recently hired minority employees usually bear the brunt of layoffs; reducing spending in this way may therefore defeat important affirmative-action features of personnel policy. Moreover, it is hard to reduce the salaries or eliminate the jobs of competent and responsible employees. Aside from humanitarian concerns, governmental agencies must be able to attract capable persons to public jobs and honor union contracts.

When there is pressure to reduce personnel expenses, one solution is to "freeze" hiring. People who leave public employment are not replaced, at least not for the duration of the freeze. The drawback of this response is that it is divorced from other policy considerations. The people who leave may cause gaping holes in the administration of important programs. The advantage of a freeze is that it reduces the complexity and political costs of making personnel decisions.

As long as employees have been hired, it makes little sense to cut their supplies or fail to maintain their equipment. Similar logic prevents the ending of partially completed projects. There is little sense, so the argument goes, in not completing a project and thereby wasting the initial investment. (The counterargument, of course, is that expenditures may simply extend a wasteful project).

Ongoing statutes fix revenue as well as expenditures, and it is often not feasible to introduce substantial statutory changes. This is true not only for the major federal provisions that define tax rates and exemptions, but also for certain statutory oddities that commit some revenues to specific purposes. Visitor fees at Grand Teton National Park, for example, automatically go for the educational expenses of the dependents of park employees; the Department of the Interior receives one-third of the revenues collected from federal grazing lands and uses them for range improvements; 30% of customs receipts automatically go to agricultural programs; revenues from gasoline taxes finance transportation policies.[32]

"Tax expenditures" occur when individuals or corporations reduce their overall income (on which taxes are levied) through the use of legal exceptions to the standard definitions of adjusted gross income. These exceptions are numerous and are known in popular parlance as tax "loopholes." They include special exclusions, exemptions, and deductions, which reduce taxable income (for example, charitable contributions, mortgage interest payments, and certain income from municipal bonds and corporate stocks); preferential rates, which reduce taxes by applying lower rates to part or all of a taxpayer's income (for example, the preferential treatment of long-term capital gains); special credits, which are subtracted from the actual taxes due (for example, the investment tax credit); and deferrals of tax, which generally allow deductions in a current year if they are properly attributable to a future year (for example, accelerated depreciation).

Early estimates of tax expenditures for fiscal year 1983 by the Brookings Institution were about $317 billion (over one-third of conventionally measured federal expenditures).[33] The actual total may considerably exceed this figure. They are of special interest to us here because there is no established procedure for reviewing tax expenditures regularly. They are written into law and remain there unless a special effort is made to alter them. As we might expect, major changes rarely occur. Thus, although the president may propose new tax expenditures to stimulate the economy, in general they are yet another constraint on his ability to manipulate the economy.

Summary

Presidents face severe constraints on their ability to manipulate the economy. They are hindered by the extent of our understanding of economics, the nature of our economic system, the structure of economic policy-making, and previous policy decisions. This is not to argue that presidents have never tried to turn the economy to their advantage. Some have undoubtedly tried. The prospects of success for these efforts, however, especially in the long run, are not great.

INFORMATION CONTROL

A technique for influencing public opinion that is much less direct than appeals to the public is information control. This comes in many forms, ranging from withholding information from the public to lying. If the public is unaware of a situation or has a distorted view of it, then the president may have more flexibility in achieving what he desires. Often the president desires public passivity as much as he wants public support.

Withholding Information

One means of influencing public opinion through information control is to withhold from the public information it needs to evaluate the president and his policies. The war in Vietnam provides many examples of the president and other high officials withholding crucial information from the American people about very important policy matters.

In 1962 the U.S. military commander in Vietnam was ordered to try to prevent reporters from learning that American soldiers were directing combat missions.[34] That same year the Pentagon for the first time revealed that there were several thousand American troops in South Vietnam. In early 1963 the public learned that there had been 11,000 U.S. military personnel there six months earlier.[35] All of this information, it must be stressed, was revealed *after* the actions were taken, precluding any chance for public debate before the soldiers were sent.

During the 1964 presidential election campaign President Johnson failed to tell the American public his administration was planning possible bombing raids and troop actions against North Vietnam.[36] Instead he publicly advocated American restraint in the war.[37] When he decided to commit a significantly greater number of troops to South Vietnam, he ordered officials to keep the decision secret and play down the change in policy. The public was not alerted to the serious military situation facing South Vietnam. No announcement was made that American troops had taken offensive combat roles in addition to their advisory functions. Similarly, efforts were made to hide the fact that the bombing of North Vietnam had changed from reprisals for specific enemy acts to a long-run strategy.[38] Throughout the 1960s and into the 1970s the CIA financed Laotian tribesmen to fight the Pathet Lao, but the American public was never notified that its tax dollars were being used for this purpose.[39] In 1969 and 1970 the Air Force engaged in a large-scale effort to conceal its secret bombing of Cambodia.

In other areas of foreign policy the public was kept equally in the dark. Americans were not informed that between 1962 and 1973 the United States engaged in covert actions to prevent Salvador Allende from coming to power in Chile and then to aid his opponents once he was elected.[40] In 1975 the U.S. secretly intervened in the civil war in Angola.[41]

Pertinent information is also withheld on domestic policies. President Nixon favored federal subsidies for the Supersonic Transport (SST) plane and therefore withheld a negative assessment of the airplane by his own advisers (done at public expense).[42] He also failed to make public a $7 million government study projecting the nation's recreational needs and presenting a detailed program to meet them.[43] In the Johnson administration attempts were made to keep secret the results of the Coleman report on educational opportunity as well as an evaluation of Head Start programs.[44]

The presidents perceived the information contained in these reports to be contrary to their self-interest. Each of these reports was eventually released, but not until members of Congress or the media had discovered them and applied pressure for their publication. The public received some of the information only after it was no longer relevant to the formulation of public policy.

The classification of information under the rubric of "national security" is a frequently used means of withholding information from the public. Most people support secrecy in handling national security affairs, especially in matters such as defense plans and strategy, weapons technology, troop movements, the details of current diplomatic negotiations, the methods and sources of covert intelligence gathering, and similar information about the defense, negotiations, and intelligence gathering of other nations. Secrecy in these matters is directly related to our national security and is essential to providing flexibility and bargaining potential in international negotiations and to maintaining our relationships with other countries.

The question arises as to whether too much information is classified and whether classification is used by the president and other high officials to influence public opinion. When officials withhold information that might aid the public in evaluating their performance in office and in answering general questions of public policy but that might embarrass them if made public, they may provide a distorted view of reality and increase or maintain support for themselves.

The classification system is set up by executive order of the president and is implemented by many thousands of bureaucrats. In 1972, after a major campaign to reduce the number of official classifiers of secrets, there were still 1,647 people in the State Department alone who could classify material.[45] Many thousands more exercise similar authority in the Defense Department, CIA, FBI, and other federal agencies. The discretion bureaucrats have in classifying information, no matter what the guidelines might say, was dramatically demonstrated in Daniel Ellsberg's trial for releasing the *Pentagon Papers,* the secret study of decision making about the war in Vietnam. The director of the study, who was responsible for its classification, testified that he was unaware of official classification guidelines and made the decision to classify it "top secret" very quickly, without regard for the government's own rules and regulations for the protection of national defense.[46]

The Ford administration found there were no clear rules for responding to congressional demands for classified documents. One committee could subpoena the same document from several different agencies, each of which would censor what it considered information too sensitive to be made public. The committee would then receive six different versions. Pasting them together, it could get most of the original document.[47] This shows the lack of consensus, even among those doing the classifying, on what should or should not be classified.

At the end of 1978 an executive order issued by President Carter and designed to limit classification and accelerate declassification took effect. The new procedures ordered by the president established narrower, more explicit criteria for restricting public access to government information. Thus, a document could be classified only if its unauthorized disclosure reasonably could be expected to cause "identifiable" damage to national security. The previous standard allowed classification if any damage could be reasonably expected.[48] President Reagan has tried to retract this policy, however.

It appears that much of what has been classified really ought not to have been. Lyndon Johnson said there was little that he knew as president that was not also in the press.[49] In 1972 Richard Nixon complained about excessive secrecy and pointed out that even the menus of official dinners for visiting heads of state came to the White House marked "top secret."[50] In the *Pentagon Papers* case discussed above, the government claimed that public disclosures of the study would cause "irreparable injury to the defense interests of the United States."[51] A decade later, however, evidence to support such a contention has not been produced.

In 1981 a former State Department official wrote:

> For several years I was in charge of the State Department bureau which was then responsible for the department's compliance with the Freedom of Information Act and Executive Orders on classification and declassification. Based on that experience, it is my firm conclusion that the government's basic problem with information is not that it releases too much, but that it classifies and withholds far too much. Despite the reforms of the past decade, the overwhelming tendency within all reaches of the federal government is to squirrel away information which properly belongs to the American people.[52]

Further reason to doubt the necessity of much classification stems from officials leaking classified information to the press for their own purposes. Although we shall discuss leaks in greater detail in Chapter 4, the following quote from a top Johnson aide indicates the extent of these leaks:

> Presidents and White House national security advisors at presidential direction have leaked more classified information since 1960 than all the disaffected State Department, Defense Department, and Central Intelligence Agency employees combined. During the Nixon administration, Henry Kissinger provided more classified information to selected reporters than they had ever before received.[53]

During part of the Nixon administration a Navy yeoman, assigned to the Washington Special Action Group's staff, "retained" copies of secret notes and minutes and gave them to the Chairman of the Joint Chiefs of Staff, Admiral Thomas Moorer.[54] The Special Action Group was a very high-level group dealing with national security matters, and at least some of the nation's highest ranking military officers evidently felt it appropriate that classification rules would not apply to them.

The classification system does more than simply deny information to foreign adversaries and the American public, as the following excerpt from congressional testimony by Rear Admiral (ret.) Gene LaRocque illustrates:

Classification is made for a variety of reasons. First, to prevent it from falling into the hands of a potential enemy; this . . . accounts for only a small portion of the material classified. Other reasons for classifying material are: to keep it from the other military services; from civilians in their own service; from civilians in the Defense Department; from the State Department; and, of course, from the Congress. Sometimes, information is classified to withhold it for later release to maximize the effect on the public or the Congress.

Frequently, information is classified so that only portions of it can be released selectively to the press to influence the public or the Congress. These time-released capsules have a lasting effect.[55]

In other words, classification is sometimes used to attempt, either directly or indirectly, to manipulate public opinion. This is also seen in the quote from the Johnson aide printed above. The president and his advisors can selectively leak classified information that will be to their advantage.

Naturally, classification may also be used to cover up mistakes. We really do not know what errors in judgment and what policies have been obscured because of being classified, but there is little doubt that many have been hidden from the public. As we might expect, national security was a rationale used by the Nixon White House to support its efforts to withhold evidence concerning the Watergate cover-up from Congress, the courts, and the American people. Ironically, Nixon earlier declared that classification "frequently served to conceal bureaucratic mistakes and prevent embarrassment to officials and administrations."[56]

"Executive privilege," whereby presidential aides are shielded from testifying before Congress, is yet another means by which the president controls the public's access to information. Although cabinet members regularly testify before Congress, Henry Kissinger, who functioned as the most important foreign policy figure besides the president in Richard Nixon's first term, refused to testify because of this doctrine. At one point Attorney General Richard Kleindienst claimed executive privilege for the entire executive branch.[57] Although he later rescinded this extreme opinion, it points up the problems of this extraconstitutional doctrine, which has no clearly delineated boundaries.[58]

De-emphasis

A president can also employ more subtle methods of manipulating information in an effort to influence public opinion. He can, for example, order that information collected by the government be de-emphasized. When the economy was not doing well in 1971, the White House ordered the Bureau of Labor Statistics to discontinue its monthly briefing of the press on prices and unemployment. Similarly, during the war in Vietnam the Defense Department gave much more attention in its public announcements to deserters from enemy forces than to deserters from the armed forces of our South Vietnamese allies. In each case the government possessed information that might negatively influence public perceptions of the president and his administration. It chose not to emphasize this "bad news."

Collection

Going a step further, a president can simply not order that information on a policy be collected. This, of course, prevents the public from fully evaluating his performance. President Johnson had invested a great deal in his Great Society domestic programs and did not want to cut back on them when large amounts of funds were needed for the war in Vietnam. Although warned by the Council of Economic Advisors at the end of 1965 of the need for a tax increase to avoid the inflation that would result from having *both* guns and butter, he refused to request one. He also refused to seek wage and price controls. Instead Johnson kept the precise costs of the war from Congress and the public.[59] No serious effort was ever made to determine the true costs of U.S. involvement in the war in Vietnam, and Americans felt the ravages of inflation for years to come.

Timing

Sometimes information is provided, but the timing of its release is used to try to influence public opinion. On November 2, 1970, the White House announced the most recent casualty figures from Vietnam. They were a five-year low and their announcement was made on Monday instead of Thursday as usual, presumably because the 1970 congressional elections were being held the next day.[60] The Carter administration revealed that the Pentagon had developed a new technology that made aircraft virtually invisible to enemy detection devices. This disclosure coincided with an administration effort during the 1980 presidential election campaign to show that it was working to strengthen national defense. Taking the opposite tactic, the Ford administration waited to announce that the country was in a recession until one week after the 1974 congressional elections.[61]

Obfuscation

Presidents and their aides may also attempt to obscure or distort the truth in order to confuse or mislead the public. President Eisenhower regularly gave purposefully ambiguous answers at his press conferences.[62] A classic example of this technique is an answer that Nixon's press secretary Ron Ziegler gave to a reporter's question about the Watergate tapes.

> I would feel that most of the conversations that took place in those areas of the White House that did have the recording system would, in almost their entirety, be in existence, but the special prosecutor, the court, and I think, the American people are sufficiently familiar with the recording system to know where the recording devices existed and to know the situation in terms of the recording process, but I feel, although the process has not been undertaken yet in preparation of the material to abide by the court decision, really, what the answer to that question is.[63]

In a similar exercise in obfuscation a U.S. spokesman in Vietnam declared that "it became necessary to destroy the town to save it."[64] In a press conference on the war held by the secretaries of state and defense, reporters were told that communist forces in Vietnam had suffered tremendous casualties and that their effectiveness had been reduced. Yet in the next sentence the secretaries announced that communist activity had "increased substantially."[65] What to make of these seemingly contradictory statements was anybody's guess.

Distortion comes in many forms. One of the most common is to provide impressive statistics without going into the details of how they were compiled. In 1982 President Reagan told the American people more than half the stores investigated by the government were selling items that were prohibited for purchase with food stamps. He omitted the fact that the stores that were investigated were ones already suspected of abuse.

President Johnson once proudly claimed that under his guidance the Eighty-ninth Congress had appropriated a record $9.6 billion for education. What he failed to tell the American public was that this impressive figure included about $2 billion for military training plus the budgets of the Library of Congress, the Agricultural Extension Service, most of the Office of Economic Opportunity, and the Smithsonian Institution.[66] Although each of these agencies or programs is related to education in one way or another, they do not fall under the heading of "education" as most people who heard the aggregate figure would define it.

Johnson used a similar tactic when he claimed that the fiscal year 1968 budget provided $26.6 billion for "poor people." Included in these figures were billions of dollars for social security benefits and veterans pensions plus funds for highway construction and urban renewal.[67] Again, these policies are not those that we generally think of as aimed at "poor people."

Presidents have also used tricks to make overall spending appear small. In his last year in office President Johnson introduced the "unified budget," which included trust funds previously *excluded* from the budget, such as those for social security, unemployment benefits, highway construction, and retirement pensions of railroad workers. The fact that the trust funds were running a surplus allowed him to cut the size of the projected federal deficit—at least on paper. (The surplus trust funds could not be used to cover the deficit in the regular budget.) President Nixon introduced the "full employment" budget in fiscal 1972. His ruse was to calculate the federal revenues not at what was expected but at what they would be if there were full employment (which there was not). This subterfuge allowed him to show a smaller overall deficit.

In more recent times presidents (and Congress) have used what are termed "off-budget" expenditures to reduce the size of the budget—on paper. These expenditures are primarily federal loans to the public for specified investment and assistance projects, federal guarantees of loans made by private issuers, and lending activities of federally sponsored enterprises such as the Farm Credit Administration, Federal Home Loan Bank system, Student Marketing Association, and the Federal National Mortgage Association. Although they involve billions of dollars of outlays, these funds are not included in the regular budget.

More dramatically, in 1981 President Reagan's budget director revealed that White House budget estimates were often designed to exaggerate the administration's budget cuts and conceal the size of the likely deficits. Part of this involved "reductions" from an artificially high expenditure base. As in previous administrations, there was both more and less to the president's budget than met the eye.[68]

It is not only what goes into compiling a "fact" that is important for the public's evaluation of it, but also the context of events in which the "fact" occurs. For example, sustained bombing of North Vietnam by the United States was begun after an attack on U.S. barracks at Pleiku, South Vietnam. The bombing was supposed to be in response to the enemy's attack on U.S. forces. However, the administration had already decided to bomb the North and was just waiting for the proper pretext.[69]

In 1964 Lyndon Johnson went before Congress to ask for a resolution supporting U.S. retaliation against North Vietnam for two attacks on U.S. ships in the Gulf of Tonkin. The Gulf of Tonkin Resolution was subsequently passed with only two dissenting votes and marked the watershed of U.S. military actions in Vietnam. As the president desired, it was passed in the context of strong public support for retailiating against "unprovoked" attacks against Americans.

The public might have been less enthusiastic in its backing of military reprisals, however, if it had known what the president knew about the context in which the North Vietnamese actions took place. First, the United States had secretly been gathering intelligence and supporting covert South Vietnamese operations against North Vietnam for several years before the incidents in the Gulf of Tonkin. Some of these activities were going on in the vicinity at the time of the attacks on the U.S. ships, and the North Vietnamese might have thought our ships were involved.[70]

The second piece of crucial contextual information that was withheld from the American people was that there was considerable reason to doubt that the second attack ever occurred! As President Johnson later said (in private, of course), "For all I know, our Navy was shooting whales out there."[71] Although it is possible that at the time the president had honestly concluded that the attack had in fact occurred,[72] there is little doubt that the public's approval of U.S. retaliatory actions would have been more restrained if it had had this information. As the authors of a leading study of the war later concluded, "the second attack . . . had quite possibly been a figment of the jittery destroyer crews' imaginations."[73]

Distortion may also be a matter of emphasis as the following statement about official U.S. statements about the war in Vietnam indicates:

When internal estimates and high-level public statements are compared . . . the two were not very far apart. With few exceptions, they went up and down together from phase to phase. U.S. leaders hedged public utterances in much the same way they hedged their internal memorandums. . . .

What, then, was the credibility gap all about? In large part, it was not really a gap but a matter of emphasis. . . . No administration would ever admit a mistake even if the mistake was self-evident. The pretense of perfect consistency had to be upheld even when inconsistency was blatant. . . .

At the same time U.S. leaders gave a creditable public accounting of their inside estimates and duly noted the long road ahead, they also fostered precisely the opposite impression—that things were going well and that the end was in sight. To be sure, the right cautionary words appeared in the formal statements, but the stress was on the brighter side, the upbeat note. In a few instances some officials made outrageously optimistic predictions . . . which tended to linger in the public mind. Of equal importance, leaders in Washington did nothing to damp down the perpetual outpouring of optimism from the field. They also went out of their way to attack deeply pessimistic press accounts of the war.[74]

When the 1968 Tet offensive began, the president wanted the U.S. commander in Vietnam to "make a brief personal comment to the press at least once each day . . . to convey to the American public your confidence in our ability to blunt these enemy moves, and to reassure the public here that you have the situation under control."[75]

Attempts to distort information are not always successful. In 1971 the United States supported a South Vietnamese invasion of Laos. It did not achieve all its goals, and the South Vietnamese retreated six weeks ahead of their own timetable for withdrawal. Nevertheless, the administration denied that there was a failure, and the deputy assistant secretary of defense for public affairs said the South Vietnamese were engaged in "mobile maneuvering" and proceeding according to plan. However, at night on television the American public could see South Vietnamese soldiers extricating themselves from an unfavorable situation, some even clinging to the skids of overloaded helicopters in an attempt to escape from their enemy.[76]

On a wider level, by 1967 two-thirds of the American people felt the Johnson administration was not telling them all it should know about the Vietnam War. In 1971 a similar percentage felt the same way about the Nixon administration.[77] Out of such attitudes emerged the credibility gap and low levels of popular standing for these presidents.

Prevarication

The most extreme form of information control is lying. Do presidents lie? The answer is yes. Let us look at some examples of lies told directly by the president or by high-level government officials speaking for the president. In the Truman administration a gap existed between what officials were telling the American people about the situation in Vietnam and what they really knew. In 1952, for example, Secretary of State Dean Acheson privately reported that it was "futile and a mistake to defend Indochina in Indochina," but the next day he publically stated that communist "aggression has been checked" and that the "tide is now moving in our favor."[78]

The Eisenhower administration falsely claimed it had no role in the 1954 coup in Guatemala. It also said first that the U-2 spy plane shot down over the Soviet Union was there by accident, and later that it was not authorized to be there. Both of these statements were false. The president was often not truthful in his responses at press conferences regarding his awareness of an issue.[79]

The Kennedy administration also told several Cold War–oriented lies. In 1961 it claimed that the U.S. had no role in the Bay of Pigs invasion of Cuba; in 1962 it said that it had no information on Soviet missiles in Cuba; in 1963 it argued that it had no role in the coup that overthrew President Diem of South Vietnam and that the CIA did not use reporters as informants. Each of these claims was untrue.[80]

The number of prevarications expanded considerably in the Johnson presidency. Thus, shortly after taking office Johnson let his secretary of defense mislead the American people about the situation in South Vietnam as the latter told the press that the South Vietnamese could cope (on the same day he told the president that South Vietnam might fall to the communists even with U.S. aid).[81]

Several interesting lies emanated from the Johnson administration in 1965. The day before he nominated Abe Fortas to the Supreme Court, Johnson told reporters he had not even considered whom to appoint.[82] The U.S. also claimed a CIA agent never offered a $5 million bribe to the prime minister of Singapore. Unfortunately for the U.S., the prime minister produced a letter of apology from Secretary of State Dean Rusk—predating the disavowal. Finally, the president justified our invasion of the Dominican Republic as necessary to save American lives because "some fifteen hundred innocent people were murdered and shot, and their heads cut off," and the United States ambassador there had phoned the president while sitting under his desk as bullets were whizzing overhead. None of this was true, nor was the claim that we were neutral. We really invaded the island to prevent a possible communist takeover.[83]

Two years later in a particularly fascinating but nevertheless tragic episode the *USS Liberty* was attacked by our Israeli allies, and 34 Americans were killed and 75 were wounded. The Pentagon explained that the ship was stationed so close to the fighting in the Arab-Israeli war in order to assist in relaying information concerning the evacuation of Americans from the Middle East and so that the moon could be used as a passive reflector for communications. This was an attempt to hide the fact that the *Liberty* was a spy ship monitoring battlefield communications.[84]

In congressional hearings in 1968 the chairman of the joint chiefs of staff lied when he testified that the joint chiefs of staff had made no recommendations for a bombing program before the Gulf of Tonkin crisis occurred.[85]

There were countless other prevarications from the Johnson White House, some large and some small. The president lied when he told reporters that he had known the massive North Vietnamese Tet offensive of 1968 was coming,[86] and about a wide range of other matters relating to the war in Vietnam;[87] when he denied that Richard Goodwin wrote speeches for him; and when he claimed that there was no connection between a price increase in aluminum and his decision to sell some of the government's stockpile of that metal. He also repeatedly lied about such matters as his appointments, his travel plans, his future policies, his acquaintance with a former protege who had gotten into trouble, his wealth, and what he drank.[88]

Continuing a pattern set in the Johnson years, the Nixon administration issued a constant stream of statements assuring the public that we were winning the war in Vietnam. These statements included inaccurate information on the effects of U.S. bombing, counts of enemy casualties, "secure" areas, U.S. losses of planes, and the capabilities of the South Vietnamese army. In 1971 the secretary of defense displayed a piece of pipe at a news conference that he said had been severed from an enemy fuel line in Laos during the U.S.-supported South Vietnamese invasion of that country. Later it was revealed that the pipe came from an earlier, unreported South Vietnamese operation in Laos.[89]

There were yet other lies. The government claimed that the U.S. had made no attempts to prevent the election of Marxist Salvador Allende as President of Chile in 1970.[90] Nevertheless, in 1977 former CIA director Richard Helms was convicted on two counts of failing to testify fully about these activities before Congress. The president lied about an entirely different matter when he said his lawyer (John Dean) had advised him that capital punishment was constitutional. Dean, however, had simply never looked into the matter.[91]

Last, but certainly not least, we must not forget Watergate. Over a period of more than two years, from mid-1972 through August 1974, the White House claimed that the president had no role in the break-in of the Democratic National Committee headquarters or its subsequent cover-up. This same claim was made on behalf of many top administration officials. As we now know the president and his chief of staff, chief domestic policy advisor, personal attorney, and White House counsel, two attorneys general, leading campaign officials, and numerous other aides were guilty of a wide variety of Watergate-related crimes. The Watergate tapes even captured the president coaching his chief of staff and White House counsel to tell investigators that they could "not recall" answers to crucial questions.[92]

Although the Ford administration was considerably more forthright with the public than its immediate predecessors, it still issued some lies. In a televised press conference following major personnel decisions in November 1975, the president, according to one of his closest aides, "resorted at least seven times to responses he could not himself have believed." These included reasons for his dismissal of the secretary of defense, who had input into various decisions, and who took the initiative in the decision to remove Vice President Rockefeller from consideration for a place on the 1976 Republican ticket. Later the president contradicted himself on the first of these responses on a nationally televised interview.[93] The president also secretly ordered the CIA to "stonewall" a congressional inquiry into possible abuses by the agency.[94]

In addition, several presidential press secretaries have reported that they were sometimes provided with less than the whole truth by the president's advisors. Thus, at times they inadvertently misled reporters because they themselves did not know the truth.[95]

There are also a range of white lies that presidents sometimes tell. Lyndon Johnson incorrectly claimed that his great-great-grandfather died at the Alamo.[96] This seems to have satisfied some personal need for the president and had little impact on public policy. It did little for his general credibility, however. Gerald Ford's press secretary told the press that the president was playing in a golf tournament in Florida only because he was attending a community leaders conference nearby. Actually, the conference was arranged as an excuse for him to play in the tournament.[97] Jimmy Carter falsely told Bill Moyers in a televised interview that he never reviewed requests to use the White House tennis courts.[98]

Information Control in Perspective

What can we conclude from our discussion of information control? Perhaps the most obvious pattern that we have found is that it is most common in the national security area. The reason is simple: it is difficult for the public to challenge official statements about events in other countries, especially military activities, which often are shrouded in secrecy. It is much easier to be skeptical about domestic activities that American reporters can scrutinize and to which they can provide alternative views. In addition, the public can relate many domestic policies to their own experiences more easily than they can relate most foreign and military policies. When officials' statements do not correspond to people's experiences, they have a built-in basis for skepticism.

Information control is employed to deny information not only to a foreign adversary, but also to the American public. In virtually all of the examples involving national security policy, from the U-2 flight over the Soviet Union to the secret bombing of Cambodia, the "enemy" knew the truth. The Soviet Union was well aware of the reconnaissance flights, and the Cambodians and North Vietnamese certainly knew that they were being bombed by the U.S. Only the American people were not told the truth.

The desires of officials to maintain public support may overlap with the subtleties, at least as they perceive them, of implementing foreign policy and result in officials keeping information from the public. In the case of both the 1969–70 bombing of Cambodia and the war in Laos, the administration misled the public to avoid fueling domestic dissent. The White House faced all it could handle. (This, of course, does not justify covert action in a democracy.) On a more substantive level, there was a desire to avoid providing North Vietnam with a pretext for increasing its military operations in these countries or forcing it to retaliate. Moreover, the president did not want to destroy what was left of the 1962 accords for Laos, and he did not want the Cambodian government to be forced to ask us to stop the bombing, in which it covertly acquiesced.[99]

Sometimes presidents and their aides deceive the public for only a short time, presumably to avoid panic or to confuse a foreign adversary, as in the Cuban missile crisis. President Kennedy had no intention of keeping the presence of Soviet missiles in Cuba a permanent secret. But in the short run he did not want the public to panic, and he did not want the Soviet Union to know that the U.S. was aware of the missiles until he had reached a conclusion about the proper response. Similarly, the Carter White House discouraged reporters from thinking that a mission to rescue the American hostages in Iran was under consideration.[100]

The White House may attempt to control information about seemingly minor matters such as a president's appointments, speeches, or trips to keep his options open until the last minute. Some presidents, most notably Lyndon Johnson, have been almost obsessive on this score. They have wanted to be able to reconsider their decisions right up until they were formally announced. Johnson also did not like to reveal his travel plans because they would give opponents a chance to plan demonstrations at his arrival. He also did not want to have to cancel public travel plans because at times such cancellations could create a false crisis atmosphere.[101] He even went so far as to cancel decisions if they became prematurely public, just to create uncertainty about leaks. Many observers felt that this was foolish behavior. His successor, Richard Nixon, gave advance notification of his travel plans without any noticeable problems, and other presidents have not found it necessary to change their speeches or appointments as a result of leaks to the press.

In most of the cases cited here attempts to mislead the public, once uncovered, have had a negative impact on the presidency and the country. We have been embarrassed before the rest of the world when caught in our lies about the U-2 flights, the Bay of Pigs invasion, and similar events. The president has been embarrassed before the country and has often developed credibility problems through deceptions on both major and minor issues. It is not at all clear that the benefits of information control are worth the costs.

No one really knows how many attempts at deception are made by government officials or how much significance these have for public policy. But in the face of numerous confirmed examples it is reasonable to assume there are many more that we do not know about. This conclusion is supported by the following two examples. In 1966 several reporters met with Assistant Secretary of Defense for Public Affairs Arthur Sylvester. One reporter raised a question about the credibility of American officials on the war in Vietnam. Sylvester responded: "Look, if you think any American official is going to tell you the truth, then you're stupid. Did you hear that?—Stupid."[102] In 1974 Senator Edward Kennedy requested information on the commitments entailed in plans for military aid to South Vietnam. When American Ambassador to South Vietnam Graham Martin heard of this, he cabled his superiors in the State Department that it would be foolish to give the senator an "honest and detailed answer."[103]

Information control is an unfortunate and, regrettably, a common technique used by presidents. Their goal is to influence public opinion by controlling the information upon which the public bases its evaluations of chief executives and their policies and upon which it determines if there is cause for concern. Although we have no way to measure the impact of these efforts, it is probably safe to say that some are successful and some lead to embarrassment and a loss of credibility for the president and his administration.

SYMBOLS

The language used in political discourse may have an influence on public opinion independent of the subject under discussion. Language is not only a vehicle for expressing ideas. Words can also shape people's ideas by affecting what is expressed and how it is remembered, by evoking emotions, and by classifying objects of attention into categories that influence how they will be evaluated and what information will be relevant to them.

One important aspect of political language is the use of symbols.[104] A symbol is something simple or familiar that stands for something complex or unfamiliar. Symbols are frequently used to describe politicians, events, issues, or some other aspect of the political world. For example, labeling one's opponents as "radicals," "obstructionists," or "free-spenders" is much simpler than providing a detailed discussion of the issue at hand. Describing a nation's purpose in war as "to make the world safe for democracy" can eliminate the need to discuss the complex decisions and uncertain implications of the war.

Naturally, symbols are not the same thing as what they describe. Otherwise they would serve no elucidating purpose. The choice of symbols inevitably highlights certain aspects of an issue or event and conceals others. The symbolic mode of political discourse, because it provides a comfortable context for viewing the world, may lead citizens to filter new information to fit the previously adopted symbols, affecting their perceptions of reality. Thus, if presidents can get a substantial segment of the public to adopt symbols favorable to them, they will be in a position to influence public opinion.

Use of Symbols

Because of the potential power of symbols in shaping public opinion, presidents have encouraged the public to adopt certain symbols as representative of their administrations. Franklin Roosevelt dubbed his administration the "New Deal," and Harry Truman termed his the "Fair Deal." Each symbol was a gross oversimplification for new and extremely complex policies, but each served to reassure many Americans that these policies were for their good. Similarly, John Kennedy's "New Frontier" and Lyndon Johnson's "Great Society" served as attractive symbols of their administrations.

Symbols are also used to describe specific policies. The draft, which forced young men to serve involuntarily in the armed forces, was rather cavalierly termed "selective service." President Johnson declared a "War on Poverty" despite the fact that many saw the "war" as more of a skirmish. President Nixon went to considerable efforts to have the public view the January 1973 peace agreement ending the involvement of American troops in Vietnam as "peace with honor," clearly a controversial conclusion. He also claimed his administration represented "law and order," a claim that is especially ironic in light of the Watergate debacle.

Perhaps the most important and effective televised address President Reagan made to the nation in 1981 was his July 27 speech seeking the public's support for his tax cut bill. In it he went to great lengths to present his plan as "bipartisan." It was crucial that he convince the public that this controversial legislation was supported by members of both parties and was therefore, by implication, fair. Despite the fact that House Democrats voted overwhelmingly against the president's proposal two days later, he described it as "bipartisan" *eleven* times in the span of a few minutes! No one was to miss the point.

As these examples indicate, symbols can be manipulated in attempts not only to lead public opinion but also to deliberately mislead it. Richard Nixon appears to have been especially blatant in this regard. During the Watergate controversy he repeatedly referred to his unwillingness to cooperate fully with Congress and the special prosecutor as necessary to protect the office of the presidency (a powerful symbol), not himself as a particular president. Earlier, he had John Dean, his counsel, come to his office and look at some budget papers on his desk as a group of college newspaper editors were ushered into the Oval Office. Dean knew nothing about the budget, but Nixon thought he looked "hippie" and that it would impress the young editors that the president had such a young aide working with him on the budget.[105]

Avoiding the wrong symbols has also occupied presidents. When Congress enacted the Model Cities program, it called the project the Demonstration Cities program. Fearing that the public might confuse the original title with the political demonstrations that were then common, President Johnson had his administration adopt the Model Cities name.[106] Part of the 1974 summit meeting between the U.S. and the Soviet Union took place at Yalta in the U.S.S.R. Because of the unfavorable connotations of Yalta, a residue of a World War II meeting there, it was officially referred to as the "Oreanda Summit." (Oreanda was the area where the dacha in which the leaders met was situated.)[107]

The White House tries to label opponents as well as policies. President Nixon's chief of staff, H. R. Haldeman, accused critics of Nixon's Vietnam peace plan as being traitors, and the president made no disclaimer. Vice President Agnew classified administration critics as "radical-liberals" and "effete snobs."

The presidency uniquely lends itself to symbolic manipulation. In his role as chief of state the president personifies the government and our nation's heritage. Presidents use this opportunity to enhance their public standing. They are frequently seen on television welcoming heads of state or other dignitaries to the White House, dedicating federal projects, speaking before national groups, or performing ceremonial functions such as laying a wreath at the Tomb of the Unknown Soldier in Arlington National Cemetery.

The president's foreign travels provide even greater opportunities to be viewed as the representative of America and as a statesman above partisan politics. As he deals with the leaders of other nations on matters of international importance and as he is greeted by cheering crowds of Egyptians, Poles, or Italians, Americans naturally take pride in him as the representative of our country, the embodiment of our goals, and the bearer of our goodwill. As we shall see, presidents are aware of this and may schedule activities so they will be covered on prime-time television.

The president also participates in many ceremonial roles dealing with domestic matters. These include having his picture taken with the winner of the national spelling bee, the teacher of the year, or the March of Dimes poster child, lighting the national Christmas tree, and issuing proclamations celebrating national holidays such as Thanksgiving and Veterans Day and lesser known celebrations such as National Pickle Week. The Nixon White House set aside about an hour on most days for the president to attend to such responsibilities in five-to-ten-minute segments, and the president's staff "was constantly looking out for events that would, by association, contribute to the President's popularity."[108] Other presidents have been eager for the same type of publicity.[109]

All of this activity as chief of state, the president hopes, will help foster the view that he is a fitting head of state and competent to run the country and make important and difficult decisions. He wants to try to relieve some of the fears and anxieties of the public and give it hope for and confidence in the future. If he is successful in projecting an image of dignity and ability, which may or may not be accurate, he will make it easier for people to vest their allegiance in him as a visible, human source of authority and to accept decisions they might otherwise oppose.

While engaging in these and other functions, the president often makes appeals to patriotism, traditions, and our history (and its greatness) to move the public to support him, reminding people of their common interests. He also frequently invokes the names of great leaders of the past, such as Lincoln or Wilson, who made difficult decisions on the basis of high principles, and relates himself or his decisions to them.

Presidents also make gestures to show that they are really "one of the people." President Carter made considerable use of this technique, desiring to be seen as a people's president. He invited hundreds of thousands of people to his inauguration and walked (instead of riding) down Pennsylvania Avenue from the Capitol to the White House after taking the oath of office. Later he conducted a "fireside chat" over national television, seated before a blazing fire and dressed casually in a sweater instead of a suit. He also staged a press conference in which private individuals could call in from around the country and directly ask him questions. On trips around the country he sometimes stayed overnight with average American families, and he held "town meetings" in which local residents could ask him questions. At the White House Carter cut down on the use of limousines and on the playing of *Hail to the Chief* when he entered rooms at public receptions. He often allowed himself to be seen wearing blue jeans.

Failure at Establishing Symbols

Despite the considerable efforts presidents make to manipulate symbols, they are not always successful. The Nixon administration tried to find a slogan that captured its essence, including the "New Federalism," the "New American Revolution," the "Generation of Peace," and the "Open Door," but none of these metaphors caught on with the press or the public.[110] Gerald Ford wore a WIN (for "Whip Inflation Now") button during a televised address before a joint session of Congress to represent his economic priorities, but it only became an object of derision. Ronald Reagan learned from his Republican predecessor and rejected acronyms for his economic programs.[111]

Many observers feel that a president's failure to lead the public to adopt broad symbols for his administration can cause severe problems in his relations with the public. According to pollster George Gallup, "people tend to judge a man by his goals, by what he is trying to do, and not necessarily by what he accomplishes or by how well he succeeds."[112]

The following passage from Gerald Ford's memoirs is revealing in this regard:

> The analysis that caught my attention came, as it so often did, from David Broder of the Washington *Post*. "How," he asked, "did a palpably honest President, who has brought his party back from its worst disgrace, find himself trailing in the race for nomination?" Then Broder answered his own question: "It is the inability of Mr. Ford to define the goals, the vision

and the purpose of his Presidency in a way that gives coherence to his administration and to his campaign."

Broder was close to the mark, but I wasn't sure that even he understood how difficult a task that was. When I became President, I didn't initiate sweeping new programs because it was a time to heal, and new programs, which had to mean more government, would have been divisive at that point.[113]

Jimmy Carter faced a great deal of criticism for lacking a unifying theme and cohesion in his programs, for failing to inspire the public with a sense of purpose, an idea to follow. Instead of providing the country with a sense of his vision and priorities, he emphasized discrete problem solving. In other words, he had an "analytic but not synthetic approach to government."[114]

At the midpoint of Carter's tenure in office former White House aide and presidential scholar Emmet John Hughes reported that

alone of all Democrats to occupy the White House since Wilson, the thirty-ninth President has felt no need to raise any such plain standard. Jimmy Carter has stayed true to the muted tone of his Inaugural Address: "I have no new dream to set forth today, but rather urge a fresh faith in the old dream." Last month, he readily conceded to his guest in the Oval Office: "I guess I may not be very good at slogans. But if you think of a good one, let me know." When asked to speak of any distant "horizon" he might hope to help the Republic reach, after his four or eight years in the White House, he pointed modestly ahead: "I would like the people to believe they have had a government that has been fair to them."[115]

In an interview following the 1980 presidential election, Carter's White House chief of staff, Hamilton Jordan, seemed to agree with the criticism of the Carter administration when he reflected:

My most basic regret is that, in doing so many things, we never clearly fixed in the public mind a sense of our priorities. We had our priorities. . . . But we never clearly presented to the American people a short agenda of our country's problems and our solutions to those problems.[116]

Some of the symbols presidents emphasize may be weak, lacking in impact on the public or in staying power. For example, symbols of the "post-imperial presidency" such as modesty, openness, and integrity, which Jimmy Carter worked hard to portray, were probably of this variety. In the crunch, the public appeared to be more interested in mastery and power. Carter was certainly judged in the press more on the basis of his skills in wielding power than by "post-imperial" concerns for democracy and morality.[117]

The effectiveness of symbols, especially weak ones, are also affected by the context in which they appear. In an interview after President Carter's term had ended, his press secretary, Jody Powell, recalled that Carter had been credited with great skills at manipulating symbols in the early part of his tenure in office, but that things changed. As Powell put it, "A president might look good in blue jeans if it is going well and not so good if things are bad."[118]

In the publicity surrounding the resignation of President Carter's close friend, Bert Lance, as director of the Office of Management and Budget, some observers saw the president's traits in a new light. His self-confidence took on an aura of stubbornness and self-deception, connoting both complacency and arrogance.[119] As we shall discuss more fully in Chapter 6, the meanings people attach to characteristics change even though the president remains the same.

Thus, the public is rather fickle regarding leadership attributes. As circumstances change, so do the public's expectations of presidents. Presidents like Gerald Ford and Jimmy Carter who entered office emphasizing one set of leadership traits may find that the useful half-lives of their images are very short and that they are perceived as lacking in leadership abilities. The potential of the media to influence the public's perceptions of the most essential characteristics and to accelerate the pace of change only makes the utility of symbols more tenuous.

Perhaps it is more difficult for presidents in times of governmental retrenchment to appear strong and decisive and thus capture the public's imagination, unless, like Ronald Reagan, they are attempting to retrench even further. Moreover, the complexity of modern problems and public policies and the many constraints on government may be increasingly difficult to explain.

Summary

The use of symbols in the attempt to influence public opinion is as old as the republic. There is always an incentive for leaders to simplify matters for the average citizen, tie their actions and policies to positive concepts, and influence future thinking about themselves and their policies. Yet the task is not easy. Successfully manipulating symbols to gain public support is just as problematic as are other means of opinion leadership.

PUBLIC RELATIONS

In its efforts to mold public opinion, the White House and subordinate departments employ public relations techniques modeled after those of commercial advertising firms. In other words, they attempt to portray the president and his administration in a positive light through publicity and the provision of information. As a top Nixon aide put it, the big job at the White House is to use the bully pulpit and mobilize public opinion. Thus, "Richard Nixon used to sit around figuring out how he could get a minute-and-a-half on the evening news."[120]

No one really knows how many federal employees work on public relations or how much money they spend. It is illegal for the government to hire "publicity experts" unless Congress specifically authorizes such positions (which it rarely does). Therefore, the various executive departments hire "information" experts and others to engage in public relations. Many of these employees answer questions from the press and the public and prepare information about government programs. Others prepare advertisements asking citizens to join in such widely supported activities as anti-littering or fire-prevention campaigns. Still others promote compliance with federal laws like those affecting fair housing or equal opportunity employment. Yet others encourage people to enlist in the Army, use ZIP codes, or ride the railroads. Nevertheless, the line between *information* and *propaganda* is vague and often crossed.

The White House as an Ad Agency

One indicator of the importance of public relations to contemporary presidents is the presence of advertising specialists in the White House. President Carter put Gerald Rafshoon, the advertising director for his 1976 campaign, on the White House staff. His role was that of a general advisor with special responsibilities for developing and coordinating public relations. These responsibilities included orchestrating the president's public appearances and scheduling and coordinating public appearances by other administration officials to help ensure that they publicized the president's policies and had maximum impact and that their public postures were consistent and not distracting.[121]

This use of public relations specialists was hardly novel. One of President Johnson's closest aides, Jack Valenti, came from the advertising business. Richard Nixon carried the hiring of public relations experts further than any other president. His chief of staff, H. R. Haldeman, his press secretary and later close advisor, Ron Ziegler, and several other aides came to the White House from advertising.[122]

Aside from serving as an indicator of the importance presidents place on public relations, the presence of these aides may influence the substance and especially the timing of policy. Since no president will admit to making policy decisions on the basis of advice from image makers, this is difficult to pin down. Carter aide Gerald Rafshoon told one reporter: "I try to tell the President how these things [policies] will be perceived, but I have nothing to do with making up policy."[123] He did, however, advise the president to take actions such as increasing the defense budget, firing his adviser on women's affairs, and resurrecting some of the trappings of the imperial presidency.[124]

Being human, all presidents are subject to the temptation to do the most popular thing. For example, a content analysis of President Johnson's public statements on Vietnam shows that he varied their content, i.e., their "hawkishness," with the audience he was addressing.[125] The potential for subordinating substance to style is clearly present.

People whose main concern is to make the president popular and whose vocational orientation is to view decisions in terms of their popular reception have regular and immediate access to the president's ear. One Nixon aide reports that White House aides were less concerned with the qualifications of Supreme Court nominee G. Harrold Carswell than with obtaining support for his confirmation.[126] Following the 1976 election President Carter's chief public opinion expert advised him to stress style and personality rather than programs.[127]

There is also the potential for running the White House like an advertising agency. Since an advertising specialist's orientation is to stress a uniform image, the power of such persons can be a centralizing force in an administration. Emphasis on "team play" inevitably leads to the discouragement of dissent and irregularity because it blunts the impact of the president's image. The parallels between this description and the Nixon White House are striking.

Spreading the Word

The primary goal of White House public relations efforts is to build support for the president and his policies. Part of this job is "getting the word out" about the president, his views, and his accomplishments. Lyndon Johnson constantly sought more publicity and even arranged to have favorable articles placed in the *Congressional Record* with prefatory remarks provided by the White House.[128]

Richard Nixon took a special interest in public relations and set up a special office of communications. It tried to stimulate books on Nixon, suggested ideas for feature articles about the president and his family, wrote speeches for leading administration officials, attempted to exercise more control over the public relations of the executive branch, held regional press briefings to publicize younger members of the administration, stacked a televised press conference with Nixon supporters, and pressured the Bureau of Labor Statistics to issue announcements of the number of new jobs created in the economy (as the unemployment rate failed to fall). The office also placed representatives of the administration on television shows and lecture platforms and dispersed information to editors, commentators, and reporters (to be discussed in Chapter 3) and to ethnic, religious, geographic, professional, and other types of groups interested in particular policies.[129]

Reaching the enormous television audience of about 50 million viewers of the evening news is especially important to the White House, and the president's staff builds his schedule around efforts to do so. As President Ford's deputy press secretary put it: "Whenever possible, everything was done to take into account the need for coverage. After all, most of the events are done for coverage. Why else are you doing them?"[130]

Public relations efforts may focus on certain presidential characteristics. Photographs portraying the president as a family man or pet owner are common. In January 1976 President Ford held a special budget briefing so he could display that he was "competent," a subject over which there had been considerable debate in the press.[131]

Many aspects of public relations were employed in the early days of the Reagan administration. The president was careful to focus clearly on his priority item: the economy. Publicity was carefully planned at the time of his first speech urging budgetary reductions. The White House coordinated its efforts with those of other relevant agencies such as the Treasury Department, the Council of Economic Advisers, and the Office of Management and Budget. Press briefings were held, and administration officials appeared on all three Sunday interview shows, Nightline, the MacNeil-Lehrer Report, and one of the morning news shows.[132] The White House paid close attention to the image of the president as well. Of special concern were efforts to overcome the impression of Reagan as remote and passive by portraying him as busy and engaged in important decision making.[133]

The president and his aides tailor messages they wish to transmit to the public to the needs of the press. President Carter emphasized short two- or three-minute statements to the White House press over longer addresses, because he knew that is all that would be shown on the evening news broadcasts.[134] Similarly, announcements are timed so that reporters can meet their papers' deadlines. Those made too late in the evening will not appear in the next morning's newspapers and those made too late in the afternoon will miss publication in the evening papers. Naturally, if the White House wants to decrease the coverage of an event, it can wait until after the evening news programs to announce it. Then it might be buried among the next day's occurrences. It can also pass the word to administration officials to avoid appearing on interview programs or holding press conferences.[135]

Media Events

In addition to general efforts to publicize the president, the White House has often staged "media events" in the hope of obtaining additional public support. In 1953 President Eisenhower, with the aid of an advertising agency, staged a televised roundtable discussion between himself and several members of his cabinet. The program was carefully rehearsed in an effort to appear spontaneous. The next year Eisenhower allowed television cameras into a cabinet meeting. Again, the meeting was planned in detail, with cabinet members given lines and cues to memorize. On a third occasion, the president appeared in a televised "dialogue" with Secretary of State John Foster Dulles, listening while Dulles reported on a recent trip. "Eisenhower's 'peace trip' to Italy, India, Greece, France, and Spain in 1959 was carefully arranged to produce television films of massive crowds welcoming Eisenhower as a hero." Dulles traveled to other countries accompanied by media aides who arranged arrival and departure statements and news conferences and encouraged the networks to attend them.[136]

John Kennedy sat for lengthy informal interviews that were taped for later use on television. He also developed the format in which network correspondents converse with the president. At the midpoint in his term, in December 1962, all the networks carried a live interview in the "conversation" format from the president's office in which he discussed his views with representatives of each of the networks. In yet another television innovation, he allowed ABC cameras to follow him as he and his brother, Attorney General Robert Kennedy, discussed how to deal with resistance to integration in Alabama. His trips to Europe in 1961 and 1963 were carefully planned to maximize their public relations potential, and films of his speeches and the crowds attending them were flown to the U.S. in time for the evening news. Members of the president's family also appeared on television. His wife led an hour-long tour of the White House on prime-time network television.[137]

Lyndon Johnson held two "conversations" with the press, insisting on editing each tape before it was shown to the public. He also became the first president to sign bills into law on live national television. For example, he journeyed to Independence, Missouri, to sign the Medicare bill in the presence of former President Truman, who had first proposed the legislation. He signed a liberalizing immigration bill in the shadow of the Statue of Liberty and the 1965 Elementary and Secondary Education Act in front of his old schoolteacher in Texas. His wife and two daughters participated in a number of informal interviews and his daughters' weddings received extensive television coverage.[138]

President Nixon was second to none in his use of media events. He engaged in live "conversations" with the press; allowed NBC television to film his activities in a day in the White House; became the first president to veto a bill on television; twice chatted informally with Barbara Walters on the "Today" show; was interviewed as a sports fan during halftime of the Texas-Arkansas football game; delivered a halftime message during a professional football game; made a "phone call" before 125 million viewers to the astronauts on the moon and personally greeted them when they landed in the Pacific; and chose to give a televised speech to students at Kansas State University, where he knew he would be enthusiastically received. The wedding reception of his daughter Tricia naturally received widespread coverage.[139]

The president's trip to China in 1972 was probably the greatest media event of all. The White House obtained agreement from the Chinese to allow live television coverage, and the networks sent three large cargo planes of equipment and more than 100 technicians, producers, and executives to do the job. Of course, the White House was not passive in obtaining media coverage. The president's plane arrived in Peking and returned to Washington during prime time. The latter was accomplished only by sitting on the ground in Anchorage, Alaska, for nine hours! The president was very much aware of the huge viewing audience. In his opening remarks at the first banquet in Peking, he referred to the fact that "more people are seeing and hearing what we say than on any other occasion in the whole history of the world."[140]

The next year the president met with French President Georges Pompidou in Iceland. The preparation for the meeting seemed to emphasize image over substance. A foreign service officer who had been assigned to work with the president's aides described their activities: "All they cared about was how things would look on television. White House aides fussed about the lighting, about who would stand where, what the background would be, and the furniture. The entire time I was assigned to the detail, no one asked me a substantive question. I'm sure they didn't care. All they seemed to care about was television."[141] In visits to other countries the White House was ever vigilant in its search for "photo opportunities" featuring the president surrounded by enthusiastic crowds. In some instances the president's limousine left the presidential motorcade and drove into crowds so the president would be seen on U.S. television enveloped by the citizens of another nation.[142]

Presidents Carter and Reagan engaged in most of the public relations activities of their predecessors and added a few innovations of their own. We have already noted in our section on symbols that Carter staged a call-in and several town meetings. He also traveled to New York City to sign the bill authorizing federal aid to the city. The White House signing of the Camp David Accords between Egypt and Israel on prime-time television was a spectacular media event. President Reagan had been in office for less than two months when NBC filmed "A Day with President

Reagan" and *Time* did a similar story. Both days were atypically active for the president.[143]

The reelection campaigns of incumbent presidents are often prime opportunities for the White House to flex its public relations muscles. The 1972 Republican National Convention was carefully planned from the public relations viewpoint. Orchestrated by the White House, it was treated as a television show and gave viewers drama, spectacle, and celebrities. Speeches were kept short and were written in advance by campaign officials to meet the president's needs. Roll calls, parliamentary debate, and other boring aspects of a convention were kept to a minimum and out of prime time. Instead the public saw a film of President Nixon's foreign trips, a pro-Nixon demonstration by young people, or some other interesting "entertainment." In other words, a minute-by-minute scenario for the convention was planned and followed.[144]

Although Gerald Ford was less in control of the Republican party in 1976 than his predecessor had been four years earlier, he and his aides still tried to fully exploit its public relations opportunities. His arrival at the convention was timed so that he was welcomed by large crowds and so that the television networks had to cut into their prime-time television offerings to cover it live on the scene. During the convention the president's television advisor made sure Ford received maximum and positive television coverage. During a movie on Ford's career *all* the lights in the auditorium were turned off so the networks were forced to carry it and not switch to interviews of delegates or campaign officials. When potentially damaging developments were taking place or during convention lulls, the Ford camp had people ready to rush before the television cameras for interviews to direct attention away from, or to spice up, the convention.[145]

In the first debate between President Ford and Jimmy Carter in the 1976 election campaign the president had prepared his opening remarks ahead of time and would have given a variation of them no matter what Carter's first remarks had been. Answers to questions were also preplanned. He was prepared to answer all questions briefly and then to slip into one of seven prepared points and use some of his prepared quotable expressions. Rehearsals were held before the debate on a replica of the stage that would be used, and these were videotaped and replayed for the president and his advisors to try to improve Ford's performance. Thus, the "spontaneous" debate was much less than it seemed.[146]

When President Nixon decided to make the first of the White House tapes public, he and his aides sought to impress the public with the extensiveness of his disclosures. Twin stacks of notebooks, each bearing the presidential seal, were displayed at the president's side as he spoke on national television. However, each of the 50 three-ring binders contained only about 25 typewritten transcript pages. The same material, when prepared for the news media, composes a single 8-by-10-inch book, 2½ inches thick. It can be purchased as a paperback in most college bookstores.

This distortion was not enough for the White House, however. Instead of simply sending a set of transcripts to all 38 members of the House Judiciary Committee, which was investigating the charges against the president, Nixon's aides delivered them in a manner that again emphasized their volume. A station wagon was driven to the front of the White House and, while reporters watched and photographers snapped pictures, the car was filled with 38 sets of transcripts plus four large briefcases containing the single set bound in notebooks. Naturally, all this filled the back of the vehicle as it drove down Pennsylvania Avenue to the Capitol.

Simulating Support

Public relations efforts sometimes go to extraordinary lengths to attempt to influence public opinion. During the 1972 presidential election campaign President Nixon's reelection committee (run from the White House) led counter-demonstrations to antiwar demonstrations; set up mock presidential elections on college campuses but kept the turnout low so that Nixon would have a greater chance of winning—and demonstrating his support among young voters; and spied on and disrupted opponents' campaigns.[147] Perhaps most intriguing was the committee's actions following the President's decision to mine Haiphong harbor. The committee spent $8,400 on telegrams that it sent to the White House (in effect, the president sent telegrams to himself) and on advertisements to make it appear as though there were widespread support for his decision. When the *New York Times* opposed the decision in an editorial, the committee placed an ad in the paper entitled "The People vs. the *New York Times.*" It was signed by ten people who supposedly spent their own money for it. Actually, the money came from the same secret fund that paid the "hush money" to the Watergate burglars.[148]

Efforts to simulate public support for the president occurred at other times. An extensive letter-writing program was organized by the Nixon White House. Women in Washington wrote fifty or sixty individualized letters each week and then sent them to Republicans around the country to be signed and mailed to various publications that had criticized the president in one way or another. One presidential aide estimated that fifteen to twenty percent of these letters were published. The White House also worked with state committees to set up grass roots letter-writing operations. Following one of the president's televised speeches on Vietnam, the White House sent itself telegrams of support. The telegrams, stacked in piles on the president's desk the morning after his speech, made for impressive wire service and television pictures, indicating intense public support for his actions. Frequently, H. R. Haldeman, the White House chief of staff, ordered individually worded telegrams sent to members of Congress from around the country thanking or criticizing them, depending upon their support of the administration. Calls and letters also went out to critics. The president himself was aware of and interested in these tactics.[149]

Another Nixon aide organized the Tell-It-To-Hanoi Committee, a front committee to raise money and sponsor advertisements that either attacked those protesting the war or supported the administration's war effort. He also organized supposedly spontaneous support for Nixon from veterans across the country in response to a speech in November 1969. Yet another aide wrote short speeches for members of Congress to make, supporting the White House and attacking opponents.[150]

Interpreting Events

Presidents also use public relations to attempt to have their interpretation of events accepted by the public. President Ford once hailed as a "hundred-percent" victory a vaguely worded promise from Congress to hold down spending. As his press secretary wrote later, the congressional action "wasn't a victory at all." Similarly, the president told his staff not to be unduly optimistic about the economy so that when things were better the White House would appear in a better light and be more credible.[151]

Sometimes efforts to have the public interpret events from a certain perspective can backfire on a president. During the war in Vietnam U.S. forces were defending an outpost at Khe Sanh. It had no special significance, but it had been built up in the public's mind as a symbol of U.S. resistance to communist forces. Thus, the military could not abandon it as unimportant and had to remain and suffer unnecessary losses.[152]

Others in an administration may also try to place their interpretations on events, and these efforts may actually be aimed at the president. Following President Johnson's famous March 31, 1968, speech in which he withdrew from the race for the presidential nomination in an effort to achieve peace in Vietnam, Secretary of Defense Clark Clifford launched a deliberate public relations campaign aimed at interpreting the president's decision in the way he wanted in order to move Johnson to the next step in deescalating the war. Clifford wanted the public to see the president's actions as a change in policy, that we had reached the upper limit of our troop commitments and bombing levels north of the twentieth parallel.[153]

Discrediting Opponents

Public relations can be used to discredit opponents as well as to build support for a president or his policies. In September 1977 White House Press Secretary Jody Powell passed along to at least two newspapers unsubstantiated allegations (which later proved to be false) that Republican Senator Charles Percy had improperly used corporate aircraft and the facilities of a Chicago bank in his 1972 reelection campaign. At the time this occurred Percy was a persistent critic of Office of Management and Budget Director and Carter confidant Bert Lance. Powell said he had not conferred with the president before passing the rumors and apologized personally to Percy and told a press conference his action had been "inappropriate, regrettable, and dumb." Earlier in the year Powell told a reporter that a close inquiry would uncover improper actions of Representative Morris Udall of Arizona regarding a water project in his state. Udall had been critical of the president's efforts to end funding for some water projects and had been a steadfast opponent of Carter for the 1976 Democratic presidential nomination.[154]

Unfortunately, this use of the press to discredit opponents is not rare. A high-ranking aide to Richard Nixon planted a story in *Life* magazine on Senator Joseph Tydings of Maryland in 1970 when the senator was up for reelection. The aide also organized a "paper" committee to run ads against Tydings on the eve of the election, with no time for reply. The story falsely accused him of financial misdeeds. These actions may well have contributed to the senator's defeat. Similarly, the White House got hold of a picture of Senator Edward Kennedy dancing with an unknown beautiful woman in Rome. This was planted in the *National Enquirer* and then picked up by other magazines. Nixon was also involved in circulating a false story about the chairman of the Federal Reserve Board desiring a raise in salary as he encouraged restraint on the part of others. During the debate over the confirmation of Nixon's appointment of G. Harrold Carswell to the Supreme Court, the White House spread word that opponent Senator Birch Bayh had once flunked his bar examination and that Senators Hubert Humphrey and George McGovern had restrictive covenants in the deeds to their homes (limiting the sale of the property to caucasians). The White House also attacked the patriotism of Senators McGovern and Mark Hatfield after they introduced a bill to force U.S. withdrawal from Vietnam.[155]

Drowning Out Opposition

Members of Congress who attempt to compete with the president in shaping public opinion may face formidable public relations obstacles. In early 1967 while Senator Robert Kennedy was preparing to deliver a speech attacking President Johnson's policy towards Vietnam, the president engaged in a whirlwind of activity to divert attention: he suddenly called a press conference to announce the progress of United States–Soviet negotiations on antiballistic missiles, gave an address on civil rights at Howard University, and delivered a speech at the Office of Education about the state of the nation's schools. At the same time, Senator Henry Jackson produced a letter from the president defending his Vietnam policy; Secretary of State Dean Rusk dismissed Kennedy's proposals as nothing new; and General William Westmoreland issued a rebuttal from South Vietnam. All of these activities and opinions were reported in the morning newspapers, which diminished the impact of the reports of Kennedy's opposition. Johnson's supporters also prolonged the debate in the Senate so Kennedy was unable to appear before television cameras in time for the evening news. An even more spectacular example of the executive's manipulation of events as a public relations move to counter opposition took place in early 1966 when the Senate Foreign Relations Committee was holding hearings on Vietnam. The hearings, which received wide publicity, were not supportive of the president's policy. He therefore hastily arranged a "summit meeting" in Honolulu with the leaders of South Vietnam.[156]

Access to the Public

Presidents have easy access to the public, especially through television. In the Eisenhower and Kennedy administrations the networks usually honored the president's request for air time, but each president had the timing of at least one speech moved back by the networks. Beginning with Lyndon Johnson, the networks gave the president virtually any time slot he asked for, and Johnson did not hesitate to preempt network programming whenever he felt the need. Often he refused to disclose the subject of his broadcast in advance. The networks even converted a small theater in the White House into a presidential television studio and had "hot" cameras manned daily so the president could go on national television at very short notice.[157] By the time of the Carter administration, however, the networks were somewhat less generous.[158]

By simply asking for coverage of a presidential speech or allowing a speech or news conference to be televised, the White House can usually gain substantial free publicity. The president can also agree to appear on a special televised interview or on one of the network programs such as "Meet the Press" (NBC), "Face the Nation" (CBS), or "Issues and Answers" (ABC). Such offers will usually be readily accepted, since the president is the premier interviewee in the country.[159]

The president may also be able to gain access to network television for others. During the 1968 Democratic National Convention, President Johnson was concerned about the possibility of the delegates passing an antiwar provision for the party platform. Therefore, he called the president of CBS and elicited a promise that Secretary of State Dean Rusk's speech defending Johnson's policies would be covered in prime time.[160] Another time he suggested that the networks give Rusk and Secretary of Defense Robert McNamara air time to discuss the war in Vietnam. Two days later they appeared on a special one-hour edition of "Meet the Press."[161]

Almost everyone agrees that the president should have access to free television air time for his major policy statements, news conferences, or national addresses, and the television networks are happy to carry these appearances. But there is a question about the president possibly having too free an access to the public, access which may be exploited for partisan or public relations purposes. Should the White House be able to decide what should be covered and what should not?

In 1974 a Twentieth Century Fund study concluded that the president's access to television was undermining the traditional balance of power in American politics and giving the president an added advantage.[162] Later that year a problem arose when the networks failed to take a White House hint and initially decided not to cover a speech by President Ford. When Ron Nessen, Ford's press secretary, made a formal request for air time, the networks reluctantly made the time available.[163] The speech turned out to be less than significant, and the networks have become a bit more selective. Nevertheless, over a six-day period in April 1977, Jimmy Carter made televised addresses to the nation and to Congress and held a televised press conference.

The problem is really one of equal time for the opposition rather than simply one of presidential access. This problem is very difficult to solve as is illustrated by the efforts of the Democratic National Committee to gain time to reply to President Nixon's decision to invade Cambodia. This was a highly controversial policy and the president made two nationally televised speeches regarding it: one at the beginning and one after it was over. Only CBS made time available to the Democrats and not all the local CBS stations carried their program. Then the Federal Communications Commission ruled that the networks had to allow Republican counterrebuttals to any Democratic rebuttals they carried. This decision was later overruled by the courts, but CBS decided not to keep fighting the FCC and antagonizing the White House (Nixon was angry at it), and further rebuttals were canceled.[164]

Currently the opposition party gets free air time to present only its own State of the Union message in reply to the president's and an occasional opportunity to comment on other speeches. Moreover, the opposition party typically receives less favorable air time than the president and often does not receive a monopoly of time on all three networks as the president does. In early 1981 the networks gave the Democrats a half hour to respond to President Reagan's televised presentation of his economic program to a joint session of Congress. Two of the networks put the Democrats opposite "Dallas," one of the most popular shows on television. When these factors are combined with the differences in prestige of the speakers, it is no surprise that the ratings of the opposition are considerably lower than the president's.

Public Relations in Perspective

We have seen that the White House engages in a wide range of public relations activities. Some are straightforward and are aimed at simply publicizing the president and his programs; others distort the truth.[165] Whatever the intentions of those engaged in public relations, we should not assume that their efforts are always properly executed.

For example, one goal of public relations is to highlight the president's priorities. There are so many demands on the president to speak, appear, and attend meetings, however, that it is impossible to organize his schedule completely around public relations or to expect that his words or actions will not distract attention from his major goals. Both of these characteristics are illustrated in the following example:

> At the beginning of a two-week period in June, 1979, for example, the President [Carter] met with a congressional delegation to try to rally its support for an expected close vote on the implementation of the Panama Canal Treaty. . . . In the course of it, Carter told two congressmen that he would "whip his [Senator Kennedy's] ass" if the latter tried to run against him. This statement became a big story on the evening news. . . . [Two days later] the President introduced his proposals for national health insurance. Before any campaign could be launched to back his legislation, the President left for Vienna to sign the SALT agreements. When he returned he addressed Congress and the nation on the subject of SALT. . . . The President's next appearance on the news took place the following day, when he spoke at a ceremony after the completion of a solar panel for the White House hot-water system. There he urged the nation to give its attention to this important alternative to oil. Three days later he left for a world economic conference.[165]

We should also remember that the public is inattentive, skeptical, and volatile, and it has alternative sources of information. This combination of characteristics inhibits the impact of public relations as much as it does other forms of opinion leadership.

PRESIDENTIAL COATTAILS

In the previous sections of this chapter we have discussed presidential attempts to influence public opinion. If these efforts are successful, the president must still use the resulting public support as a resource to influence others more directly involved in governing, such as members of Congress. A special type of presidential influence on public opinion is presidential coattails. These occur when voters cast their ballots for congressional candidates of the president's party because they support the president. The advantage for the president is that public support may be directly translated into governing support if members of his party are elected on the basis of his coattails. Thus, coattails have great potential utility for presidents.

Presidential coattails are part of the lore of American politics. Politicians project them in their calculations, journalists attribute them in their reporting, historians recount them, and political scientists analyze them. Yet we really know little about coattails. Most significantly, we have limited understanding of how they affect the outcomes in congressional elections. From the perspective of the president, this is *the* crucial question regarding coattails.

Helping members of his party to win election can be a substantial blessing to the president in his ceaseless search for support in Congress. Party members are more likely to give him their support. Coattails are also a tangible indicator of the president's support in the public and his ability to influence its behavior, something of interest to members of both parties. Our focus here is on coattails from the presidential perspective, and we investigate whether presidential coattails provide the increment of votes that determine the winners in House seats in presidential election years.

Previous Research

There have been two principal categories of coattails studies. The first has relied upon survey research and has focused on the question of voter motivations. This research has attempted to determine the boundaries of the potential percentage of coattail voters across the country. A "coattail vote" has usually been defined as one where a person voted for a congressional and presidential candidate of the same party and voted for the former primarily on the basis of the personal appeal of the presidential candidate of the same party and not on the basis of party identification.[167]

Studies based on survey data have not been able to determine the impact of coattail votes on election outcomes because they are based on national population samples. We lack comprehensive survey data for individual congressional districts. These studies have also faced severe difficulties in separating various motivations for behavior when party identification and candidate and issue appeal overlap, as they often do. Finally, it is generally not possible for one survey to determine the office a voter decided upon first (a crucial factor in coattail voting is that the presidential candidate must be decided upon first). Expensive panel studies following voters' decision making over time are required for this, and they are rarely available. Even panel studies cannot solve the problem of simultaneous decisions.

A second category of coattail studies has used aggregate voting data to focus on the impact of coattail voting on congressional election outcomes. Yet these studies have relied upon crude indicators of impact such as comparing the results in congressional districts for presidential and congressional candidates of the same party to discover the extent to which one ran ahead of the other;[168] whether both won or lost, or whether they split the district;[169] the relationship between the vote percentages of the two candidates;[170] the likelihood of a congressional candidate winning his district if his presidential running mate received a certain percentage of the vote;[171] and whether both candidates in a district gained or lost over previous elections.[172]

The principal disadvantage of these studies is that they do not (and cannot) examine voter motivations. This is important, for very different motivational factors can produce similar election results.[173] There are many reasons for voting a straight ticket, the appeal of a presidential candidate being only one. Others include party loyalty, individual issue appeals, and individual candidate appeals. Additional problems in interpreting election results arise from the fact that it does not necessarily take much split-ticket voting to produce split results in a congressional district.[174] And the extent of coattails is not clear from the degree to which a president runs ahead of his congressional running mates.[175]

Some work has attempted to overcome the problems inherent in past aggregate voting studies by correlating congressional election outcomes (i.e., which party won a House seat) with the president's vote percentage in each House district while controlling for the expected party vote of the president's party in each district.[176] Controlling for constituency party strength allows one to take advantage of the more sophisticated technique of regression analysis while dealing with voters' motivations by removing the contribution of party voting to congressional electoral outcomes. At the same time, one can avoid the problems of drawing inferences from split election results or the extent to which a president ran ahead of his congressional running mates.

The results of these efforts are not entirely satisfactory, however. There is only one figure (an unstandardized regression coefficient) to summarize the impact of presidential coattail votes on House electoral outcomes for each presidential election. We are unable to attribute a particular electoral victory to coattail voting. Also, the unstandardized regression coefficients are estimates of the probability of a president's vote aiding the election of his congressional running mates. In other words, a 1% increase in the president's vote in a district increases the probability of a House candidate of his party winning election by a certain percentage. Probability statements are certainly an improvement over previous research, but they still leave us unable to reach concrete conclusions about the impact of presidential coattails on outcomes in individual congressional elections. We need to determine whether *specific elections* are won due to presidential coattail votes.

Hypothesis

Our focus here, then, is on the question of coattail victories for House seats. A coattail victory is defined as a victory for a representative of the president's party in which presidential coattail votes provide the increment of the vote necessary to win the seat. Obviously, if coattail votes determine which candidate wins a seat, they will be more significant than if they only raise a winner's vote percentage a few points. (Presidential coattails may also increase the vote of losing candidates as well as that of winners, but in such situations they obviously do not affect election outcomes.)

If a large number of seats are determined by presidential coattails, the implications for public policy can be substantial. New House members, who might be brought in on a president's coattails, are primary agents of policy changes because incumbents tend not to alter the voting patterns they have established in previous years.[177] Carrying new representatives to victory on his coattails can be an extremely useful resource for a president interested in altering public policy.

In addition, representatives of the president's party generally support the administration's programs more than do opposition party members.[178] Once again, coattails, whether they bring in new members or preserve the seats of incumbents, can have significant payoffs for the president. Moreover, it is possible that those members of the president's party who won close elections may provide him an extra increment of support out of a sense of gratitude for the votes they perceive they received due to presidential coattails or out of a sense of responsiveness to their constituents' support for the president.

To have influence on congressional election outcomes presidential coattails have to be quite strong, i.e., there has to be a large number of coattail votes in a district. Most House seats are safe for one party because of the balance of party affiliates in the district and the power of incumbency. The only way for a president's coattail vote to influence election outcomes in these districts is usually for a large number of affiliates of the other party to vote for both the president and a nonincumbent House candidate of the president's party based on their support for the president. This number must be large enough to win the district from the dominant party. A president's coattails may also save a seat for a representative of his party who previously won election in a district where the other party was dominant in terms of party identifiers. Finally, presidential coattails may make the difference in a highly competitive race in a district with a close balance between the parties. Since we should not expect these situations to occur very often, we hypothesize that there will be relatively few presidential coattail victories.

Results

A discussion of the methodology and analysis used to determine the number of coattail victories can be found in the appendix. The results of these computations are shown in Table 2.3. Over the eight presidential elections from 1952 through 1980, there was a total of 76 coattail victories or an average of 9.5 per election. The largest number of coattail victories (17) occurred in the Johnson landslide of 1964, and the fewest (4) resulted from Jimmy Carter's narrow victory in 1976. The only coattail victory of a Democratic president in the South occurred in 1964.

Presidential coattails are usually discussed in the context of picking up seats for the president's party. It is interesting to note that one of President Carter's four coattail victories in 1976 saved a seat for an incumbent. Maintaining a seat may be just as important as winning a new one, but it is not what the conventional wisdom leads us to expect.

It is also important to note that in the other 75 coattail victories there was no incumbent in the race. Thus, the potential for presidential coattails to affect the winners in House races is limited almost exclusively to

TABLE 2.3   COATTAIL VICTORIES

Year	President	No. of Coattails	President Tied or Ran Behind
1952	Eisenhower	13	0
1956	Eisenhower	8	0
1960	Kennedy	7	6
1964	Johnson	17	2
1968	Nixon	10	9
1972	Nixon	12	1
1976	Carter	4	3
1980	Reagan	5	1

open seats. With the impact of incumbency removed, there is more room for other factors, such as presidential preferences, to play a role in influencing votes.

Warren Miller has pointed out that a president's running ahead of a House candidate is not necessarily evidence of strong coattails.[179] Indeed, it may be evidence of weak coattails since the president was not able to bring the congressional candidate up to his vote percentage. Our analysis allows us to examine the reverse side of this point. As the last column of Table 2.3 shows, in 22 of the 75 coattail victories the president ran behind or tied with his House running mate. This generally occurred in the context of a very close presidential election (1960, 1968, 1976). Thus, it is not absolutely necessary for the president to run ahead in a district to have an impact on congressional electoral outcomes. In a close race a very small percentage of the vote can be crucial, and the president may generate coattail votes no matter what vote percentage he receives.

Discussion

We have examined coattails from a different perspective than is found in previous studies. By focusing on the effects of coattails on election outcomes rather than on the percentage of voters nationwide who cast coattail votes or comparisons between congressional and presidential votes in representatives' districts, we are able to throw new light on the critical question of what difference they make to the president. Of course, the conventional wisdom provides us little in the way of expectations about the influence of coattails on electoral victories with which to compare our results. There has been some discussion of the decline of coattails, however.[180] Our findings support such a conclusion, but the number of coattail victories is too small to reach firm conclusions about trends.

How one evaluates an average of 9.5 coattail victories in a presidential election depends somewhat on one's perspective. Nine and a half is about 2% of the total number of House seats up for election; this is not an impressive figure. On an absolute scale, presidential elections have little impact on the results of elections for the House. On the other hand, from the perspective of the president, some coattails are better than none, and the 13 coattail victories in the 1952 elections made the difference in giving President Eisenhower a majority in the House. Nevertheless, coattail victories are rather scarce, and the last two presidential elections produced only half of the average for the past eight elections.

Thus, presidents cannot expect to carry like-minded running mates into office to provide additional support for their programs. Rather than being amenable to voting for the president's policies due to shared convictions, representatives are freer to focus on parochial matters and to respond to narrow constituency interests. Similarly, although we cannot know the extent to which representatives have felt gratitude to presidents for the aid of their coattails and thus given the White House additional support on the House floor in the past, we do know that any such gratitude is rarely warranted. The more representatives are aware of the independence of their elections from the president's, the smaller the increment of support due to gratitude should be.

CONCLUSION

Presidents are not content to follow public opinion. In their search for public support they invest substantial amounts of time, energy, ingenuity, and manpower in techniques that include direct appeals to the public, manipulation of the economy, use of symbols, information control, and public relations. Some of this activity is quite legitimate, and some is not.

There is no guarantee of success in these efforts, however, and they often fail to achieve their desired effects. As President Carter's press secretary, Jody Powell, put it:

> Communications and the management of them, the impact is marginal. The substance of what you do and what happens to you over the long haul is more important, particularly on the big things like the economy. . . . Poor communications comes up after a problem is already there, if an economic program doesn't work, if it is ill-conceived, or if circumstances change. . . . The ability to turn a sow's ear into silk purses is limited. You can make it into a silkier sow's ear, that's all.[181]

Nevertheless, presidents continue to employ these tactics, adding their own wrinkles to those of their predecessors as they seek public support.

APPENDIX: MEASURING PRESIDENTIAL COATTAILS

Our primary focus is on the effect of the presidential vote on the congressional vote, but there are other influences on the latter that we must consider. Because both the presidential and congressional votes in a constituency are directly influenced by the level of support for each party, we must control for this impact in order to assess the contribution of the president's vote to a representative's vote. Fortunately, as noted above, a measure of constituency party strength is available to us. Because the details of the measure are presented elsewhere,[182] we can briefly summarize it here. Essentially, we triangulate the measurement of constituency party strength by averaging election results for president, senator, and representative in elections immediately previous to the presidential and congressional elections under study. This triangulation of measurement allows us to average out the results of deviant elections. Special care is taken to avoid reciprocal causation and problems in measurement arising from changing district boundaries due to reapportionment.

A second factor that may influence outcomes in congressional elections systematically is incumbency. Incumbents have won over 90% of the House seats they contested since 1952 and have generally won by large margins since the mid-1960s.[183] Incumbents have several advantages in running for reelection, including superior access to campaign funds, free mailings, inexpensive television and radio tapes, opportunities to provide particularized benefits in the form of casework service and pork-barrel projects for their constituents, and a staff paid from public funds. Although the exact relationship between the electoral advantages of incumbency and electoral outcomes remains unclear, scholars have found that incumbents carry a several-percentage-point advantage into their election campaigns.[184]

In recent years the advantages of incumbency seem to have increased[185] as representatives have employed computerized mailings targeted at specific groups, expanded their staffs, devoted more time to electoral activities, and taken advantage of the increased scope of government to provide discrete benefits for their constituents.[186] These efforts seem to be paying off. Research has shown that name recognition (as opposed to name recall) of incumbents is high (and much higher than for challengers), and to be recognized is generally an electoral advantage. Moreover, representatives have been able to isolate themselves from the low esteem in which Congress as an institution is held by the public. Incumbents continue to be reelected by wide margins, apparently because they are evaluated more on the basis of constituency service and personal qualities and characteristics than on policy decisions, and their challengers tend to be obscure and inexperienced.[187]

To control for the impact of incumbency we have coded each election for the House as "1" (incumbent) or "0" (no incumbent), depending on whether an incumbent of the president's party was in the race. Using a dummy variable to represent incumbency is superior to using an interval measure because the electoral advantages of incumbency accrue to representatives very early in their careers and then level off or even decline in future elections.[188]

There are, of course, many other factors in addition to constituency party strength and incumbency that influence the outcomes of congressional elections, including individual personalities, local scandals, campaign efforts, volatile local issues, and population shifts in congressional districts. Because of the idiosyncratic nature of such influences, however, we cannot control for them in any systematic way, and there is no reason to think that they systematically affect the relationship between the presidential and congressional votes.

The first step of the analysis is to eliminate all representatives who won election by 90% or more of the vote, since these seats were actually or effectively uncontested and coattails must be irrelevant to the election results. We then focus only on the electoral percentages of candidates, both winners and losers, of the president's party, because we cannot sensibly argue that presidential coattails aid candidates of the *other* party. Losing presidential candidates may have coattails of their own, of course, but here we are interested only in the congressional election outcomes affected by the winning presidential candidate's coattails because of the implications of this for the president's ability to govern.

We also must take into consideration that Democratic candidates have traditionally won almost all of the House seats in the South because of the one-party system that characterized that region. Since Democrats have won almost all the House seats regardless of the success of the Democratic presidential nominee, we would expect coattails to be weak in the South. There has been little potential for the president's vote to affect election outcomes for Southern House seats. The lack of correlation between the electoral results in presidential and House races in the South may weaken the relationships for the country as a whole and mask stronger relationships that exist in the North. Thus, because the South is such an anomaly in constituency party strength, it is important that we analyze the eleven states of the Confederacy separately from the rest of the country in years in which a Democrat won the presidency (1960, 1964, and 1976).

Our basic task is to isolate the impact of the presidential vote on the congressional vote and then see if this impact is critical in determining the outcomes of elections for the House. What seems to be the easiest approach is to place constituency party strength, incumbency, and the president's vote in an equation as independent variables and regress them with the congressional vote. By controlling for constituency party strength and incumbency, we would obtain an estimate of the impact of the presidential vote on the congressional vote.

Unfortunately, there are two fundamental problems with such a strategy, one theoretical and one methodological. To place all three variables in the same equation, we would have to presume that the three independent variables (constituency party strength, incumbency, and presidential vote) affect the congressional vote simultaneously. They do not, as we know, because constituency party strength and incumbency occur prior to the presidential vote, and constituency party strength influences it as well as the congressional vote. Thus, constituency party strength is causally and temporally prior to presidential vote, and we must allow it to account for as much variation in the congressional vote as possible before we examine the impact of the presidential vote. Equally important, constituency party strength and presidential vote are highly correlated and regression inappropriately apportions the variance in the congressional vote they appear to explain, artificially reducing the true impact of constituency party strength and increasing that of the presidential vote. Thus, to avoid both these problems we must calculate the impact of the president's vote on the congressional vote by following the procedure presented below.

It is clear, then, that we cannot have the three independent variables in the same equation. Instead, we will do the next best thing and see how the presidential vote correlates with what is left unexplained by constituency party strength and incumbency (i.e., the residual). In this manner we can still estimate the impact of presidential vote on the congressional vote.

For each presidential election the congressional vote percentage (CV) for those of the president's party is regressed on constituency party strength (CPS) and incumbency (I). From these regressions we derive constants and unstandardized regression coefficients (b) representing the impact of these variables on the congressional vote in each presidential election. These are used in equation (1) below.

The contributions of constituency party strength and incumbency to the vote of *each* candidate of the president's party is estimated for each presidential election through the use of equation (1).

(1) $CV_1 = a + b_1 \cdot CPS + b_2 \cdot I$

where CV_1 = congressional vote percentage

b_1 = unstandardized regression coefficient for the relationship between CPS and CV

CPS = constituency party strength

b_2 = unstandardized regression coefficient for the relationship between I and CV

I = incumbency

The resulting figure for each candidate of the president's party represents the vote we can expect each would have received on the basis of constituency party strength and incumbency alone, without help from the president's coattails.

As the R^2s in Table 2.4 indicate, most of the variance in the percentage of the congressional vote received by the candidates of the president's party is explained by constituency party strength and incumbency. This

TABLE 2.4 PERCENT OF VARIANCE IN CONGRESSIONAL VOTE
EXPLAINED BY EQUATION (1)

Election	R^2	N
1952	.68	333
1956	.78	361
1960 (ND)	.77	316
(SD)	.71	41
1964 (ND)	.76	313
(SD)	.49	67
1968	.79	386
1972	.71	366
1976 (ND)	.66	303
(SD)	.61	75
1980	.74	380

ND = Northern Democrats
SD = Southern Democrats

is consistent with Hinckley's conclusion that "once party and incumbency influences are identified, there is not much variation left to explain."[189] This does not bode well for the importance of the presidential vote in explaining the congressional vote, but we must investigate further to learn whether the presidential vote provides the increment of vote necessary to explain electoral victories.

To answer this question we must regress the residuals in each district with the president's vote in that district and obtain an unstandardized regression coefficient for each election representing the relationship between the presidential vote and that portion of the congressional vote that remains unexplained by equation (1). As the R^2s in Table 2.5 indicate, these relationships are generally weak and are often close to zero.

We then multiply the unstandardized regression coefficients by the residual for each candidate of the president's party. The resulting figure is the percentage of the candidate's vote that we can attribute to the president's coattails. We have one more step, however. We must subtract this percentage from the total vote percentage of each candidate. If the remaining vote percentage is sufficient for a candidate's victory, we conclude that the outcome is not dependent upon the president's coattails. For example, we may find that a winning candidate received 4% of the vote due to presidential coattails. If this candidate received a total of 60% of the vote, then 56% of the total vote (60% − 4%) was due to factors other than presidential coattails. Since 56% is sufficient to win an election, the outcome of the election was not determined by presidential coattails.

TABLE 2.5 CORRELATION BETWEEN PRESIDENTIAL VOTE AND
RESIDUALS OF EQUATION (1)

Election	R^2
1952	.19
1956	.11
1960 (ND)	.10
(SD)	.00
1964 (ND)	.07
(SD)	.17
1968	.10
1972	.07
1976 (ND)	.04
(SD)	.00
1980	.03

ND = Northern Democrats
SD = Southern Democrats

NOTES

1. My italics. Emmet John Hughes, "Presidency vs. Jimmy Carter," *Fortune*, December 4, 1978, pp. 62, 64.
2. Jon Margolis, "Polls Show Americans Have Changed Their Minds Since Reagan's Election," Bryan–College Station *Eagle*, March 21, 1982, p. 11A.
3. Newton Minow, John B. Martin, and Lee M. Mitchell, *Presidential Television* (New York: Basic Books, 1973), p. 33.
4. William Safire, *Before the Fall: An Inside View of the Pre-Watergate White House* (New York: Doubleday, 1975), p. 537.
5. David Wise, *The Politics of Lying: Government Deception, Secrecy, and Power* (New York: Vintage, 1973), pp. 377–78.
6. Doris Kearns, *Lyndon Johnson and the American Dream* (New York: Harper and Row, 1976), p. 303.
7. Minow, et al., *Presidential Television*, p. 47.
8. Gerald R. Ford, *A Time to Heal* (New York: Harper and Row and Reader's Digest, 1979), pp. 261–62, 376–77.
9. James Fallows, "The Passionless Presidency: The Trouble with Jimmy Carter's Administration," *Atlantic Monthly*, May 1979, p. 44.
10. Richard M. Nixon, *RN: The Memoirs of Richard Nixon* (New York: Grosset and Dunlap, 1978), pp. 726, 731–32.
11. Richard E. Neustadt, *Presidential Power: The Politics of Leadership from FDR to Carter* (New York: Wiley, 1980), pp. 73–78.
12. "Prime Concern," *Newsweek*, December 19, 1977, p. 17.
13. Arthur M. Schlesinger, Jr., *A Thousand Days: John F. Kennedy in the White House* (Boston: Houghton Mifflin, 1965), p. 715. He, his wife, and his aides made hundreds of traditional speeches over the radio, however. See Minow, et al., *Presidential Television*, pp. 30–32.

14. Herbert G. Klein, *Making It Perfectly Clear* (Garden City, N.Y.: Doubleday, 1980), p. 428. See Richard Nixon's fifth television interview with David Frost for the former president's view on going to the people too often.
15. Safire, *Before the Fall*, p. 187. See also Henry Kissinger, *White House Years* (Boston: Little, Brown, 1979), pp. 504–5, 515.
16. Minow, et al., *Presidential Television*, p. 30; Elmer E. Cornwell, Jr., *The Presidency and the Press* (Morristown, N.J.: General Learning Press, 1974), p. 10.
17. "Carter Fails to Educate Public on Energy Crisis," *New Orleans Times-Picayune*, April 30, 1978, section 1, p. 21. For examples from other presidents see Walter Bunge, Robert Hudson, and Chung Woo Suh, "Johnson Information Strategy for Vietnam: An Evaluation," *Journalism Quarterly* 45 (Autumn 1968), pp. 419–25; Halford Ross Ryan, "Harry S. Truman: A Misdirected Defense for MacArthur's Dismissal," *Presidential Studies Quarterly* 11 (Fall 1981), pp. 576–82.
18. Eugene J. Rossi, "Mass and Attentive Opinion on Nuclear Weapons Tests and Fallout, 1954–1963," *Public Opinion Quarterly* 29 (Summer 1965), pp. 280–97.
19. Robert S. Erikson, Norman R. Luttbeg, and Kent L. Tedin, *American Public Opinion: Its Origins, Content, and Impact*, 2nd ed. (New York: Wiley, 1980), p. 144.
20. John E. Mueller, *War, Presidents and Public Opinion* (New York: Wiley, 1973), pp. 69–74.
21. Lee Sigelman, "Gauging the Public Response to Presidential Leadership," *Presidential Studies Quarterly* 10 (Summer 1980), pp. 428–29; Lee Sigelman, "Rallying to the President's Support: A Reappraisal of the Evidence," *Polity* 11 (Summer 1979), pp. 542–61.
22. Michael Wheeler, *Lies, Damn Lies, and Statistics: The Manipulation of Public Opinion in America* (New York: Liveright, 1976), pp. 146–47.
23. Carey Rosen, "A Test of Presidential Leadership of Public Opinion: The Split-Ballot Technique," *Polity* 6 (Winter 1973), pp. 282–90.
24. Sigelman, "Gauging the Public Response."
25. "Most Utah Residents Say 'No' to MX Missile Deployment," Bryan–College Station *Eagle*, September 15, 1981, p. 5A.
26. Lee Sigelman and Carol K. Sigelman, "Presidential Leadership of Public Opinion: From 'Benevolent Leader' to Kiss of Death?", *Experimental Study of Politics* 7 (No. 3, 1981), pp. 1–22.
27. See, for example, "An Editors' Report on the Yankelovich, Skelly and White 'Mushiness Index,' " *Public Opinion*, April–May 1981, pp. 50–51.
28. Theodore H. White, *Breach of Faith* (New York: Dell, 1976), pp. 415–16.
29. Edward R. Tufte, *Political Control of the Economy* (Princeton, N.J.: Princeton University Press, 1978).
30. David G. Golden and James M. Poterba, "The Price of Popularity: The Political Business Cycle Reexamined," *American Journal of Political Science* 24 (November 1980), pp. 696–714; Nathaniel Beck, "Presidential Influence on the Federal Reserve in the 1970s," *American Journal of Political Science* 26 (August 1982), pp. 415–45.
31. "Real Earnings in February 1981," *United States Department of Labor News*, March 24, 1981, p. 2.

32. Murray L. Weidenbaum, "Institutional Obstacles to Reallocating Government Expenditures," in Robert H. Haveman and Julius Margolis, eds., *Public Expenditures and Policy Analysis* (Chicago: Markham, 1970), pp. 243–44.
33. Joseph A. Pechman, ed., *Setting National Priorities: The 1983 Budget* (Washington, D.C.: Brookings Institution, 1982), Appendix B.
34. William McGaffin and Erwin Knoll, *Anything but the Truth* (New York: Putnam's, 1968), p. 79.
35. Wise, *Politics of Lying*, p. 57.
36. Leslie H. Gelb with Richard K. Betts, *The Irony of Vietnam: The System Worked* (Washington, D.C.: Brookings Institution, 1979), pp. 103–4; *The Pentagon Papers* (New York: Bantam, 1971), chap. 5.
37. See, for example, John M. Orman, *Presidential Secrecy and Deception: Beyond the Power to Persuade* (Westport, Conn.: Greenwood Press, 1980), p. 98.
38. Gelb with Betts, *Irony of Vietnam*, p. 315; Wise, *Politics of Lying*, pp. 66–69; Robert L. Gallucci, *Neither Peace nor Honor: The Politics of American Military Policy in Viet-Nam* (Baltimore: Johns Hopkins University Press, 1975), pp. 40–41; Herbert Y. Schandler, *The Unmaking of a President: Lyndon Johnson and Vietnam* (Princeton, N.J.: Princeton University Press, 1977), pp. 15, 21–22; Hugh Sidey, *A Very Personal Presidency: Lyndon Johnson in the White House* (New York: Atheneum, 1968), p. 180; Larry Berman, *Planning a Tragedy: The Americanization of the War in Vietnam* (New York: Norton, 1982), p. 57.
39. Orman, *Presidential Secrecy*, pp. 99–106; William Colby, *Honorable Men: My Life in the CIA* (New York: Simon and Schuster, 1978), chap. 6.
40. Kissinger, *White House Years*, chap. 17; Colby, *Honorable Men*, pp. 303–5, 380; Henry Kissinger, *Years of Upheaval* (Boston: Little, Brown, 1982), chap. 9.
41. See Morton H. Halperin and David H. Hoffman, *Top Secret: National Security and the Right to Know* (Washington, D.C.: New Republic Books, 1977), pp. 21–24.
42. "SST Report," *Congressional Quarterly Weekly Report*, August 28, 1971, p. 1830.
43. Jack Anderson, "A Blueprint for Recreation," *Washington Post*, July 21, 1974, section C, p. 7.
44. James S. Coleman, *Policy Research in the Social Sciences* (Morristown, N.J.: General Learning Press, 1972), pp. 13–14.
45. United States Department of State, *Freedom of Information* (Washington, D.C.: U.S. Government Printing Office, 1974).
46. " 'Top Secret' Tag Routine Jury is Told," *Washington Post*, April 24, 1973, section A, pp. 1, 15.
47. Ron Nessen, *It Sure Looks Different from the Inside* (Chicago: Playboy Press, 1978), p. 61.
48. "New Rules for Classifying Information Set by Carter," *Congressional Quarterly Weekly Report*, July 8, 1978, p. 1747.
49. Patrick J. McGarvey, *C.I.A.: The Myth and the Madness* (Baltimore: Penguin Books, 1973), pp. 31–32.
50. Wise, *Politics of Lying*, p. 101.
51. William E. Porter, *Assault on the Media: The Nixon Years* (Ann Arbor, Mich.: University of Michigan Press, 1976), p. 88.
52. Hodding Carter III, "Less Freedom of Information Means Less Freedom," *Wall Street Journal*, May 25, 1981, p. 23. See also the testimony of William G.

Florence before the House Subcommittee on Foreign Operations and Government Information, June 24, 1971, cited in Richard L. Worsnop, "Secrecy in Government," *Editorial Research Reports*, August 18, 1971, p. 648; Theodore C. Sorenson, *Watchmen in the Night* (Cambridge, Mass.: MIT Press, 1975), p. 104; McGarvey, *C.I.A.*, p. 233; Nessen, *It Sure Looks Different From the Inside*, pp. 351–52; Michael Baruch Grossman and Martha Joynt Kumar, *Portraying the President: The White House and the News Media* (Baltimore: Johns Hopkins University Press, 1981), p. 179; Klein, *Making It Perfectly Clear*, p. 186; Hoyt Purvis, ed., *The Presidency and the Press* (Austin, Tex.: Lyndon B. Johnson School of Public Affairs, 1976), pp. 32, 44.

53. Joseph A. Califano, Jr., *A Presidential Nation* (New York: Norton, 1975), p. 193.

54. Porter, *Assault on the Media*, pp. 141–42; John Ehrlichman, *Witness to Power: The Nixon Years* (New York: Simon and Schuster, 1982), pp. 303–10.

55. Quoted in Norman Dorsen and Stephen Gillers, eds., *None of Your Business: Government Secrecy in America* (New York: Penguin Books, 1974), p. 73.

56. Carter, "Less Freedom of Information Means Less Freedom," p. 23.

57. Raoul Berger, *Executive Privilege: A Constitutional Myth* (Cambridge, Mass.: Harvard University Press, 1974), pp. 254–55.

58. For a full discussion of this question, see *Ibid.*

59. Kearns, *Lyndon Johnson*, pp. 296–97. See also p. 281.

60. Wise, *Politics of Lying*, p. 452.

61. Nessen, *It Sure Looks Different*, p. 76.

62. Fred I. Greenstein, "Eisenhower as an Activist President: A Look at New Evidence," *Political Science Quarterly* 94 (Winter 1979–80), pp. 588–90.

63. Israel Shenker, "Obfuscation Foes Against Ziegler and an Air Attaché," *New York Times*, November 28, 1974, section 1, p. 35. See also Klein, *Making It Perfectly Clear*, p. 204.

64. Don Oberdorfer, *TET!* (Garden City, N.Y.: Doubleday, 1971), p. 185.

65. Schandler, *Unmaking of a President*, p. 49.

66. McGaffin and Knoll, *Anything but the Truth*, p. 162.

67. *Ibid.*

68. William Greider, "The Education of David Stockman," *Atlantic Monthly*, December 1981, p. 51.

69. Gelb with Betts, *Irony of Vietnam*, p. 105; Wise, *Politics of Lying*, p. 41; Townsend Hoopes, *The Limits of Intervention*, rev. ed. (New York: McKay, 1973), p. 30.

70. Gelb with Betts, *Irony of Vietnam*, pp. 102–3; *Pentagon Papers*, chap. 3 and pp. 259–60; Wise, *Politics of Lying*, pp. 62–66; Joseph C. Goulden, *Truth Is the First Casualty* (Chicago: Rand McNally, 1969), chap. 3 and pp. 122–41; Colby, *Honorable Men*, pp. 170–71.

71. Quoted in Goulden, *Truth is the First Casualty*, p. 160. See also pp. 142–80 and Wise, *Politics of Lying*, pp. 62–65.

72. See, for example, *Pentagon Papers*, pp. 262–63.

73. Gelb with Betts, *Irony of Vietnam*, p. 104.

74. *Ibid.*, pp. 320–21.

75. Schandler, *Unmaking of a President*, p. 83.

76. A similar sequence of events occurred during the 1968 Tet battle. See Oberdorfer, *TET!*, p. 159.
77. Mueller, *War, Presidents and Public Opinion*, pp. 112–13.
78. Gelb with Betts, *Irony of Vietnam*, pp. 48–49, 311.
79. Greenstein, "Eisenhower as an Activist President," p. 588.
80. Gelb with Betts, *Irony of Vietnam*, pp. 86–91; Wise, *Politics of Lying*, pp. 58–59; *Pentagon Papers*, chap. 4; Colby, *Honorable Men*, p. 377; Berman, *Planning a Tragedy*, pp. 23–29.
81. Paul Freedenberg, *The Rhetoric of Vietnam: Reaction to Adversity* (Unpublished dissertation, University of Chicago, 1972), p. 48; "Secretary McNamara Reports on the Situation in Vietnam," *Department of State Bulletin*, January 13, 1964, p. 46.
82. Sidey, *Very Personal Presidency*, pp. 172–73.
83. *Ibid.*, p. 178; Wise, *Politics of Lying*, pp. 60–61.
84. Goulden, *Truth is the First Casualty*, pp. 100–4; Phil G. Goulding, *Confirm or Deny* (New York: Harper and Row, 1970), chap. 4.
85. Gelb with Betts, *Irony of Vietnam*, p. 104, fn. 31.
86. *Pentagon Papers*, p. 592.
87. David Halberstam, *The Powers That Be* (New York: Knopf, 1979), pp. 475–77.
88. Sidey, *Very Personal Presidency*, chap. 7.
89. Wise, *Politics of Lying*, pp. 71–72.
90. On this, see Colby, *Honorable Men*, pp. 303–4, 380.
91. John Dean, *Blind Ambition: The White House Years* (New York: Simon and Schuster, 1976), p. 138.
92. *The White House Transcripts* (New York: Bantam Books, 1974), p. 171.
93. Robert T. Hartmann, *Palace Politics: An Inside Account of the Ford Years* (New York: McGraw-Hill, 1980), pp. 369, 376–77; Ford, *Time to Heal*, p. 330. See also Hartmann, p. 229.
94. Colby, *Honorable Men*, pp. 16–17, 19.
95. Nessen, *It Sure Looks Different*, p. 132, 203, 352; J. F. terHorst, "What the Press Must Do," *Newsweek*, December 9, 1974, p. 15; Purvis, *The Presidency and the Press*, pp. 34, 36, 38; Jerald F. terHorst, *Gerald Ford and the Future of the Presidency* (New York: The Third Press, 1974), pp. 234–35. See also Nessen, p. 351.
96. Christian, *The President Steps Down*, pp. 219–20.
97. Nessen, *It Sure Looks Different*, p. 351. See also pp. 29–30, 36.
98. Fallows, "Passionless Presidency," p. 38.
99. See, for example, Kissinger, *White House Years*, pp. 252, 453.
100. Dick Kirschten, "A Little Humor, a Little Humility Help Powell Weather Stormy Seas," *National Journal*, July 26, 1980, p. 1230.
101. On Johnson, see Califano, *Presidential Nation*, pp. 221–22; George Christian, *The President Steps Down: A Personal Memoir of the Transfer of Power* (New York: Macmillan, 1970), p. 227.
102. Quoted in McGaffin and Knoll, *Anything but the Truth*, p. 86. See also other comments by Sylvester, quoted in Theodore C. Sorenson, *Kennedy* (New York: Harper and Row, 1965), p. 321.
103. Carl P. Leubsdorf, "Kennedy Tells of Envoy Cable," *New Orleans Times-Picayune*, April 3, 1974, sec. 1, p. 3.

104. For interesting and insightful studies of political symbols, see Murray Edelman, *The Symbolic Uses of Politics* (Urbana, Ill.: University of Illinois Press, 1964); Murray Edelman, *Politics as Symbolic Action: Mass Arousal and Quiescence* (Chicago: Markham, 1971); Murray Edelman, *Political Language: Words That Succeed and Policies That Fail* (New York: Academic Press, 1977).
105. Dean, *Blind Ambition*, p. 134.
106. Edward C. Banfield, "Making a New Federal Program: Model Cities, 1964–68," in *Policy and Politics in America*, ed. by Allan P. Sindler (Boston: Little, Brown, 1973), p. 140.
107. Nixon, *RN*, p. 1029.
108. Frederic V. Malek, *Washington's Hidden Tragedy: The Failure to Make Government Work* (New York: Free Press, 1978), pp. 28–29.
109. See, for example, "An LBJ Portrait, Warts and All," *Newsweek*, January 20, 1975, p. 22. See Merlin Gustafson, "Our Part-time Chief of State," *Presidential Studies Quarterly* 9 (Spring 1979), pp. 163–71, for the argument that the chief-of-state role is not burdensome on the president and that he should be fully involved in it.
110. Jeb Stuart Magruder, *An American Life: One Man's Road to Watergate* (New York: Pocket Book, 1975), pp. 163–64; Klein, *Making It Perfectly Clear*, pp. 323–24.
111. "RWR's Own New Deal," *Newsweek*, March 2, 1981, p. 23.
112. Quoted in Thomas E. Cronin, "The Presidency Public Relations Script," in Rexford G. Tugwell and Thomas E. Cronin, eds., *The Presidency Reappraised* (New York: Praeger, 1974), p. 171.
113. Ford, *Time to Heal*, pp. 384–85.
114. Bert A. Rockman, "Constants, Cycles, Trends, and Persona in Presidential Governance: Carter's Trouble Reviewed" (paper presented at the Annual Meeting of the American Political Science Association, Washington, D.C., 1979), p. 44. Fallows, "Passionless Presidency," pp. 42–43.
115. Hughes, "Presidency vs. Jimmy Carter," p. 63.
116. "Jordan Takes Stock as He Packs Up His Memories," *New York Times*, December 4, 1980, p. 22.
117. Bruce Miroff, "The Media and Presidential Symbolism: The Woes of Jimmy Carter" (paper presented at the Annual Meeting of the American Political Science Association, New York, September 1981), pp. 20–21.
118. Michael Baruch Grossman and Martha Joynt Kumar, "Carter, Reagan, and the Media: Have the Rules Changed or The Poles of the Spectrum of Success?" (paper presented at the Annual Meeting of the American Political Science Association, New York, September 1981), p. 17.
119. Miroff, "The Media and Presidential Symbolism," p. 14.
120. John Ehrlichman, presentation at the Annual Meeting of the American Political Science Association, New York, September 1981. See also Kissinger, *Years of Upheaval*, pp. 77, 95; Ehrlichman, *Witness to Power*, pp. 263–64, 266–67 for comments on Nixon's interest in and attention to public relations.
121. "Rafshoon and Co.," *Newsweek*, January 29, 1979, pp. 22–23; "Carter's non 'good ole boy,'" *Houston Chronicle*, September 3, 1978, sec. 1, p. 14; Dom Bonafede, "Has the Rafshoon Touch Left Its Mark on the White House?" *National Journal*, April 14, 1979, pp. 588–93; Dom Bonafede, "Carter Sounds

Retreat from 'Cabinet Government,'" *National Journal*, November 18, 1978, p. 1857; Grossman and Kumar, *Portraying the President*, pp. 99, 219.

122. Magruder, *American Life*, p. 6.

123. Bonafede, "Rafshoon and Co.," p. 22.

124. Sidney Blumenthal, *The Permanent Campaign: Inside the World of Elite Political Operatives* (Boston: Beacon Press, 1980), pp. 50–51; David L. Paletz and Robert M. Entman, *Media—Power—Politics* (New York: Free Press, 1981), p. 74.

125. Lawrence C. Miller and Lee Sigelman, "Is the Audience the Message? A Note on LBJ's Vietnam Statements," *Public Opinion Quarterly* 42 (Spring 1978), pp. 71–80.

126. Magruder, *An American Life*, p. 129.

127. See James T. Wooten, "Pre-Inaugural Memo Urged Carter to Stress Style Over Substance," *New York Times*, May 4, 1977, p. 1.

128. Wise, *Politics of Lying*, p. 41; William C. Spragens and Carole Ann Terwood, *From Spokesman to Press Secretary: White House Media Operations* (Washington, D.C.: University Press of America, 1980), p. 41; Grossman and Kumar, *Portraying the President*, p. 118.

129. Minow, et al., *Presidential Television*, p. 66; James Keogh, *Nixon and the Press* (New York: Funk and Wagnalls, 1972), p. 39; Magruder, *An American Life*, pp. 85–89, 109–10, 119–20, 163; Grossman and Kumar, *Portraying the President*, p. 296; Halberstam, *The Powers That Be*, pp. 698–99; Klein, *Making It Perfectly Clear*, pp. 129, 185, 203, 307.

130. Grossman and Kumar, *Portraying the President*, pp. 29, 45–46.

131. *Ibid.*, p. 234.

132. Grossman and Kumar, "Carter, Reagan, and the Media," p. 14.

133. Elizabeth Drew, "A Reporter At Large: Early Days," *New Yorker*, March 16, 1981, pp. 85–86. On similar activities in 1982, see Albert R. Hunt, "GOP Seen Winning Partisan Advantage, For Now, From Collapse of Budget Talks," *Wall Street Journal*, April 30, 1982, p. 18.

134. Martha Joynt Kumar and Michael Baruch Grossman, "The Manager of the Message: The Press Secretary to the President of the United States" (paper presented at the Annual Meeting of the Southern Political Science Association, New Orleans, 1977), p. 27.

135. Christian, *President Steps Down*, p. 198.

136. Minow, et al., *Presidential Television*, pp. 36–37.

137. *Ibid.*, pp. 41–43.

138. *Ibid.*, pp. 46–47.

139. *Ibid.*, pp. 56–57, 62, 64–65; William Small, *To Kill a Messenger* (New York: Hastings House, 1970), pp. 238–42.

140. Minow, et al., *Presidential Television*, pp. 66–67. See also Kissinger, *White House Years*, pp. 757, 761, 1054–55.

141. Grossman and Kumar, *Portraying the President*, p. 236.

142. Kissinger, *White House Years*, pp. 630, 925, 1268.

143. Elizabeth Drew, "A Reporter At Large: Early Days," p. 86.

144. Magruder, *An American Life*, pp. 310–11.

145. Nessen, *It Sure Looks Different*, pp. 227, 241–42. But the president was not in complete control, giving his acceptance speech at 11:40 P.M. E.S.T.

146. *Ibid.*, pp. 262–63, 265.

147. Magruder, *American Life*, pp. 89, 187, 244–45, chaps. 8–9.
148. Carl Bernstein and Bob Woodward, *All the President's Men* (New York: Warner, 1975), pp. 293–94.
149. Magruder, *American Life*, pp. 62, 92–93, 111; Grossman and Kumar, *Portraying the President*, p. 292.
150. Klein, *Making It Perfectly Clear*, pp. 118, 120, 279.
151. Nessen, *Sure Looks Different*, pp. 88–89.
152. Schandler, *Unmaking of a President*, p. 91.
153. *Ibid.*, pp. 313–19.
154. Charles Mohr, "Powell Apologizes for Attempting to Spread Rumor Harmful to Percy," *New York Times*, September 15, 1977, pp. 1, 62.
155. Magruder, *American Life*, pp. 77, 130, 149; Klein, *Making It Perfectly Clear*, pp. 281, 285–87.
156. Bruce Ladd, *Crisis in Credibility* (New York: New American Library, 1968), pp. 174–75; Chester L. Cooper, *The Lost Crusade: America in Vietnam* (New York: Dodd, Mead, 1970), p. 301; Herbert M. Baus and William B. Ross, *Politics Battle Plan* (New York: Macmillan, 1968), pp. 313–14.
157. Minow, et al., *Presidential Television*, pp. 35, 44–45; Wise, *Politics of Lying*, p. 374.
158. See Blumenthal, *The Permanent Campaign*, p. 50.
159. For example, see Nessen, *Sure Looks Different*, p. 219.
160. Wise, *Politics of Lying*, pp. 362–67.
161. Minow, et al., *Presidential Television*, p. 46.
162. *Ibid.*, especially chap. 3.
163. Nessen, *It Sure Looks Different*, pp. 75–76; "President vs. Network," *Newsweek*, October 2, 1974, p. 91.
164. Minow, et al., *Presidential Television*, p. 135; Lawrence F. O'Brien, *No Final Victories: A Life in Politics from John F. Kennedy to Watergate* (New York: Ballantine Books, 1975), pp. 281–85; Klein, *Making It Perfectly Clear*, p. 289.
165. For other examples see William L. Rivers, *The Opinionmakers* (Boston: Beacon Press, 1967), pp. 120–21, chap. 3.
166. Grossman and Kumar, *Portraying the President*, pp. 99–100. See also p. 314.
167. See Warren E. Miller, "Presidential Coattails: A Study in Political Myth and Methodology," *Public Opinion Quarterly* 19 (Winter 1955–56), pp. 353–68; Angus Campbell and Warren E. Miller, "The Motivational Basis for Straight and Split Ticket Voting," *American Political Science Review* 51 (June 1957), pp. 293–312; William B. Moreland, "Angels, Pinpoints, and Voters: The Pattern of a Coattail," *American Journal of Political Science* 17 (February 1973), pp. 170–76; Herbert M. Kritzer and Robert B. Eubank, "Presidential Coattails Revisited: Partisanship and Incumbency Effects," *American Journal of Political Science* 23 (August 1979), pp. 615–26; Gary C. Jacobson, "Presidential Coattails in 1972," *Public Opinion Quarterly* 40 (Summer 1976), pp. 194–200.
168. Charles Press, "Voting Statistics and Presidential Coattails," *American Political Science Review* 52 (December 1958), pp. 1041–50.
169. Milton C. Cummings, Jr., *Congressmen and the Electorate: Elections for the U.S. House and the President, 1920–1964* (New York: Free Press, 1966), chaps. 1 and 2.
170. Malcolm Moos, *Politics, Presidents, and Coattails* (Baltimore: Johns Hopkins

University Press, 1952), pp. 110–11; Jacobson, "Presidential Coattails in 1972."

171. Milton C. Cummings, Jr., "Nominations and Elections for the House of Representatives," in Milton C. Cummings, Jr., ed., *The National Election of 1964* (Washington, D.C.: Brookings Institution, 1966), pp. 231–33.

172. Charles Press, "Presidential Coattails and Party Cohesion," *Midwest Journal of Political Science* 7 (November 1963), pp. 320–35.

173. Miller, "Presidential Coattails," p. 368; Campbell and Miller, "The Motivational Basis for Straight and Split Ticket Voting."

174. Cummings, *Congressmen and the Electorate*, p. 51; Frank B. Feigert, "Illusions of Ticket Splitting," *American Politics Quarterly* 7 (October 1979), pp. 470–88.

175. Miller, "Presidential Coattails," pp. 354–56.

176. George C. Edwards III, "Impact of Presidential Coattails on Outcomes in Congressional Elections," *American Politics Quarterly* 7 (January 1979), pp. 94–108; George C. Edwards III, *Presidential Influence in Congress* (San Francisco: W. H. Freeman, 1980), pp. 70–78.

177. See, for example, Aage R. Clausen, *How Congressmen Decide* (New York: St. Martin's, 1973); Aage R. Clausen and Carl E. Van Horn, "The Congressional Response to a Decade of Change: 1963–1972," *Journal of Politics* 29 (August 1977), pp. 624–66; David W. Brady and Naomi B. Lynn, "Switched Seat Congressional Districts: Their Effect on Party Voting and Public Policy," *American Journal of Political Science* 17 (August 1973), pp. 528–43; Herbert Asher and Herbert Weisberg, "Voting Change in Congress: Some Dynamic Perspectives on an Evolutionary Process," *American Journal of Political Science* 22 (May 1978), pp. 391–425; Walter J. Stone, "The Dynamics of Constituency: Electoral Control in the House," *American Politics Quarterly* 8 (October 1980), pp. 399–424. On the Senate, see Keith T. Poole, "Dimensions of Interest Group Evaluation of the U.S. Senate, 1969–1978," *American Journal of Political Science* 25 (February 1981), pp. 49–67.

178. Edwards, *Presidential Influence in Congress*, pp. 58–62.

179. Miller, "Presidential Coattails," pp. 354–56.

180. See, for example, Edwards, *Presidential Influence in Congress*, pp. 70–78.

181. Grossman and Kumar, "Carter, Reagan, and the Media," pp. 18, 26.

182. Edwards, *Presidential Influence in Congress*, pp. 72–73; Edwards, "Impact of Presidential Coattails"; George C. Edwards III, "Presidential Electoral Performance as a Source of Presidential Power," *American Journal of Political Science* 22 (February 1978), pp. 152–68.

183. David R. Mayhew, "Congressional Elections: The Case of the Vanishing Marginals," *Polity* 6 (Spring 1974), pp. 295–317.

184. Robert S. Erikson, "The Advantage of Incumbency in Congressional Elections," *Polity* 3 (Spring 1971), pp. 395–405; Robert S. Erikson, "Malapportionment, Gerrymandering, and Party Fortunes in Congressional Elections," *American Political Science Review* 66 (December 1972), pp. 1234–45; Robert S. Erikson, "A Reply to Tidmarch," *Polity* 4 (Summer 1972), pp. 527–29; Thomas E. Mann, *Unsafe at Any Margin: Interpreting Congressional Elections* (Washington, D.C.: American Enterprise Institute, 1978); James L. Payne, "The Personal Electoral Advantage of House Incumbents, 1936–1976," *American Politics Quarterly* 8 (October 1980), pp. 469–72; Barbara

Hinckley, "House Re-elections and Senate Defeats: The Role of the Challenger," *British Journal of Political Science* 10 (October 1980), pp. 452–58; Barbara Hinckley, *Congressional Elections* (Washington, D.C.: Congressional Quarterly, 1981), pp. 37–40. But see Melissa P. Collie, "Incumbency, Electoral Safety, and Turnover in the House of Representatives, 1952–1976," *American Political Science Review* 75 (March 1981), pp. 119–31.

185. Richard Born, "Generational Replacement and the Growth of Incumbent Reelection Margins in the U.S. House," *American Political Science Review* 73 (September 1979), pp. 811–17.

186. See, for example, "Computers and Direct Mail Are Being Married on the Hill to Keep Incumbents in Office," *Congressional Quarterly Weekly Report*, June 21, 1979, pp. 1445–52; "For Many Incumbents Running for Reelection Is Now a Full-Time Job," *Congressional Quarterly Weekly Report*, July 7, 1979, pp. 1350–57; Albert D. Cover, "One Good Term Deserves Another: The Advantages of Incumbency in Congressional Elections," *American Journal of Political Science* 21 (August 1977), pp. 523–41; Albert D. Cover and David R. Mayhew, "Congressional Dynamics and the Decline of Competitive Congressional Elections," in Lawrence C. Dodd and Bruce I. Oppenheimer, eds., *Congress Reconsidered* (New York: Praeger, 1977); Richard F. Fenno, Jr., *Home Style: House Members in Their Districts* (Boston: Little, Brown, 1978); Morris P. Fiorina, *Congress: Keystone of the Washington Establishment* (New Haven: Yale University Press, 1977); Glenn R. Parker, "The Advantage of Incumbency in House Elections," *American Politics Quarterly* 8 (October 1980), pp. 449–64.

187. Fiorina, *Congress;* John A. Ferejohn, "On the Decline in Competition in Congressional Elections," *American Political Science Review* 71 (March 1977), pp. 166–76; Glenn R. Parker and Roger H. Davidson, "Why Do Americans Love Their Congressmen So Much More Than Their Congress?" *Legislative Studies Quarterly* 4 (February 1979), pp. 53–61; Candice Nelson, "The Effects of Incumbency Voting in Congressional Elections, 1964–1974," *Political Science Quarterly* 93 (Winter 1978–79), pp. 665–78; Kent L. Tedin and Richard W. Murray, "Public Awareness of Congressional Representatives: Recall Versus Recognition," *American Politics Quarterly* 7 (October 1979), pp. 509–17; Alan I. Abramowitz, "A Comparison of Voting for U.S. Senator and Representative in 1978," *American Political Science Review* 74 (September 1980), pp. 633–40; Hinckley, "House Re-elections and Senate Defeats"; Barbara Hinckley, "The American Voter in Congressional Elections," *American Political Science Review* 74 (September 1980), pp. 641–50; Thomas E. Mann and Raymond E. Wolfinger, "Candidates and Parties in Congressional Elections," *American Political Science Review* 74 (September 1980), pp. 617–32; Hinckley, *Congressional Elections*, pp. 40–53; Gary C. Jacobson, "Incumbents' Advantages in the 1978 Congressional Elections," *Legislative Studies Quarterly* 6 (May 1981), pp. 183–200; Morris P. Fiorina, "Some Problems in Studying the Effects of Resource Allocation in Congressional Elections," *American Journal of Political Science* 25 (August 1981), pp. 543–67; Diana Evans Yiannakis, "The Grateful Electorate: Casework and Congressional Elections," *American Journal of Political Science* 25 (August 1981), pp. 568–80; Glenn R. Parker, "Interpreting Candidate Awareness in U.S. Congressional Elections," *Legislative Studies Quarterly* 6 (May 1981), pp. 219–34; Edie N. Goldenberg and Michael

W. Traugott, "Normal Vote Analysis of U.S. Congressional Elections," *Legislative Studies Quarterly* 6 (May 1981), pp. 247–58; Albert Cover and Bruce S. Brauberg, "Baby Books and Ballots: The Impact of Congressional Mail on Constituent Opinion," *American Political Science Review* 76 (June 1982), pp. 347–59. But see John R. Johannes and John C. McAdams, "The Congressional Incumbency Effect: Is It Casework, Policy Compatibility, or Something Else?", *American Journal of Political Science* 25 (August 1981), pp. 512–42; John C. McAdams and John R. Johannes, "Does Casework Matter? A Reply to Professor Fiorina," *American Journal of Political Science* 25 (August 1981), pp. 581–604.

188. Mann, *Unsafe at Any Margin,* p. 87; Richard Born, "House Incumbents and Inter-Election Vote Change," *Journal of Politics* 39 (November 1977), pp. 1008–34. But see John R. Alford and John R. Hibbing, "Increased Incumbency Advantage in the House," *Journal of Politics* 43 (November 1981), pp. 1042–61.

189. Hinckley, *Congressional Elections,* p. 76.

CHAPTER THREE

THE PRESIDENT AND THE PRESS

Despite all their efforts to lead public opinion, presidents do not directly reach the American people on a day-to-day basis. It is the press that provides citizens with most of what they know about the chief executive, his policies, and their consequences. The media also interprets and analyzes presidential activities, even the president's direct appeals to the public.

The press is thus the principal intermediary between the president and the public, and relations with the press are an important aspect of the president's efforts to lead public opinion. If the press portrays the president in a favorable light, he will face fewer obstacles in obtaining public support. If, on the other hand, the press is hostile toward his administration, the president's task will be more difficult.

Because of the importance of the press to the public presidency, the White House goes to great lengths to encourage the media to project a positive image of the president and his policies. These efforts include coordinating the news, holding press conferences, and providing a range of services such as formal briefings, interviews, photo opportunities, background sessions, travel accommodations, and daily handouts. On occasion it also resorts to attempts to punish the press for coverage the president perceives as unfair, unfavorable, or both.

In this chapter we examine the nature and structure of presidential relationships with the press, emphasizing both the context of these relationships and the White House's attempts to obtain favorable coverage. In the next chapter we discuss issues in presidential-press relations, especially the nature and consequences of media coverage of the presidency.

BACKGROUND

Today we are accustomed to turning to our newspapers or television sets to conveniently learn about what the president has said or done. Things have not always been this way. Before the Civil War newspapers were generally small, heavily partisan, and limited in circulation. Between 1860 and 1920 a number of changes occurred that forever altered the relationships between the president and the press.

Several technological innovations, including the electric printing press, the telegraph, the typewriter, the telephone, linotype, and wood-pulp paper, made it both possible and economical to produce mass circulation newspapers carrying recent national news. Aside from the sales efforts of the newspapers themselves, the increasing literacy of the population helped to create a market for these papers.

The increased interest in national affairs as a result of the new importance of the national government also helped newspapers. The government began to significantly regulate the economy with the Interstate Commerce Commission and its antitrust efforts. The United States expanded its role in world affairs with the Spanish-American war and World War I. Both of these events kindled support for and great interest in the activities of the government in Washington. The increased interest in national affairs was also caused by the renewed prominence of the presidency following an era of congressional ascendency. Theodore Roosevelt took an activist view of the presidency and exploited the new opportunities to reach the public provided by the mass circulation press. He used the White House as a "bully pulpit" to dramatize himself and the issues in which he was interested. He sought and gained extensive access to the press in order to forge a more personal relationship with the American people.

Ever since the first Roosevelt occupied the White House, news about the president has played an increasingly prominent role in the printed press, both in absolute terms and relative to coverage of Congress or the national government as a whole. Recent research has found that almost three-fourths of national government news in the 1970–74 period focused on the president.[1]

Presidents have found that they need the press because it is their primary link to the people. The press, in turn, finds coverage of the president indispensable in satisfying its audience and in reporting on the most significant political events. The advent of radio and television has only heightened these mutual needs.

THE ADVERSARIAL RELATIONSHIP

The history of presidential-press relations has not involved unlimited goodwill. President George Washington complained that the "calumnies" against his administration were "outrages of common decency" motivated by the desire to destroy confidence in the new government.[2] John Adams was so upset at criticism in the press that he supported the Sedition Act and jailed some opposition journalists under its authority.

Thomas Jefferson, certainly one of our greatest defenders of freedom, became so exasperated with the press as president that he argued that "even the least informed of the people have learned that nothing in a newspaper is to be believed . . . and I therefore have long thought that a few prosecutions of the most prominent offenders would have a wholesome effect." He also felt that "newspapers, for the most part, present only the caricature of disaffected minds. Indeed, the abuses of freedom of the press have been carried to a length never before known or borne by any civilized nation." These observations, it should be noted, come from the man who earlier had written that "were it left to me to decide whether we should have a government without newspapers or newspapers without a government, I should not hesitate to prefer the latter."[3]

Theodore Roosevelt had newspaper publisher Joseph Pulitzer (for whom the Pulitzer prizes are named) indicted for criminal libel (the charges were eventually dismissed). Woodrow Wilson complained that "I have almost come to the point of believing nothing that I see in the newspapers." Franklin Roosevelt invented a Dunce Cap Club to which he banished annoying reporters, and once awarded the Iron Cross to a reporter whose stories he felt were aiding the Nazis.[4]

In more recent years Harry Truman said he was "saving up four or five good, hard punches on the nose" for reporters that he thought had been unfair to him.[5] President Kennedy was often upset at the press for one thing or another, one time cutting off contact with one of his closest friends, a journalist, for three months because of what he perceived as the latter's indiscretion in a story.[6] Another time he canceled all twenty-two White House subscriptions to the *New York Herald Tribune* because he thought it had not been fair to his administration. Perhaps his attitude can be summed up in his famous 1962 reply to a question during a press conference that he was "reading more and enjoying it less."[7]

When President Johnson was enjoying a favorable press, he told a visiting journalist one day: "I trust the press. I trust you just as much as I trust my wife." But when things got bad, he swung to the other side of the scale and exaggerated just as much. "They warp everything I do, they lie about me and about what I do, they don't know the meaning of truth. They are liars and cheats. . . . They behave vulgarly."[8] In a news conference near the end of his tenure as president, Richard Nixon complained that he had "never heard or seen such outrageous, vicious, distorted reporting in 27 years of public life."[9] President Carter often had abrasive relations with the media.[10]

While all presidents have supported the abstract right of the press to criticize them freely, most have not found this criticism very comfortable while in office. They have viewed some of the press as misrepresenting (perhaps maliciously) their views and actions, failing to perceive the correctness of their policies, and dedicating themselves to impeding the president's goals.

Some of the reaction of the press to such charges is summed up in a statement by J. F. terHorst: "As President Ford's press secretary, I learned firsthand what I had always suspected—every President would like the press to serve as a cheerleader. But a truly free press does not have an obligation to support government policies; indeed it has an obligation to refrain from support. Otherwise it is only a propaganda arm of the government."[11] In addition, many journalists complain of presidents' inaccessibility to the press and their attempts to manipulate and even restrict it.

No matter who is in the White House or who reports on him, presidents and the press tend to be in conflict. Presidents are inherently policy advocates. They will naturally assess the press in terms of its aiding or hindering their goals.[12] The press, on the other hand, has the responsibility for presenting reality. While the press may fail in its efforts, it will assess itself on that criterion. The president wants to control the amount and timing of information about his administration, while the press wants all the information that exists without delay. As long as their goals are different, presidents and the press are likely to be adversaries.

THE WHITE HOUSE PRESS

Who are the reporters that regularly cover the White House? The regulars represent diverse media constituencies. These include daily newspapers like the *Washington Post* and the *New York Times*, weekly newsmagazines like *Time* and *Newsweek*, the wire services like the Associated Press

(AP) and United Press International (UPI), newspaper chains like Hearst, Scripps-Howard, Newhouse, and Knight, the television and radio networks, the foreign press, and "opinion" magazines like the *New Republic*. In addition, photographers, columnists, television commentators, and magazine writers are regularly involved in White House–press interactions. In 1981 about 1,700 persons had White House press credentials.[13] Fortunately, not everyone shows up at once. About 60 reporters and 15 photographers regularly cover the White House, and this number increases to more than 100 when an important announcement is expected.[14]

The great majority of daily newspapers in America have no Washington correspondents, much less someone assigned to cover the White House. The same is true of almost all of the country's individual television and radio stations. These papers and stations rely heavily upon the AP and UPI wire services, each of which cover the White House continuously and in detail with three fulltime reporters. We shall have more to say about the implications of this situation in the next chapter.

PRESIDENTIAL PRESS SECRETARY

The White House's relations with the media occupy a substantial portion of the time of a large number of aides. The authors of the leading study on presidential-press relations have estimated that about one-third of the high-level White House staff are directly involved in media relations and policy and that most of the staff are involved at some time in influencing the media's portrayal of the president.[15]

The person in the White House who most often deals directly with the press is the president's press secretary. Probably the central function of press secretaries is to serve as conduits of information from the White House to the press. They must be sure that clear statements of administration policies have been prepared on important policy matters. The press secretaries usually conduct the daily press briefings, giving prepared announcements and answering questions. In forming their answers they often do not have specific orders on what to say or not to say.[16] They must be able to think on their feet to ensure that they accurately reflect the president's views. Sometimes these views may be unclear, however, or the president may not wish to articulate his views. Therefore, press secretaries may seem to be evasive or unimaginative in public settings. They also meet individually with reporters in private meetings, where the information provided can be more candid and speculative.[17]

To be effective in the conduit role the press secretary must maintain credibility with reporters. Credibility rests on at least two important pillars: (1) truth and (2) access to and respect of the president and senior

White House officials. If a press secretary is viewed as not telling the truth or as not being close to top decision makers (and therefore not well informed), he will not be an effective presidential spokesman because the press will give little credence to what he says. Credibility problems have arisen for several press secretaries, including Ron Ziegler (Nixon) and Ron Nessen (Ford) due to the first and second pillars, respectively.[18]

Press secretaries also serve as conduits from the press to the president. They must sometimes explain the needs of the press to the president. For example, all of Johnson's press secretaries tried to convince the president to issue advance information on his travel plans to the press. When he refused, they provided it anyway and then had it expunged from the briefing transcript so the president would not see it. Press secretaries also try to inform the White House staff of the press's needs and the rules of the game, and they help reporters gain access to staff members.[19]

Press secretaries are typically not involved in substantive decisions, but they do give the president advice, usually on what information should be released, by whom, in what form, and to what audience. They also advise the president on rehearsals for press conferences and on how to project his image and use it to his political advantage.[20]

COORDINATING THE NEWS

Since the time of William Loeb, Theodore Roosevelt's press secretary, the White House has attempted to coordinate executive branch news. Franklin Roosevelt's press secretary, Steven Early, saw the whole administration as a public relations effort. But it was Dwight Eisenhower's press secretary, James Hagerty, who made the greatest efforts at coordinating executive branch news for the benefit of the White House. He met regularly with departmental press officers, scanned departmental news bulletins before their release, and advised cabinet members on their public relations problems. He also required White House aides to channel their press contacts through him, funneled favorable announcements through the White House and unfavorable ones through the departments, and monitored the volume and flow of news so as to be in a position to prevent the overlap or blanketing of one source by another. Most of the information on the administration was provided directly by the press office or in interviews scheduled and monitored by Hagerty.[21]

All of these activities made the press highly dependent upon the White House's account of events and policies and hindered reporters from obtaining more complete and perhaps contrasting views from the rest of the executive branch. This, of course, hardly distressed the White House. Coordinated management increases the probability of news reflecting positively on the president.

Subsequent presidents have been interested in achieving these goals, although none have made efforts as systematic or successful as those of the Eisenhower administration. These later presidents have attempted to coordinate executive branch news. They have assigned aides to clear the appointments of departmental public affairs officials, keep in touch with the officials to learn what news is forthcoming from the departments, and meet with them to explain the president's policy views and try to prevent conflicting statements emanating from the White House and other units of the executive branch. Specialists have had responsibility for coordinating national security news.[22]

Of course, such tactics do not always work. President Ford wanted to announce the success of the *Mayaguez* operation from the White House, but he found to his disappointment that the Pentagon had already done so, making any presidential announcement anticlimactic.[23] At the beginning of his second year in office President Reagan issued an order that required advance White House approval of television appearances by cabinet members and other top officials,[24] but it soon lapsed.

Coordinating the news from the White House itself has also been a presidential goal. Presidents have sometimes monitored and attempted to limit the press contacts of White House aides, who have annoyed their bosses by using the media for their own purposes, but these efforts have been sporadic and largely fruitless.[25] On the other hand, the Nixon administration made great strides in coordinating the offices with publicity functions within the White House, attempting to present the news in the most favorable light, such as preventing two major stories from breaking on the same day, smothering bad news with more positive news, and timing announcements for maximum effect.[26]

NEWS SUMMARY

All recent presidents, including Eisenhower, who had a reputation to the contrary, have read several newspapers each day, especially the *New York Times* and the *Washington Post*. Kennedy and Johnson were also very attentive to television news programs. Johnson had a television cabinet with three screens so he could watch all three networks at once. But even this was not enough to satisfy his thirst for news. He also had teletypes that carried the latest reports from the AP and UPI wire services installed in the Oval Office, and he monitored them regularly.[27] The president was thus not isolated from the news, which at the end of his tenure often emphasized criticism of his policies.[28]

President Nixon rarely watched television news and did not peruse many newspapers or magazines, but he was extremely interested in press coverage of his administration. He had his staff prepare a daily news summary, which ranged from 20 to 30 pages, of about 50 newspapers, 30 magazines, television news, and the AP and UPI news wires. Often this summary triggered ideas for the president, who gave orders to aides to follow up on something he read. The news summary also went to about 50 top White House assistants.[29]

Presidents Ford, Carter, and Reagan continued the news summary and circulated it to about 150 top officials in their administrations. Under Carter the summary was reduced to about 15 pages, but the number of newspapers surveyed was increased to about 75.[30]

The Carter White House also instituted a magazine survey. In 1977 the White House Press Office reported that it regularly received and reviewed the following 37 magazines.[31]

Atlantic	*New Times*
Broadcasting	*New West*
Business Week	*New York*
Columbia Journalism Review	*New York Review of Books*
Ebony	*The New Yorker*
The Economist	*People*
Encore	*Playboy*
First Monday	*Progressive*
Human Events	*Psychology Today*
Manchester Guardian	*Rollcall*
More	*Rolling Stone*
Mother Jones	*Saturday Review*
Ms.	*Science*
The Nation	*Sports Illustrated*
National Journal	*Texas Monthly*
National Review	*TV Guide*
National Spotlight	*U.S. News and World Report*
The New Republic	*Washington Monthly*
	Washingtonian

We can be sure that in addition to the magazines listed above, large circulation news magazines such as *Time* and *Newsweek* are read in the White House. Thus, President Carter received a review of a large and eclectic sample of opinion in the nation's magazines. Each week he would ask his staff to provide him with three or four complete articles for more detailed consideration.[32]

The Carter White House also developed a weekly summary of Jewish publications when it became concerned about a possible backlash within the American Jewish community against the administration's Middle East policy. The news summary reviewed U.S. Jewish publications and

The *Jerusalem Post* and went to the president and several senior assistants.[33]

Since the news summaries provide much of what the president knows about the media and in turn influence his dealings with it, they should accurately reflect press coverage. White House aides and observers have regularly claimed that the news summaries contain criticism as well as praise of the president from the nation's press, although there are differences of opinion over whether the Nixon news summaries were too partisan.[34] Even the inclusion of criticism does not necessarily guarantee that the news summaries are not biased. Any attempt to balance negative and positive coverage may provide the president with a distorted picture —press reactions may be skewed in one direction, and therefore the news summaries ought to reflect this.

PRESS CONFERENCES

The best-known direct interaction between the president and the press is the presidential press conference. In this section we shall describe the press conference in recent American history and evaluate its utility for informing the public about the president and his policies. In doing so we shall see that the president is in a strong position to manipulate press conferences to his advantage and that the press does a relatively poor job in questioning the president, all of which decreases the probabilities of press conferences serving as a useful source of information.

The frequency of press conferences has varied over time. Franklin Roosevelt held about seven a month; Truman cut this figure in half. Eisenhower further reduced their frequency, holding about two press conferences each month, a rate maintained by Kennedy, Johnson, and Carter, and somewhat bettered by Ford. The deviant case was Richard Nixon, who held only about one press conference every two months.[35] Ronald Reagan held only seven formal press conferences in his first year in office, despite his press secretary's promise at the beginning of his term that the president would hold formal televised press conferences "no less than once a month,"[36] but he increased the rate somewhat in his second year.

Such figures should not be accepted at face value, however. What presidents count as press conferences varies considerably. Eisenhower, Kennedy, Nixon, and Carter included in their totals only meetings with the press of which the press was given advance notice, that were open to any accredited reporter, and that were held in formal settings. Johnson, on the other hand, counted as press conferences meetings called without notice, some on Saturday morning at which he responded to questions while walking around the White House grounds, and three sessions on the same day at which he answered a total of thirteen questions. Gerald Ford counted meetings with reporters at campaign stops in his list of conferences. He held only fourteen press conferences within the traditional definition.[37]

The figures for average frequency of press conferences may conceal wide fluctuations in the time between conferences. Johnson's average of more than two press conferences per month hides the fact that during 40% of the months of his tenure he held one or no press conferences. From August 29 to December 6, 1965, while America was escalating the war in Vietnam, the president held no press conferences at all.[38] Similarly, Richard Nixon held no press conferences from March 15 to August 22, 1973, a period of over five months! This of course was the time of the Senate Watergate hearings.

The fluctuations in the regularity of press conferences are not as easy to explain as we might expect. Presidents do not hold fewer press conferences as they stay in office longer, as a hypothesis of increasing isolation may suggest. Although they sometimes avoid holding press conferences during difficult situations, as we noted in the previous paragraph, they tend to hold *more* conferences under these circumstances, evidently trying harder to reach the public. Nor do presidents change the substance of their news conference statements in relation to their popularity.[39]

Naturally, the more time that has elapsed between press conferences, the more events and governmental actions that will have transpired since the last press conference. The more that has transpired, the more wide-ranging the questions asked of the president are likely to be. And the more wide-ranging the questions, the more superficial the coverage of any one topic is likely to be.

The notice presidents provide of their upcoming press conferences is no more uniform than their frequency of holding them. Lyndon Johnson was famous for his short-notice press conferences, in which he gathered whatever reporters were available in his office or the Cabinet Room or took them on a walk around the White House grounds. Although this informal atmosphere was possibly more conducive to in-depth questioning, reporters had little time to prepare questions and many reporters missed these opportunities to question the president.[40] President Ford held impromptu sessions with reporters in the White House Rose Garden that were announced only minutes in advance and in which his press secretary decided which subjects were appropriate and when questioning should stop. Even though press conferences were scheduled several weeks in advance on President Carter's calendar, reporters were often not informed of the date until one or two days in advance.[41]

The short notice for many press conferences has advantages for presidents. If press conferences are not publicly scheduled until shortly before they take place, it is easier for presidents to cancel them if they find it convenient. In addition, short notice gives reporters less time to prepare questions that will be informative for the American people. Moreover, many specialty reporters who cover all of Washington, who can ask detailed questions, and who can be less concerned with remaining on good terms with the president will miss impromptu press conferences.

Another factor that has perhaps reduced the utility of the press conferences for eliciting useful information about government has been their increasing size. Theodore Roosevelt began the practice of press conferences by inviting a small, select group of reporters to talk with him. Wilson welcomed all accredited news representatives to his press conferences, although the number of reporters remained small. Franklin Roosevelt had throngs of reporters surrounding his desk in the Oval Office and engaged in extensive give-and-take with reporters. Harry Truman, however, moved his press conferences to the Indian Treaty Room, an auditorium in the Executive Office Building across the street from the White House. Presidents have since generally employed a large room (such as the State Department auditorium or the East Room in the White House) for press conferences, usually relying upon public address systems.

The increased number of reporters covering press conferences and the setting in which they take place has inevitably made them more formal. More reporters mean more persons with different concerns and thus less likelihood of follow-up questions to cover a subject in depth. Spontaneity in questions and answers has largely been lost.

Presidents have taken other steps that have contributed to the formalization of press conferences. Beginning with Truman, they have undergone formal briefings and "dry runs" in preparation for questions that might be asked. Presidents have asked their aides and the departments and agencies to submit to them possible questions and suggested answers, and sometimes they call for further information. In 1982 President Reagan began holding full-scale mock news conferences. Guessing at questions is not too difficult. There are obvious areas of concern, and questions raised at White House and departmental briefings and other meetings with reporters provide useful cues. The president also can anticipate the interests of individual reporters, and he has discretion over whom to recognize.[42] Needless to say, spontaneity has been reduced under the burden of these preparations.

Over time presidential press conferences have also become more public. Until the Eisenhower presidency a non-quotation rule was in effect. But early in his term the *New York Times* began printing a transcript of the press conferences that quoted the questions asked of the president and prefaced his answers with "the President said that he . . ." This preserved the letter, if not the spirit, of the non-quotation rule.

Also, early in Eisenhower's term a tape was made of a press conference and broadcast over the radio (some snippets of conferences had been broadcast in Truman's administration). Obviously, this limited the significance of the non-quotation rule. In January 1955 a pretaped press conference was televised, and this became a frequent occurrence. While the White House reserved the right to edit the tape, it rarely exercised this option. Verbatim transcripts of the press conferences were also published. The final steps in this process were taken by John Kennedy, who allowed live telecasts of his press conferences, and Richard Nixon, who innovated with televised press conferences in the evening.

The change in the nature of the presidential press conferences from semiprivate to public events has diminished their utility in transmitting information from the president to the press. Since every word they say is transmitted verbatim to millions of people, contemporary presidents cannot speak as candidly as, say, Franklin D. Roosevelt could. Nor can they speculate freely about their potential actions or evaluations of persons, events, or circumstances. Instead, they must choose their words carefully, and their responses to questions are often not terribly enlightening.

These problems are aggravated by the fact that the public nature of presidential press conferences provides an additional opportunity for the presidency to influence public opinion directly. When President Kennedy allowed his press conferences to be televised live, he also tried hard to insure a large audience for them.[43] The reason is obvious: the press had become a prop in the president's efforts to reach the public.

Of course, if they feel it is not to their advantage to have their press conferences televised, presidents can choose not to. President Johnson felt he did not come across well on television and had only 24 of his press conferences broadcast.[44] Nixon steadily reduced the number of televised press conferences in his first term. In his first four years he held 9, 6, 9, and 7 conferences, respectively, but only 8, 4, 3, and 1 of them were televised.[45]

Other problems also diminish the prospects of press conferences serving as a device for compelling the president to explain himself to the public. The disallowance of follow-up questions up to Ford's presidency hindered in-depth responses and made it easier for presidents to evade the intent of questions. Even now it is unusual for a reporter to follow up on his or her own question. In addition, some reporters are instructed by their editors and publishers to ask questions of local interest, questions in which no other reporter is likely to be interested. Other reporters have prepared their one allowable question in advance and even practiced asking it. They are not likely to switch to a follow-up question at the last minute. The odds are very great against two or three of these or other reporters having similar questions and being called on in a row.[46]

Presidents since Truman have frequently begun their press conferences with carefully prepared opening statements. Examples include

President Kennedy's 1962 blast at the steel companies for raising their prices (eventually leading to the increases being rescinding) and President Carter's five-minute monologue on his administration's accomplishments in a televised press conference during the 1980 presidential election. These statements have given presidents an opportunity to reach the public on their own terms. Opening statements have also further reduced the opportunities for questions while at the same time focusing questions on issues of the president's choosing (contained in the statement). In a study of the press conferences of Presidents Kennedy, Nixon, Ford, and Johnson, the author found that less than 10% of the words of the first three presidents were taken up in their formal announcements. The formal announcements of Johnson, on the other hand, composed 38% of his press conference words. As we might expect, Johnson was also more successful than other presidents in eliciting questions relevant to his opening statements.[47] Other presidents have typically been able to focus only between 10% and 15% of their press conference questions on their opening statement.[48]

Because the president is in control of his press conference, he can avoid the harder questions. Sometimes presidents state that they will not entertain questions on certain topics (Kennedy on the Bay of Pigs or Eisenhower on the U-2 incident). They may also evade questions with clever rhetoric or simply answer with a "no comment." Or they can use a question as a vehicle to say something they planned ahead of time. If necessary they can reverse the attack and focus on the questioner or, conversely, they can call on a friendly reporter for a "soft" question. Eisenhower used a skilled evasiveness and impenetrable syntax to avoid direct answers to embarrassing or politically sensitive questions,[49] something not unusual among presidents.[50] Presidents Harding and Coolidge required questions to be written and presented in advance. Wilson sharply reduced the number of press conferences after a couple of years in office. President Nixon added a new wrinkle in avoiding unpleasant questioning when in early 1973 he held a press conference in which he spoke at Camp David, the presidential retreat in the Catoctin Mountains in Maryland, while reporters listened to a loudspeaker at the White House.

Presidents and their staffs have sometimes found it convenient to plant questions with the press. In other words, they end up asking themselves questions. This practice started at least as early as Franklin Roosevelt. Eisenhower and Johnson especially followed this practice.[51]

How does a question get planted? The process is really not very involved. One such instance during President Nixon's term occurred when a friendly reporter approached press secretary Ronald Ziegler at a bar in San Clemente near the president's home and asked, "What's on the President's mind?" Ziegler said he would let him know, and the next day he suggested that a question on Nixon's efforts to bring government to the people might be useful. At the ensuing press conference the reporter asked the following question:

> Mr. President, this press conference in Los Angeles is sort of a climax to a series of activities that you have described as bringing the government to the people, such as your recent meetings in Louisville, Fargo, Salt Lake City, and your work at the Western White House at San Clemente. What benefits do you see to you and to the country from such activities?[52]

Needless to say, the president did not have a difficult time answering this "cream puff."

Many of the questions asked of the president involve trivial topics. Nixon aide John Ehrlichman said the President's press conferences had "a lot of flabby and fairly dumb questions."[53] This point was dramatically demonstrated in a press conference President Nixon held with media executives on prime-time national television in November 1973. He had indicated that he was anxious to answer a question regarding charges that he had increased milk-price supports in return for campaign contributions from dairy groups. With time for only one more question, the final questioner asked the president about his retirement plans. Exasperated, Nixon agreed to answer this trivial question if the questioner would ask him about milk-price supports. To answer the extra question Nixon had to suffer the additional indignity of telling the networks over national television to delay their regularly scheduled programs and give him more time. In sum, the president ended up asking himself a question for which he had obviously prepared an answer.

President Ford was also frustrated by the questions asked of him at press conferences. After his first press conference he reflected:

> In general I was disappointed by the questions that were raised. The White House press corps didn't seem interested in finding out how I planned to deal with the substantive issues that confronted me. They just wanted to know what I was going to do about Nixon, and I thought they had wasted my time.[54]

One reason for the emphasis on the trivial in questioning is deference to the president. Reporters meet the president in his territory, not theirs, and dutifully rise when he enters the room. An adversarial relationship may exist outside the press conference, but it is rarely reflected during the sessions themselves. The author of a study of press conferences between 1961 and 1975 found only two occasions in fifteen years when the number of hostile questions asked by reporters at any press conference exceeded three.[55]

Perhaps the White House press should adopt the view of Peter Lisagor, one of the leading White House correspondents of his time:

> I don't even think a note of irreverence at press conferences, of whatever kind, is either disrespectful or boorish. After all, the President is under no compulsion to seek office and he gets a fairly good wage for it. In most cases he clawed and struggled to be elected, and he knew in advance that he would be held accountable, not only every four years but constantly.[56]

Various efforts at symbolic manipulation have also become part of presidential press conferences. President Nixon dispensed with a lectern, evidently to appear more informal, candid, and impressive. At the first press conference of his successor, Gerald Ford, reporters' chairs were placed closer to the podium to decrease the "distance" from the president. The blue curtain that Nixon had used as a backdrop was removed because it looked stagy and imperial. Instead, Ford stood before open doors to create a friendlier atmosphere and an obvious contrast with the siege mentality of the previous administration.[57]

The artificial nature of press conferences, especially on television, may lead to distortions. On the one hand, a truly spontaneous answer to a question may be candid, but it also may be foolish or expose the president's ignorance of an area. Generalizations based on such a reply may be inaccurate because the "real" president may be well-informed and require more than a few seconds to think about a complex problem. On the other hand, some presidents may be glib, charming, and attractive, and therefore perform well in a spontaneous press conference, but really not be very competent. The advent of television has further increased the potential for distortion since a president's physical attractiveness, delivery, and flair for the dramatic may leave more of an impression on the public's mind than the substance of his answers.

Press conferences also have the potential for verbal slips on the part of the president, with the possibility of broad consequences. This is one of the reasons President Nixon felt press conferences were not the place to enunciate, much less develop, policy.[58] President Harding demanded written questions in advance after he inaccurately described the provisions of a treaty in a press conference. President Nixon once slipped by declaring that mass murderer Charles Manson was guilty while his trial was in progress. His comment did not affect the trial, but it brought the president a substantial amount of unfavorable publicity for being injudicious. The most famous verbal slip was probably President Truman's response to a question regarding the use of atomic weapons in the Korean War. The president replied that they were always under consideration, and this only served to confuse and alarm everyone involved, including our allies.[59] President Truman's slip also reflects the difficulty of handling "yes/no" questions on delicate matters.

Reading the transcript of a press conference also can be misleading. The official transcripts prepared by the White House clean up sentence structure, make additions to and subtractions from the president's replies, and correct his errors, such as mistaking a senator's or a country's name or a fact about a policy.

In sum, presidential press conference are often not very informative. In the more formal and less spontaneous press conferences that characterize the more recent era, the president has a substantial opportunity to control the image he projects. He often begins with a prepared announcement, his answers to most questions are equally prepared, and he has leeway on when he will hold the conference and whom he will call upon. While the press conference does provide the president an opportunity to focus national attention upon himself, stimulate public opinion, and criticize or support various political actors, and while the pre-conference briefing may serve as a useful device for informing the president across a broad spectrum of issues, we cannot depend upon it for revealing the real president, and the nature of television may distort more than it reveals.

SERVICES FOR THE PRESS

In order to get their messages across to the American people and to influence the tone and content of the press's presentation of those messages, presidents have provided services for the press ranging from background briefings and exclusive interviews to press releases, photographs, and logistical support.

Franklin Roosevelt established the background briefing, in which the president gave reporters material that they could use as long as it was not attributed to the White House. He also established "off the record" briefings to provide reporters with material that they could not print but that would serve to inform them. Today briefings may be "on the record" (remarks may be attributed to the speaker), "on background" (a specific source cannot be identified but the source's position and status can—such as a "White House source"), "deep background" (no attribution), or "off the record" (the information reporters receive may not be used in a story).

For purposes of convenience we shall term all sessions between White House officials (including the president) and the press that are not "on the record" as "backgrounders." All recent presidents, especially Johnson and Ford, have engaged in background discussion with reporters, although President Nixon's involvement was rare. Some presidents, especially Eisenhower and Nixon, have relied heavily upon their principal foreign policy advisers to brief reporters on foreign affairs.[60]

The most common type of presidential discussion with reporters on a background basis is a briefing. In these sessions the president typically explains a policy's development and what it is expected to accomplish. Interestingly, the president does not appear to stress the substance of policy. He seldom makes "hard" news statements in background briefings because this would irritate absent members of the press. The reporters watch the president perform, and since the president controls the conditions of these briefings, the chances of making a favorable impression are good.[61]

Reporters tend to view middle-level aides as the best information sources. They have in-depth knowledge about the substance of programs, and they are free from the constraints of high visibility, so they are in a good position to provide useful backgrounders. Backgrounders are particularly important for these officials because presidents are generally intolerant of staff members who seek publicity for themselves, and most interviews with White House staff are on this basis. (Sometimes aides say more than their superiors would like in order to prod the president in a particular policy direction.)[62]

Backgrounders have a number of advantages for the White House.[63] Avoiding direct quotation allows officials to speak on sensitive foreign policy and domestic policy matters candidly and in depth, something domestic politics and international diplomacy would not tolerate if speakers were held directly accountable for their words. The White House hopes such discussions will help it communicate its point of view more clearly and serve to educate journalists, perhaps preparing them for future policies, and make them more sympathetic to the president's position in their reporting. An impressive performance in a background session can show the White House to be competent and perhaps elicit the benefit of the doubt in future stories. Moreover, background sessions can be used to scotch rumors and limit undesirable speculation about presidential plans and internal White House affairs.

Backgrounders also may be aimed at the public (in the form of trial balloons that the White House can disclaim if they meet with disapproval) or at policymakers in Washington.[64] They may also be directed at other countries. To discourage the Soviet Union's support of India in its war with Pakistan, Henry Kissinger told reporters in a backgrounder that the Soviet policy might lead to the cancellation of President Nixon's trip to Moscow. Since the statement was not officially attributed to Kissinger, it constituted less of a public threat to the Soviet Union, while at the same time it communicated the president's message.[65]

Reporters have generally been happy to go along with protecting the identities of "spokesmen" and "sources" (although an experienced observer can identify most of them), because the system provides them more information than they would have without it. This increases the information available to the public, and it probably helps advance journalistic careers as well.[66]

Backgrounders, of course, have also provided the White House opportunities to disseminate misleading or self-serving propaganda anonymously. Sometimes this comes in the form of intramural warfare, as was especially common in the Ford administration but also appeared in the Nixon and earlier administrations.[67]

More significantly, the rules regarding quotation and attribution increase the ability of the White House to control the press's portrayal of it. As one Ford White House official commented: "We are trying to make them [the press] use what we want them to use, not what they want. That is what we are trying to do, and it often works."[68]

Some in the press see backgrounders as having negative implications for good reporting. According to one leading Washington journalist,

> Watergate and the saga of Woodward and Bernstein give a false impression of the Washington press corps. Its reputation for tenacious independence and unremitting criticism of government officials is, at best, a recent phenomenon and generally undeserved. For years the relationship developed between the working press and Washington officials had been comfortable. The press cooperated—indeed, it often helped draft the rules—in mutually advantageous private meetings, during which public officials advanced positions—many dubious, many purely political—under a cloak of anonymity. These "background" meetings . . . became grist for the Washington press mill and indispensable for Washington officials. The press was their willing accomplice in government secrecy, trial balloons, and justifications for policy failures.[69]

In addition to the more informal sessions discussed above, briefings are held each weekday for the White House press (they were held twice daily until the Nixon administration). In the daily briefings reporters are provided with information about appointments and resignations; presidential decisions to sign or not to sign routine bills and explanations for his actions; and the president's schedule (whom he will see that day, what meetings he has, what his future travel plans are, and when the press can see him). More significantly from the standpoint of the press, the briefing provides presidential reactions to events, the White House "line" on issues and whether it has changed, and a reading of the president's moods and ideas. This information is obtained through prepared statements or answers to reporters' queries. Responses to the latter are often prepared ahead of time by the White House staff. All of this, of course, also provides the press with an opportunity to have the president's views placed on the public record, which eases the burdens of reporting.[70]

Usually the president's press secretary or his deputy presides over these briefings, although sometimes the president participates. White House staff members and executive branch officials with substantial expertise in specific policy areas such as the budget or foreign affairs sometimes brief the press and answer questions at the daily briefing or at special briefings, especially when the White House is launching a major publicity campaign.[71]

Interviews with the president and top White House staff members are a valuable commodity to the press, and sometimes the White House uses them for its own purposes. Immediately following the 1972 presidential election Richard Nixon granted an exclusive interview to Garnett Horner of the *Washington Star*. This not only rewarded the *Star* for its favorable treatment, but it also "punished" the *Washington Post* for its opposition to the President.[72] In 1980 Jimmy Carter was angered by the *Boston Globe*'s pro-Kennedy slant. Thus, his staff arranged an exclusive presidential interview with the *Globe*'s rival, the *Boston Herald American*.[73] In a less subtle move, President Nixon traded an exclusive interview to Hugh Sidey of *Time* for a cover story on him. The president did not like Sidey, and this was the only time he saw him alone in 5½ years. It was a straight exchange with the conditions (which are typical for a cover story) negotiated ahead of time. In order to obtain an interview with President Ford even the venerable Walter Cronkite agreed to use only questions the president could handle easily. At other times the White House may give exclusives to a paper like the *New York Times* in return for getting a story in which it is interested a prominent place in the paper.[74]

Some presidents, such as Gerald Ford, are very accessible to the press, granting many interviews and photo opportunities and including journalists as social guests at the White House. Even after announcing his defeat in the 1976 election, Ford shook hands with the reporters present. His candidness, accessibility, and warmth helped maintain generally good press relations.[75] John Kennedy also saw reporters often and maintained very good press relations.[76]

Lyndon Johnson was also very accessible to the press and included its members in White House social activities.[77] Nevertheless, his relations with the press, especially at the end of his term, were very strained. This was primarily due to the "credibility gap" that we discussed in Chapter 2.

Richard Nixon generally chose to remain inaccessible to the press, holding few press conferences or interviews and seldom permitting questions from the press when he appeared at public ceremonies.[78] Remaining aloof, he depended upon indirect, staff-mediated relations. When speechwriter William Safire defended Nixon's increased accessibility to the press in late 1970 and early 1971, the president became upset and cancelled his next press conference. He did not even want to appear to be more accessible, lest that imply he had been inaccessible before; he was sensitive to the charge of image-making. The hapless Safire was ignored in the White House for three months after his efforts at defending his boss and was given no assignments.[79]

Providing the press exclusive information may be as ingratiating as an exclusive interview. Lyndon Johnson used this to distract reporters from more embarrassing stories. For example, because he was concerned over the critical stories of a certain reporter, he gave the reporter access to briefings and interviews on administration plans. This gave the journalist a head start over his peers and, feeling that he was trusted and highly valued by the administration, he devoted himself to writing uncritical page one stories describing the president's policy plans. At other times the White House may trade advance notice of a story for information reporters possess about developments elsewhere in the government that are not clear to the president and his staff.[80] President Johnson tried to encourage reporters to overlook his personal indiscretions with promises that he would treat them well if they did.[81]

Recent presidents, with the exception of Richard Nixon, have regularly cultivated elite reporters and columnists, the editors and publishers of leading newspapers, and network news producers and executives with small favors, social flattery, and small background dinners at the White House. (Nixon turned these chores over to top aides.) Indeed, since the 1960s the White House has had first a special person and then an office for media liaison to deal directly with the representatives of news organizations, such as editors, publishers, and producers, in addition to the press office that deals with reporters' routine needs.[82]

There are many additional services that the White House provides for the press. It gives reporters transcripts of briefings and presidential speeches and daily handouts announcing a myriad of information about the president and his policies, including advance notice of travel plans and upcoming stories. Major announcements are timed to accommodate the deadlines of newspapers, magazines, and television networks.[83]

Photographers covering the president are highly dependent on the White House press office, which provides facilities for them on presidential trips and arranges photo sessions, making sure they will produce the most flattering shots of the president (such as Johnson's left profile). President Reagan even prohibited impromptu questions from reporters at these sessions. Moreover, the official White House photographers provide many of the photographs of the president that the media use. Naturally, these are screened so that the president is presented favorably.[84]

When the president goes on trips, at home or abroad, extensive preparations are made for the press. These preparations include arranging transportation and lodging for journalists, installing equipment for radio and television, securing phones for reporters, erecting platforms for photographers, preparing a detailed account of where and with whom the president will be at particular times, providing elaborate information about the countries the president is visiting, forming pools to cover the president closely (as in a motorcade), scheduling the press plane to arrive before the president's so the press can cover his arrival, and, in the past, even offering discounts for the families of journalists who accompanied the president to vacation spots like Florida, Palm Springs, and Vail.

As many of these services suggest, the press is especially dependent upon the White House staff in covering presidential trips, particularly foreign trips. The number of sources of information is generally reduced, as is the access of the press to the principal figures they wish to cover. Thus the president's aides are in a good position to manipulate press coverage to their advantage. Coverage of foreign trips is generally favorable, although less so than in the past now that reporters with expertise in foreign affairs accompany the president, and the press points out the relationship of the trip and its goals and accomplishments to the president's domestic political problems.[85]

Even in Washington, however, reporters are very much in a controlled environment. They may not freely roam the halls of the White House, interviewing whomever they please. They are highly dependent upon the press office for access to officials, and about half their interviews are with the press secretary and his staff. Much of their time is spent waiting for something to happen or watching the president at formal or ceremonial events. Since most news stories about such occurrences show the president in a favorable light, the press office does everything possible to help reporters record these activities. Similarly, the White House is happy to provide photographs featuring the president's "warm," "human," or "family" side. These please editors and the public alike.[86]

Briefings, press releases, and the like have advantages for the White House as well as for the press. They can be used to divert the media's attention from embarrassing matters, as when President Ford's press secretary held a briefing on the president's energy speech to distract the press from the story of missing gifts that former President Nixon had received from other countries.[87] The Reagan White House adopted a strategy of blitzing the media with information to divert its attention after the press raised questions about the president's sleeping through Libyan attacks on U.S. forces off the coast of Africa.[88]

More frequently, the White House, by adopting an active approach to the press, gains an opportunity to shape the media's agenda for the day. Through announcements and press releases it attempts to focus attention on what will reflect positively on the president. Many times these generate questions from reporters and subsequent news stories. This is especially likely to be true for representatives of the smaller papers who have few resources and are thus heavily dependent upon White House–provided news.[89] Moreover, since White House reporters, especially the wire services, are under pressure to file daily "hard news" reports, the White House is in a strong position to help by providing such information, much of it trivial and all of it designed to reflect positively on the president. As a Ford official put it: "You can predict what the press is going to do with a story. It is almost by formula. Because of this they are usable."[90]

Briefings also provide the White House with an opportunity to obtain reporters' reactions to its actions and proposals. Presidents Johnson and Nixon were particularly interested in what happened at the briefings.[91]

Many observers, including journalists, feel that the press tends to parrot the White House line, so conveniently provided at a briefing or in a press release, especially early in a president's term. The White House has taken advantage of this through several techniques including releasing information about or offering unsubstantiated rebuttals to important stories just before deadlines, thus preventing the press from checking or analyzing the statements; releasing stories on Saturday afternoon when reporters specializing in a policy area are off-duty and when agency officials with whom statements could be verified are at home; and President Carter's use of 2- or 3-minute statements that could get on the evening news programs uncut and without excessive interpretation.[92] The pressure among journalists to be first with a story exacerbates the potential for White House manipulation inherent in this deferential approach, as concerns for accuracy give way to career interests.[93]

Presidents have undoubtedly hoped that the handouts, briefings, and other services they and their staffs provide for reporters will gain them some goodwill. They may also hope that these services will keep the White House press from digging too deeply into presidential affairs. Author Richard Reeves observed: "Ron Nessen's [Gerald Ford's press secretary] job is to keep the White House press corps occupied, dumb and happy. He runs an adult day care center. If he were not there doling out a daily ration of front page headlines and 90-second television spots, all those reporters, many of them talented men and women, might be prowling around the government talking to people in, say, the State or Defense Departments, people who know what is going on."[94] Former White House counsel John Dean reports that in the fall of 1972, White House reporters were not happy with press secretary Ron Ziegler's answers to the hard questions asked at the daily briefings regarding the Watergate break-in, but their unhappiness was not reflected in their stories.[95] It is worth noting that the Watergate cover-up was not discovered by the White House press but primarily by obscure reporters far removed from the heady atmosphere and the soft job of covering the president.

From a related perspective, Nixon White House communications director Herbert Klein has written that the White House must keep reporters interested in the president's agenda, because bored journalists are more negative in their reporting and may base their stories on trivial incidents like the president stumbling on a plane.[96]

Despite the wide range of services the White House provides the press, presidents cannot routinely buy it off.[97] Nevertheless, observers have found that this does sometimes occur. When Ronald Reagan went to Jamaica and Barbados in early 1982, his aides were concerned that the press would produce stories suggesting the president's trip might be less work than frolic. They invited the press to bring their families along, and 27 press-corps members accepted the offer, paying for their family members. As one White House official explained, "We figured it would be a lot harder for them to write vacation stories if they were vacationing themselves." The gambit appears to have worked, as most coverage emphasized the president at work rather than at play.[98]

In addition, the White House controls a commodity of considerable value to the press: information on the president's personal life. Most reporters are under pressure to provide stories on the minutiae of the president's life, no matter what he does. Some White House aides have found that the provision of such information can co-opt journalists or sidetrack them from producing critical stories. Some reporters will exploit the opportunity to please their editors instead of digging into more significant subjects; others reciprocate their favorable treatment by the White House with positive stories about the president.[99]

SERVICING THE LOCAL MEDIA

Seeing yet another opportunity to influence the press, the White House has provided services for the local as well as the national and Washington-based media. For example, John Kennedy had intimate luncheons with the editors of small-town and weekly newspapers in which the guests could ask any questions they desired but could not report the president's responses. What they could report was the setting and circumstances of their meeting and their impressions of the president as a person. These were almost always favorable.[100]

Relations with the local media took a significant step forward in the Nixon administration. In an effort to bypass the more liberal national press and to develop goodwill, President Nixon held briefings for local news executives given by himself or senior administration officials. He also sent administration briefing teams around the country to discuss his legislative proposals with local media representatives. They found the local press very responsive to this attention, often giving the president substantial publicity and using the White House story ideas and sometimes even the background materials it provided.[101]

Although Nixon's motivations were undoubtedly heavily partisan, subsequent presidents learned that dealing directly with the nonnational press was very useful in obtaining coverage of the president's message in the local and specialty media. Once the Washington press reports an issue, it tends to drop it and move on to the next one, yet repetition is necessary to convey the president's views to the generally inattentive public we discussed in Chapter 1. Moreover, the Washington press tends to place more emphasis on the support or opposition to a program than on its substance, which the White House wants to communicate.[102]

The Nixon White House, for example, drew up a list of about 150,000 entries, broken down into numerous categories such as daily newspapers, ethnic groups, and geographical locations.[103] Special mailings of news releases and documents to newspapers, television and radio stations, journal writers, private individuals, and citizens groups were also made. In one two-week period during April 1971, the Nixon White House prepared 16 mailings and sent materials to 146,000 groups, publications, or individuals. These materials included booklets on environmental policy and government reorganization to 1,100 reporters and news organizations, a statement by the president opposing abortion to 198 Catholic media and organizations, labor policy information to 1,364 labor and finance writers, a senior-citizens proclamation to 100,000 groups concerned with the aging, and a copy of a James Kilpatrick column to 9,273 academics and Republicans.[104] Local press executives also received White House notes and Christmas cards.

Seven years later the Carter White House sent out 21 items between mid-August and mid-September 1978. Two observers reported:

Five items appeared to be "backgrounders," explaining issues such as inflation, aviation policy, and hospital cost containment. These were sent to the entire mailing list, which consisted of 6,500 news organizations, interest groups, and individuals. Three items were sent to a list of 525, which included columnists and large dailies, newspapers with a circulation of more than 100,000. Six items, including transcripts of briefings and photographs, were sent to 100 Jewish media outlets (September, 1978, was the month of the Camp David meetings that President Carter had with Egyptian President Anwar Sadat and Israeli Prime Minister Menachem Begin). Three were sent to a black media list of 260, 2 to a Hispanic media list of 350, and 1 to a Greek media list of 15. Altogether, 36,120 pieces were sent out during the month, 260 of them photos and 700 of them in Spanish. This total was slightly above the June through September monthly average of 35,551 items.[105]

Thus the Nixon efforts at dealing with the local press were continued and expanded. Gerald Ford invited local news announcers to the White House for taped personal interviews to be used exclusively in their home stations. He also held press conferences for reporters from the local press.[106]

Every other week President Carter had local newspapers and broadcast journalists come to Washington to meet him and be briefed by administration officials. The information provided in these meetings was not released to the general press for 24 hours so that the out-of-town journalists could file their exclusive stories. Carter also had a list of 2,000 editors and broadcasters for White House mailings.[107]

Technology has provided the White House with yet additional opportunities to service the local press. By 1972 almost all the cabinet departments had installed Spotmaster machines, which hold radio tapes that radio or television stations can rebroadcast via telephone as "live" interviews with top officials. At the end of 1978 the White House began to provide 30- and 40-second taped radio spots free of charge to radio stations that called a toll-free White House number. The two to four spots recorded each day are written and recorded by a member of the White House staff. At first they gave no indication that they were being supplied by the White House itself, but after complaints a subtle sign-off of "for the White House" was added.

Presidents who engage in servicing (and lobbying) the local media undoubtedly hope that they will receive a sympathetic hearing from journalists grateful to be invited to the White House and perhaps susceptible to presidential charm. They also hope that by providing information directly to the local media they can evade the closer scrutiny of the Washington-and New-York-based national media, with its greater resources to challenge White House versions of events and policies and to investigate areas of government not covered by briefings or press releases. Naturally, they hope they can also create some goodwill that will be reflected in news stories on the local level.

HARASSMENT OF THE PRESS

The White House can wield the stick as well as offer the carrot. While the Nixon administration did not ignore the latter, it emphasized the former—with a vengeance. The president and his aides were obsessed with the media and spent a disproportionate amount of time dealing with it, and they allowed the personalities and views of reporters to cloud their view and affect their working relationship with the press.[108]

Nixon felt that the media represented "the greatest concentration of power in the United States."[109] White House chief of staff Bob Haldeman stated that the power of the press was and is "awesome."[110] The president regularly spoke of the press (to his staff) as the "enemy," as something to be hated and beaten. According to one of his speechwriters, William Safire, this attitude was "neither justified nor defensible." It went beyond a feeling of ideological bias, institutionalized opposition, or concern for information contrary to the public good. It was hatred.[111]

Columnist Jack Anderson described Nixon's relations with the press as follows: "Richard Nixon repels the press. He's openly hostile. He spits in their eye. He thumbs his nose at them, and they respond as human beings do, by writing tougher stories than they might otherwise have done." At the end of direct American involvement in the Vietnam war he told reporters: "We finally have achieved a peace with honor. I know it gags some of you to write that phrase, but that is true."[112]

Open hostility, however, was not the full story of the Nixon White House's relations with the press. The attitudes described above led to harassment of the press and attempts to pressure it into quiescence. These attempts took many forms. One was sending Vice President Spiro Agnew to make speeches highly critical of the printed and electronic press as early as November 1969. Agnew opposed television commentators' spot critiques of presidential addresses. He also criticized the network reporters for being prejudiced against the president and unrepresentative of the American people, and for distorting the news and emphasizing negative instead of positive events.

Although Agnew was the one speaking, responsibility for his attacks was clearly in the Oval Office.[113] The same themes were repeated by other administration officials and by the president himself in a steady stream of complaints about the networks' news coverage.[114]

There is evidence that these efforts were partly successful. One study found that television reporters reduced the amount of personal interpretation of news events following the administration's criticism.[115] In June 1973, CBS stopped its spot analyses of presidential speeches, but five months later it resumed them. On the other hand, CBS earlier announced a policy of giving free access to the airwaves to the opposition (i.e., the Democrats), something ABC and NBC said had been their policy all along.[116]

Agnew and the White House also criticized the printed media for bias, distortion, negativism, and monopolization of local news outlets and for being unrepresentative of the American people. As with the television networks, complaints were made directly to the news organizations and reporters as well as to the public.[117] Some papers, such as the *New York Times* and the *Washington Post*, prime targets in the White House attack, became more careful in their coverage and began including more conservative material. The *Times* hired Nixon speechwriter William Safire as a columnist. Both papers also began to print corrections of some of their factual errors.[118] Nevertheless, they led the charge in the Watergate investigation.

It is significant that the Nixon White House was not at all bothered by press treatment that was favorable to it. When it attacked the networks, it focused more on CBS and NBC than ABC, whose coverage was more favorable. When the Nixon White House criticized newspapers, it concentrated its wrath on the "Eastern" press, especially the *Washington Post* and *New York Times*, the two most prominent newspapers in the country. The editorial pages of both these papers are oriented toward a liberal, Democratic viewpoint. Most other papers, however, are not. Nixon was quite content to receive their support and was not concerned that the liberal point of view was not better represented in their coverage of the news.

It is also worth noting that the "instant analysis" of President Nixon's speech by network commentators that was the immediate cause of Vice President Agnew's famous Des Moines speech in November 1969 was really not "instant" at all. Reporters had the speech five hours before it was given and received a follow-up briefing by administration officials, including Henry Kissinger, three hours ahead of time.[119] The White House was opposed merely to the criticism in the analyses.

The Nixon administration did not limit its efforts at harassing the press to mere criticism. According to chief of staff Haldeman, Nixon often ordered him to "go after" reporters—orders he said he ignored. One instance in which he did *not* ignore such an order was regarding CBS reporter Daniel Schorr, who was often critical of the administration. Haldeman asked for the FBI's file on Schorr, and a full FBI field investigation of the reporter took place. When this became public, the White House lied and said it was considering Schorr for a job! Other reporters had their phones wiretapped or their taxes audited. CBS reporter Dan Rather was called to the White House and criticized by Haldeman and John Ehrlichman. They also complained to his superiors. Les Whiten, columnist Jack Anderson's associate, was arrested by the FBI after receiving some documents. (A grand jury refused to indict him.) Anderson was both bugged and tailed.[120]

In a clever but deceitful tactic the White House had letters, ostensibly from Nixon-haters, sent to two prominent columnists who wrote exclusively about the president. The "authors" of the letters thanked the columnists for their "scathing attacks" on the president. The intention was to force the columnists to consider their biases toward Nixon, at least as the White House saw them, and the letters may have had a modest effect.[121]

Sometimes efforts were made to punish or intimidate an entire newspaper. When the Long Island newspaper *Newsday* investigated the president's close friend Bebe Rebozo in 1971, Nixon got angry. The reporter who supervised the investigation, the publisher, and the editor had their taxes audited by the IRS, as did the newspaper itself. The timing of these audits is suggestive. *Newsday* was also cut off from privileged White House information, and its Washington bureau chief was struck from the list of those accompanying the president on his historic visit to China in 1972.[122]

Richard Nixon hated no paper more than the *Washington Post*, and his administration took special pains to give it a hard time. Witness the following conversation between the president and his chief of staff captured on the White House tapes:

> The President: The main thing is the *Post* is going to have damnable, damnable problems out of this one. They have a television station and they're going to have to get it renewed.
> Haldeman: They've got a radio station, too.
> The President: Does that come up, too? . . . It's going to be goddam active here. . . . Well, the game has to be played awfully rough.[123]

The frightening thing is that the president was serious. One of the *Post*'s TV stations, Channel 10 in Miami, was challenged (unsuccessfully) in its license renewal by Nixon associates as early as 1970.[124]

When the Nixon administration perceived that the *Post*'s investigation of Watergate was a real threat, the White House began excluding it from covering social events at the Executive Mansion, and many on the White House staff refused to talk to the *Post*'s veteran White House correspondent, Carroll Kilpatrick. Presidential aide Charles Colson told a reporter for the *Washington Star*, the *Post*'s chief competitor, that after the 1972 election the White House planned to deny news to the *Post* while providing it freely to the *Star*. In addition, several persons long associated with the president filed challenges with the Federal Communications Commission to the license renewals for another of the *Post*'s television stations in Florida.[125]

The technique of cutting off access of critical newspapers to administration sources seems to have been ordered fairly routinely by Nixon. The success of these efforts, however, was limited, as White House sources continued to talk to reporters and the orders "wore off" after a while or were carefully eroded by top presidential aides.[126]

Other techniques were used to harass "unfriendly" newspapers. The *Times* and the *Post* were excluded from some briefings. The *Boston Globe* was excluded from Nixon's China trip.[127] Likewise Vice President Agnew excluded some papers from covering one of his foreign trips. Press Secretary Ron Ziegler punished some reporters by leaving them out of White House pools.[128] Attorney General John Mitchell made a short-lived threat to subpoena the records of reporters who gave black militants what he considered undue coverage.[129]

Television received special attention from the Nixon White House. The day after a Nixon speech on Vietnam in November 1969, Dean Burch, Chairman of the Federal Communications Commission—a supposedly independent agency—called the presidents of CBS, NBC, and ABC on behalf of the White House and requested transcripts of the news analyses done after the speech. He also called some local television stations to ask about their editorials on the speech. Several White House aides made similar calls at various times. The next year Charles Colson, special counsel to the president, met separately with the heads of the three networks to discuss their news coverage of the administration and to urge that they eliminate loyal-opposition responses to the president or else the White House would seek to force them to by law.[130]

As time went on, things got even tougher. The networks were threatened with the loss of the five highly profitable local television stations they each owned and antitrust suits were instituted against them. Immediately after the 1972 election, Colson called the president of CBS and told him things would get worse for his network if it did not "play ball" with the administration. According to later testimony Colson allegedly said in substance, "We'll bring you to your knees in Wall Street and on Madison Avenue."[131]

Less direct efforts to intimidate the media were also made. Clay Whitehead, the head of the president's Office of Telecommunications Policy, told local station owners that they would be held responsible for the fairness (undefined) of network news at license renewal time. He wanted to pressure the local affiliates into exerting pressure on the networks to be less critical of the administration.[132]

Presidential aides put pressure on the Public Broadcasting Service to cancel funds for news programs such as those hosted by William F. Buckley, Bill Moyers, and Elizabeth Drew and to dismiss Sander Vanocur as news director of the National Public Affairs Center for Television. The White House wanted less public television air time devoted to news coverage and analysis, and it wanted the news programs that were presented to be local (and therefore probably more favorable to the administration).[133]

Richard Nixon engaged in a war with the press throughout his tenure in office. As we noted earlier, all presidents are angered by the press at one time or another. Sometimes they have attempted to interfere with its carrying out its duties. Kennedy pressed the *New York Times* to pull reporter David Halberstam out of Vietnam (from which he had been sending back pessimistic, but generally accurate, reports), and Johnson attempted to have a wire service correspondent in Vietnam replaced. He also cut off access to reporters and columnists, even very prominent ones, who irritated him, and he badgered and bullied reporters.[134]

Presidents have also frequently criticized the press, phoning reporters or the networks with their complaints. Nevertheless, they remained on generally good terms with the press. While Johnson might be furious at a reporter one day, he might invite the same person to lunch the next day. He might even appoint him to a government position (as he appointed John Chancellor, a frequent nemesis, to head the Voice of America).[135]

President Carter's press secretary, Jody Powell, also took many swipes at the press, complaining to various reporters about what he considered inaccurate reports. Sometimes his language was quite strong, but his disarming personality and his ability to recover quickly from bursts of anger took some of the sting out of his criticisms. He felt that "you ought to be able to respond forcefully to stories that you think are off-base, and both government and press ought to be grown up enough not to take it personally." Like Johnson, he could be critical on one day and cordial on the next.[136]

Nixon added an extra dimension to the adversarial relations between the president and the press. He preferred to bludgeon the press into submission. Failing that, he tried to discredit the press by creating doubt in the public's mind that the press was treating his administration fairly.[137] He hoped that the public would pay less attention to the press criticism of him and his policies, and he would also have an acceptable excuse to avoid meeting directly with them.

CONCLUSION

The mass media play a prominent role in the public presidency, providing the public with most of its information about the White House and mediating the president's communications with his constituents. Presidents need the press in order to reach the public, and presidential-press relations are an important complement to the chief executive's efforts at leading public opinion. Through attempting to coordinate news, holding press conferences, and providing a wide range of services for the press, the White House tries to influence its portrayal in the news. On occasion, the inevitable adversarial nature of presidential-press relations leads to open warfare and various forms of harassment of the press.

Among the things that most infuriate presidents are leaks and what they perceive as biased reporting. Other observers have criticized the press for the trivial, superficial nature of its coverage of the presidency. In the next chapter we turn our attention to these issues in presidential-press relations.

NOTES

1. Elmer E. Cornwell, Jr., "Presidential News: The Expanding Public Image," *Journalism Quarterly* 36 (Summer 1959), pp. 275–83; Alan P. Balutis, "The Presidency and the Press: The Expanding Presidential Image," *Presidential Studies Quarterly* 7 (Fall 1977), pp. 244–51. See also Herbert J. Gans, *Deciding What's News* (New York: Vintage, 1979), p. 9.

2. Richard Harris, "The Presidency and the Press," *New Yorker*, October 1, 1973, p. 122; Dom Bonafede, "Powell and the Press—A New Mood in the White House," *National Journal*, June 25, 1977, p. 981.

3. Harris, "The Presidency and the Press," p. 122; Peter Forbath and Carey Winfrey, *The Adversaries: The President and the Press* (Cleveland: Regal Books, 1974), p. 5.

4. David Wise, *The Politics of Lying: Government Deception, Secrecy, and Power* (New York: Vintage, 1973), pp. 458–59.

5. Bonafede, "Powell and the Press," p. 987.

6. Benjamin Bradlee, *Conversations with Kennedy* (New York: Norton, 1975), especially p. 25.

7. Wise, *The Politics of Lying*, pp. 460, 479–80.

8. Hugh Sidey, *A Very Personal Presidency: Lyndon Johnson in the White House* (New York: Atheneum, 1968), p. 163.

9. *Nixon: The Fifth Year of His Presidency* (Washington, D.C.: Congressional Quarterly, 1974), p. 177-A.

10. Michael Baruch Grossman and Martha Joynt Kumar, "Carter, Reagan, and the Media: Have the Rules Changed or the Poles of the Spectrum of Success?" (paper delivered at the Annual Meeting of the American Political Science Association, New York, September 1981), p. 10.

11. "What the Press Must Do," *Newsweek*, December 9, 1974, p. 15.

12. See, for example, George Christian, *The President Steps Down: A Personal Memoir of the Transfer of Power* (New York: Macmillan, 1970), p. 190.

13. Dick Kirschten, "Life in the White House Fish Bowl—Brady Takes Charge as Press Chief," *National Journal*, January 31, 1981, p. 180.

14. Michael Baruch Grossman and Martha Joynt Kumar, *Portraying the President: The White House and the Media* (Baltimore: Johns Hopkins University Press, 1981), p. 135.

15. *Ibid.*, pp. 84, 116.

16. One exception might have been Ron Ziegler. See Jeb Stuart Magruder, *An American Life: One Man's Road to Watergate* (New York: Pocket Books, 1975), p. 70.

17. Grossman and Kumar, *Portraying the President*, p. 141.

18. *Ibid.*, pp. 151–54.

19. *Ibid.*, pp. 145–46.

20. *Ibid.*, p. 145.

21. *Ibid.*, pp. 22–23, 142, 184–85, 278; Elmer E. Cornwell, Jr., *The Presidency and the Press* (Morristown, N.J.: General Learning Press, 1974), p. 17.

22. Bonafede, "Powell and the Press," p. 985; Grossman and Kumar, *Portraying*

the President, pp. 93, 95–96, 101–02, 122–23, 142; Herbert G. Klein, *Making It Perfectly Clear* (Garden City, N.Y.: Doubleday, 1980), pp. 185, 203; Theodore C. Sorenson, *Kennedy* (New York: Harper and Row, 1965), p. 318.

23. Ron Nessen, *It Sure Looks Different from the Inside* (Chicago: Playboy Press, 1978), pp. 127–28.
24. Walter S. Mossberg, "Reagan Prepares Curbs on U.S. Officials to Restrict News Leaks on Foreign Policy," *Wall Street Journal*, January 13, 1982, p. 7.
25. Grossman and Kumar, *Portraying the President*, pp. 142, 148–49, 277.
26. Magruder, *An American Life*, pp. 3, 91–92; William Safire, *Before the Fall: An Inside View of the Pre-Watergate White House* (New York: Doubleday, 1975), p. 361. Earlier presidents had, of course, tried this as well. See, for example, Sorenson, *Kennedy*, pp. 318–20.
27. Christian, *The President Steps Down*, pp. 6–7; Grossman and Kumar, *Portraying the President*, p. 53; Fred I. Greenstein, "Eisenhower as an Activist President: A Look at New Evidence," *Political Science Quarterly* 94 (Winter 1979–80), p. 578; Hoyt Purvis, ed., *The Presidency and the Press* (Austin, Texas: Lyndon B. Johnson School of Public Affairs, 1976), p. 11; David Halberstam, *The Powers That Be* (New York: Knopf, 1979), p. 388.
28. See, for example, Herbert Y. Schandler, *The Unmaking of a President: Lyndon Johnson and Vietnam* (Princeton, N.J.: Princeton University Press, 1977), p. 256.
29. Klein, *Making It Perfectly Clear*, pp. 197, 418; Grossman and Kumar, *Portraying the President*, pp. 103–4; Safire, *Before the Fall*, pp. 342–43; Wise, *The Politics of Lying*, p. 345; Richard M. Nixon, *RN: The Memoirs of Richard Nixon* (New York: Grosset and Dunlap, 1978), p. 355; William E. Porter, *Assault on the Media: The Nixon Years* (Ann Arbor, Mich.: University of Michigan Press, 1976), p. 35; James Keogh, *President Nixon and the Press* (New York: Funk and Wagnalls, 1972), p. 70.
30. Bonafede, "Powell and the Press," p. 986.
31. Grossman and Kumar, *Portraying the President*, p. 103; "White House Reading List Includes 38 Magazines," *Folio*, October 1977, p. 23.
32. Bonafede, "Powell and the Press," p. 986.
33. "A Jewish News Wrap-up," *Newsweek*, August 29, 1977, p. 14.
34. For example, see William Safire, "Last Days in the Bunker," *The New York Times Magazine*, August 18, 1974, p. 6; Klein, *Making It Perfectly Clear*, pp. 322, 418; Grossman and Kumar, *Portraying the President*, pp. 102–4; James Gerstenzang, "News Summary Aids Carter," *New Orleans Times-Picayune*, March 9, 1977, section 1, p. 7; Saul Kohler, "Ford Knows What's Said," *New Orleans Times-Picayune*, September 15, 1974, section 1, p. 8.
35. Wise, *The Politics of Lying*, p. 359; Grossman and Kumar, *Portraying the President*, p. 245.
36. Kirschten, "Life in the White House Fish Bowl," p. 180.
37. Grossman and Kumar, *Portraying the President*, pp. 245–46. See also William W. Lammers, "Presidential Press Conference Schedules: Who Hides and When?", *Political Science Quarterly* 96 (Summer 1981), pp. 262–63.
38. Grossman and Kumar, *Portraying the President*, pp. 244–45.

39. Lammers, "Presidential Press Conference Schedules," pp. 261–78; Jarol B. Manheim and William W. Lammers, "The News Conference and Presidential Leadership of Public Opinion: Does the Tail Wag the Dog?", *Presidential Studies Quarterly* 11 (Spring 1981), pp. 177–88.
40. See Christian, *The President Steps Down*, pp. 198–99; William C. Spragens, "The Myth of the Johnson 'Credibility Gap,' " *Presidential Studies Quarterly* 10 (Fall 1980), pp. 629–35.
41. Grossman and Kumar, *Portraying the President*, pp. 139, 243, 247.
42. See, for example, *ibid.*, pp. 140, 427–28; Christian, *The President Steps Down*, p. 199; Keogh, *Richard Nixon and the Press*, p. 49; Gerald R. Ford, *A Time to Heal* (New York: Harper and Row, 1979), p. 157; "Dress Rehearsals to Prep the President," *Newsweek*, May 24, 1982, p. 23.
43. Newton Minow, John B. Martin, and Lee M. Mitchell, *Presidential Television* (New York: Basic Books, 1973), p. 39.
44. Cornwell, *The Presidency and the Press*, p. 19.
45. Wise, *The Politics of Lying*, pp. 456–57. See the comments in Henry Kissinger, *White House Years* (Boston: Little, Brown, 1979), pp. 316, 319 on the stress Nixon experienced in press conferences.
46. Wise, *The Politics of Lying*, pp. 466–67; Edward R. Morgan, Max Ways, Clark Mollenhoff, Peter Lisagor, and Herbert G. Klein, *The Presidency and the Press Conference* (Washington, D.C.: American Enterprise Institute, 1971), p. 5.
47. Jarol B. Manheim, Book Review, *Presidential Studies Quarterly* 9 (Fall 1979), p. 486.
48. Jarol B. Manheim, "The Honeymoon's Over: The News Conference and the Development of Presidential Style," *Journal of Politics* 41 (February 1979), p. 66.
49. *Ibid.*, pp. 64–66.
50. Greenstein, "Eisenhower as an Activist President," pp. 587–90.
51. Grossman and Kumar, *Portraying the President*, pp. 140–41, 287, 428–29; Wise, *The Politics of Lying*, pp. 469–71; Sorenson, *Kennedy*, p. 318.
52. Wise, *ibid.*, p. 471.
53. John Ehrlichman, *Witness to Power: The Nixon Years* (New York: Simon and Schuster, 1982), pp. 285–87. See also, Morgan, et al., *The Presidency and the Press Conference*, pp. 5, 12; David L. Paletz and Robert M. Entman, *Media—Power —Politics* (New York: Free Press, 1981), p. 61.
54. Ford, *A Time to Heal*, p. 158.
55. Manheim, "The Honeymoon's Over," pp. 60–61.
56. Morgan, et al., *The Presidency and the Press Conference*, p. 16.
57. Ford, *A Time to Heal*, pp. 156–57.
58. Keogh, *President Nixon and the Press*, pp. 44–45.
59. Wise, *The Politics of Lying*, pp. 461–63.
60. *Ibid.*, pp. 420–42; Grossman and Kumar, *Portraying the President*, pp. 122–23, 165–67; Christian, *The President Steps Down*, p. 187; Dick Kirschten, "Questions and Answers," *National Journal*, February 7, 1981, p. 237; Kissinger, *White House Years*, p. 302.
61. Grossman and Kumar, *Portraying the President*, pp. 165, 167–68.

62. *Ibid.*, pp. 60, 169–71, 185–86, 203.
63. See *ibid.*, pp. 161–62, 164, 167–68; Nessen, *It Sure Looks Different*, p. 64; Klein, *Making It Perfectly Clear*, pp. 429–30.
64. Ehrlichman, *Witness to Power*, p. 122.
65. Doris A. Graber, *Mass Media and American Politics* (Washington, D.C.: Congressional Quarterly Press, 1980), p. 207.
66. Grossman and Kumar, *Portraying the President*, pp. 160–61.
67. *Ibid.*, p. 162.
68. Quoted in *ibid.*, p. 227.
69. Haynes Johnson, *In the Absence of Power: Governing America* (New York: Viking Press, 1980), pp. 97–98. See also Wise, *The Politics of Lying*, pp. 442–46.
70. Grossman and Kumar, *Portraying the President*, pp. 32–33, 40.
71. *Ibid.*, pp. 87, 122–23, 165, 169–70.
72. *Ibid.*, pp. 67, 284.
73. "Carter Gets Even with the *Boston Globe,*" *Newsweek*, February 25, 1980, p. 21.
74. Grossman and Kumar, *Portraying the President*, pp. 59–60, 63–64, 280–81.
75. Nessen, *It Sure Looks Different*, pp. 319, 332, 349–50; John Herbers, *No Thank You, Mr. President* (New York: Norton, 1976), p. 181.
76. Sorenson, *Kennedy*, p. 318; Cornwell, *The Presidency and the Press*, p. 17.
77. Christian, *The President Steps Down*, p. 230.
78. Grossman and Kumar, *Portraying the President*, p. 246.
79. Safire, *Before the Fall*, pp. 349–51.
80. Grossman and Kumar, *Portraying the President*, pp. 88, 287–88.
81. Sidey, *A Very Personal Presidency*, p. 172.
82. Dom Bonafede, "Has the Rafshoon Touch Left Its Mark on the White House?", *National Journal*, April 14, 1979, p. 591; Grossman and Kumar, *Portraying the President*, pp. 25–26, 89, 166, 207–9, 284–87.
83. Grossman and Kumar, *Portraying the President*, pp. 44, 49.
84. *Ibid.*, pp. 56, 78–80.
85. *Ibid.*, pp. 235–38.
86. *Ibid.*, pp. 44, 228, 232, 270–71; Stephen Hess, *The Washington Reporters* (Washington, D.C.: Brookings Institution, 1981), p. 60.
87. Nessen, *It Sure Looks Different*, p. 18.
88. Dom Bonafede, "The Washington Press—It Magnifies the President's Flaws and Blemishes," *National Journal*, May 1, 1982, pp. 767–71.
89. Grossman and Kumar, *Portraying the President*, pp. 33, 140. See also "Meeting the Press," *Public Opinion*, December–January 1982, p. 10.
90. Paletz and Entman, *Media—Power—Politics*, pp. 55–56. See also Halberstam, *The Powers That Be*, p. 244; Ehrlichman, *Witness to Power*, pp. 264, 266–67.
91. Grossman and Kumar, *Portraying the President*, pp. 33, 88, 142.
92. Hess, *The Washington Reporters*, p. 60; Paletz and Entman, *Media—Power—Politics*, p. 72; Grossman and Kumar, *Portraying the President*, pp. 49, 274–79; Herbers, *No Thank You, Mr. President*, pp. 41–42, 58, 182; Hodding Carter III, "The El Salvador Crusade," *Wall Street Journal*, March 19, 1981, p. 25.
93. On this see Purvis, *The Presidency and the Press*, p. 61; Grossman and Kumar, *Portraying the President*, p. 182.

94. Dom Bonafede, "Nessen Still Seeks 'Separate Peace' with Press," *National Journal*, October 11, 1975, p. 1412. See also Purvis, *The Presidency and the Press*, p. 12.
95. John Dean, *Blind Ambition: The White House Years* (New York: Simon and Schuster, 1976), p. 127.
96. Klein, *Making It Perfectly Clear*, p. 427.
97. Grossman and Kumar, *Portraying the President*, pp. 171–72, 311; Christian, *The President Steps Down*, pp. 186–87.
98. "Playing the Holiday Gambit," *Newsweek*, April 19, 1982, p. 27.
99. Grossman and Kumar, *Portraying the President*, pp. 231, 276–77. See also Porter, *Assault on the Media*, pp. 239–41.
100. Grossman and Kumar, *Portraying the President*, p. 164.
101. *Ibid.*, pp. 90–91; Klein, *Making It Perfectly Clear*, p. 202; Magruder, *An American Life*, pp. 3, 112–13, 166.
102. Grossman and Kumar, *Portraying the President*, p. 90.
103. Magruder, *An American Life*, pp. 109–11.
104. Klein, *Making It Perfectly Clear*, pp. 185, 195; Grossman and Kumar, *Portraying the President*, p. 296. See also Grossman and Kumar, p. 91.
105. Grossman and Kumar, *Portraying the President*, p. 92.
106. Nessen, *It Sure Looks Different*, p. 350; Robert Locander, "Carter and the Press: The First Two Years," *Presidential Studies Quarterly* 10 (Winter 1980), p. 114.
107. Bonafede, "Powell and the Press," p. 986.
108. Klein, *Making It Perfectly Clear*, pp. 69, 76.
109. Fifth interview with David Frost.
110. H. R. Haldeman, *The Ends of Power*, p. 244.
111. See Safire, *Before the Fall*, especially pp. 75, 321–23, 341–65. See also Ehrlichman, *Witness to Power*, p. 264.
112. Forbath and Winfrey, *The Adversaries*, p. 12.
113. Haldeman, *The Ends of Power*, p. 243; Safire, *Before the Fall*, pp. 352–53; Magruder, *An American Life*, p. 63; Klein, *Making It Perfectly Clear*, p. 168.
114. See, for example, Klein, *Making It Perfectly Clear*, p. 353; Magruder, *An American Life*, pp. 99–100; Wise, *The Politics of Lying*, pp. 339, 379–99; Porter, *Assault on the Media*, pp. 48–49.
115. Dennis T. Lowrey, "Agnew and the Network TV News: A Before/After Content Analysis," *Journalism Quarterly* 48 (Summer 1971), pp. 31–41.
116. Porter, *Assault on the Media*, pp. 64, 204, 209.
117. See, for example, Wise, *The Politics of Lying*, p. 356; Magruder, *An American Life*, pp. 99–100; Klein, *Making It Perfectly Clear*, p. 353.
118. Porter, *Assault on the Media*, pp. 198–201.
119. *Ibid.*, pp. 43–44; Klein, *Making It Perfectly Clear*, pp. 170, 201.
120. Haldeman, *The Ends of Power*, pp. 244–45 (Haldeman argues that the full field investigation of Schorr was due to a mistake in communications); Safire, *Before the Fall*, pp. 354–55, 357; Wise, *The Politics of Lying*, pp. 379–93; Porter, *Assault on the Media*, pp. 40–41, 112, 142–44, 178–79; Klein, *Making It Perfectly Clear*, p. 214; Magruder, *An American Life*, pp. 62–63; Timothy Crouse, *The Boys on the Bus* (New York: Random House, 1973), p. 255; Thomas Whiteside, "Annals of Television: Shaking the Tree," *New Yorker*, March 17, 1975, p. 84.

See also Ehrlichman, *Witness to Power*, pp. 277–83 for his version of pressure on Rather's superiors.

121. Magruder, *An American Life*, p. 112.

122. Porter, *Assault on the Media*, pp. 126–30, 184; Safire, *Before the Fall*, p. 614; Wise, *The Politics of Lying*, pp. 317–26.

123. *Comparison of White House and Judiciary Committee Transcripts of Eight Recorded Presidential Conversations*, Hearings before the Committee on the Judiciary, House of Representatives, 93rd Congress, 2nd Session, p. 5.

124. Porter, *Assault on the Media*, pp. 53, 169.

125. *Ibid.*, pp. 174, 194; Whiteside, "Annals of Television," p. 66; Wise, *The Politics of Lying*, pp. 402–3; Carl Bernstein and Bob Woodward, *All the President's Men* (New York: Warner, 1975), pp. 246–47.

126. Klein, *Making It Perfectly Clear*, pp. 325, 405; Crouse, *Boys on the Bus*, pp. 220–22; Herbers, *No Thank You, Mr. President*, p. 58; Safire, *Before the Fall*, pp. 345–46, 353; Ehrlichman, *Witness to Power*, pp. 264, 275; Kissinger, *Years of Upheaval*, p. 95.

127. Porter, *Assault on the Media*, pp. 194–95.

128. Herbers, *No Thank You, Mr. President*, pp. 85–86.

129. "Mitchell Assures Newsmen on Files," *New York Times*, February 6, 1970, pp. 1, 40.

130. Wise, *The Politics of Lying*, p. 397; Porter, *Assault on the Media*, pp. 45–48; Whiteside, "Annals of Television," pp. 42, 46; Klein, *Making It Perfectly Clear*, pp. 173–74, 211–12, 291. Klein, pp. 173–74, 211, argues that it was a mistake to call the television networks after Nixon's Vietnam speech, but, as the White House routinely requested editorial reactions from television and radio stations and newspapers, he did not realize this request was unusual or would be seen as intimidation.

131. Whiteside, "Annals of Television," pp. 61, 77–78, 80; Porter, *Assault on the Media*, pp. 158–59; Klein, *Making It Perfectly Clear*, pp. 212–13. Klein, p. 217, denies the antitrust suits were motivated by political considerations.

132. Whiteside, "Annals of Television," p. 70; Porter, *Assault on the Media*, p. 173; Klein, *Making It Perfectly Clear*, p. 292; Safire, *Before the Fall*, p. 353; Wise, *The Politics of Lying*, p. 403.

133. Klein, *Making It Perfectly Clear*, p. 224; "Government Interference in Public Broadcasting Disclosed," *Congressional Quarterly Weekly Report*, March 24, 1979, p. 533.

134. Paletz and Entman, *Media—Power—Politics*, pp. 61–62; Halberstam, *The Powers That Be*, pp. 436–37, 547–48; Joseph A. Califano, Jr., *A Presidential Nation* (New York: Norton, 1975), p. 117.

135. Halberstam, *The Powers That Be*, pp. 359–61, 389, 433, 437, 441–42, 490; Paletz and Entman, *Media—Power—Politics*, p. 61; Christian, *The President Steps Down*, p. 230; Cornwell, *The Presidency and the Press*, p. 17; Wise, *The Politics of Lying*, pp. 369–74; Forbath and Winfrey, *The Adversaries*, p. 11; Whiteside, "Annals of Television," p. 59.

136. "Jody Faces Life," *Newsweek*, September 19, 1977, pp. 119–20.

137. Safire, *Before the Fall*, p. 354.

CHAPTER FOUR

ISSUES IN PRESIDENTIAL-PRESS RELATIONS

In the previous chapter we focused on the context, structure, and nature of presidential-press relations from the perspective of the White House. In addition to the chief executive's efforts to influence the media, there is another side of this relationship we must examine: the content of the news. Ultimately, it is the written and spoken word that concerns the president. Leaks of confidential information and what is seen in the White House as superficial and biased reporting exacerbate the tensions inherent in presidential-press relations.

Presidents commonly view the press as a major obstacle to their obtaining and maintaining public support. As we have already seen, criticism of media coverage as being trivial and distorted and as violating confidences is a standard feature of most administrations. The White House feels that this type of reporting hinders its efforts to develop public appreciation for the president and his policies.

We know little about the nature of press coverage of the presidency and even less about its effects on the public. Nevertheless, it is essential that we attempt to organize what we know and look at its implications for the public presidency.

In this chapter we examine some of the most prominent issues in presidential-press relations. These include leaks, biased reporting, superficial coverage, and their effects. First, we discuss each of these issues separately to put them in perspective. Then we turn to a case study of network television coverage of President Carter's 1979 "crisis of confidence" speech and the subsequent alterations in his cabinet to more fully examine the issues of biased and trivial reporting.

LEAKS

After one month in office President Carter was told that the *Washington Post* was going to print a story about the CIA making payments to Jordan's King Hussein. Although the White House asked the paper not to publish the story, it did so on the very day Secretary of State Cyrus Vance was going to meet Hussein about the Middle East peace problems.[1] A few months later Carter was angered over stories that he was disappointed with various members of his Cabinet. He told White House staffers that those who were spreading such rumors should resign or be fired.[2] A year and a half later he was again upset, this time by a series of unauthorized and frequently contradictory statements from unnamed "administration officials" that Carter felt had confused public perceptions of U.S. foreign policy. He summoned State Department and National Security Council officials and berated them for their poor judgment and told them to stifle all press comments on sensitive policy matters.[3] In each case, it should be noted, Carter did not blame the press or in any way try to intimidate it.

President Carter was hardly the first president to be upset by leaks. Sometimes they can be potentially quite serious, as when the U.S. negotiating strategy in the first SALT talks was disclosed during the Nixon administration. When the *Pentagon Papers* were leaked to the public, President Nixon felt that there was a danger that other countries would lose confidence in our ability to keep secrets and that information on the delicate negotiations then in progress with China might also be leaked, endangering the possibility of rapprochement.[4] At other times they are just embarrassing, as when internal dissent in the administration is revealed to the public. President Johnson feared that leaks would signal what he was thinking and that he would lose his freedom of action as a result.[5]

In early 1982 President Reagan read the riot act to his cabinet, denouncing leaks as one of the major problems facing the administration. He was particularly concerned about leaks regarding his upcoming budget proposals for defense spending, a number of foreign policy matters, and the urban enterprise zones proposal that he wanted to save for his State of the Union message.[6] The president's frustration is evident in the quip with which he opened a press conference held at about the same time: "I was going to have an opening statement, but I decided that what I was going to say I wanted to get a lot of attention so I'm going to wait and leak it."[7]

Who Leaks?

Who leaks? The best answer is "everybody."[8] According to former press secretary Ron Nessen:

> Sometimes it's nobody. Sometimes it's an assistant to an assistant who doesn't really know what's going on, but is ashamed to admit that to the reporter. Sometimes it's the guy at a senior staff meeting who complains the loudest about the s.o.b. leaking stories to the press. And sometimes it's you. Some statements you make in public, on the record, are reported as the backstage whispers of an unnamed source. The correspondent hides you behind this cloak of anonymity to make his story more credible, since nobody believes the official spokesman these days but everybody trusts an unidentified source.[9]

Presidents themselves leak, sometimes inadvertently. Once when John Kennedy was angry at a leak, he ordered his press secretary to trace its source. It was Kennedy.[10] As Lyndon Johnson once put it: "I have enough trouble with myself. I ought not to have to put up with everybody else too."[11]

Top presidential aides may also reveal more than they intend. When a leak regarding President Reagan's willingness to compromise on his 1981 tax bill appeared in the *New York Times*, White House aides traced down the source of the story and found it was budget director David Stockman.[12] A year earlier a leak revealing secret CIA arms shipments to Afghan rebels was attributed to the office of the president's chief national security advisor.[13]

Most leaks, however, are deliberately planted.[14] As one close presidential aide put it, "99 percent of all significant secrets are spilled by the principals or at their direction."[15] Presidents are included in those who purposefully leak. *Newsweek* used to hold space open for the items John Kennedy would phone in to his friend Benjamin Bradlee right before the magazine's deadline.[16]

Reasons for Leaks

There are many reasons for leaks. They may be used as trial balloons to test public or congressional reaction to ideas and proposals or to stimulate public concern about an issue. Both the Ford and Carter White House used this technique to test reaction to a tax surcharge on gasoline. When the reaction turned out to be negative, they denied ever contemplating such a policy. At other times reporters who will use information to write favorable articles on a policy receive leaked information.[17]

Diplomacy is an area in which delicate communications play an important role. Leaks are often used to send signals to other nations of our friendship, anger, or willingness to compromise. At the same time they provide the president the opportunity to publicly disavow or reinterpret what some might view as, for example, an overly "tough" stance or an unexpected change in policy.

Leaks may also be used to influence personnel matters. The release of information can force a reluctant official to resign and thus save the problems accompanying firing him by letting him know his superiors wish him to leave. The release of information on an appointment before it is made places the president in an awkward position and can help ensure that he follows through on it or prematurely deny he has such plans.[18] Both the supporters and opponents of Henry Kissinger employed these tactics prior to his appointment as secretary of state.[19]

Some leaks are designed to force the president's hand on policy decisions. During the Indian-Pakistani War, President Nixon maintained a publicly neutral stance but was really favoring Pakistan. When this was leaked there was inevitably pressure to be neutral in action as well as in rhetoric.[20] In mid-1978 an article appeared in the *Washington Post*, apparently based on leaks from an administration official in favor of a strategic arms limitation agreement, stating that President Carter had decided to freeze U.S. efforts to pursue a new treaty. This prompted Carter to denounce the report and go on record in favor of the negotiations.[21]

Conversely, in the case of Lyndon Johnson, a leak that he was thinking about a decision could ensure that he would take no such action. For example, when the *Washington Post* reported the president was going to appoint Walter Washington as mayor of Washington, D.C., he held up the announcement for months. On the other hand, when it was reported that he was thinking of replacing FBI Director J. Edgar Hoover, Johnson called a press conference and announced Hoover had a permanent position. When it was reported that he was going to send Vice President Humphrey to Vietnam to assess U.S. policy, the mission was cancelled. Because of Johnson's approach to dealing with leaks, some officials tried to kill appointments or decisions they opposed by leaking information to reporters.[22]

Leaks may serve a number of other functions for individuals. They may make one feel important or help one gain favor with reporters. Leaks may also be used to criticize and intimidate personal or political adversaries in the White House itself or protect and enhance reputations. In the Ford administration, White House counsel Robert Hartman and chief of staff Richard Cheney often attacked each other anonymously in the press. Several members of the White House staff attacked Press Secretary Ron Nessen in an effort to convince the president to replace him.[23] When negotiations with North Vietnam broke down in late 1972, White House aides employed leaks to dissociate the president from his national security advisor.[24]

Presidents sometimes leak information for their own political purposes. Lyndon Johnson approved the declassification and leaking of a top secret document written by a former Kennedy administration State Department official showing his predecessor's administration's complicity in the overthrow and death of President Ngo Diem of South Vietnam in 1963. Roger Hilsman, the former official, was a critic of Johnson's Vietnam policy and an advisor to Robert Kennedy, who had decided to oppose Johnson for the Democratic presidential nomination in 1968. Thus, the president wanted to discredit them. When Hilsman tried to defend himself, other documents were leaked to counter his arguments. Another time Johnson had information leaked to one reporter who was sitting in for the regular reporter (whom Johnson did not like) in an attempt to show the newspaper they worked for that the stand-in could do a better job.[25] Johnson also leaked information on nuclear weapons to answer Barry Goldwater in the 1964 presidential election.[26]

Richard Nixon's White House tried to establish a pipeline into columnist Jack Anderson's office, directly offering information or indirectly trying to plant stories. Two stories provided by the White House were on tax investigations of potential presidential candidate George Wallace and his brother and on allegations (erroneous) about George McGovern's campaign treasurer.[27] Another time a Nixon aide leaked a false story to the *Wall Street Journal* that the president was considering seeking legislation to reduce the independence of the Federal Reserve Board and that the board's chairman, Arthur Burns, was a hypocrite because he sought a personal salary increase while he was asking the rest of the country to dampen its demands. The UPI received a somewhat similar story.[28] All of this was an attempt to make Burns more responsive to White House demands. The Nixon White House often employed leaks as a political tactic.[29]

In all of these cases it is government officials using the press for their purposes and not vice versa. Although reporters may well be aware of being used, the competitive pressure of the news business makes it difficult for them to pass up an exclusive story.[30] Nevertheless, most good reporting, even investigative reporting, does not rely heavily upon leaks. Instead, reporters put together stories by bits and pieces.[31] According to the coordinator of the *Washington Post*'s special Watergate staff:

> The *Post*'s early Watergate coverage, in my view, resulted from anything but leaks. From the beginning, what leaks we got were attempts to steer us away from the true story. . . . Instead our reportage consisted of hard footwork on the part of Woodward and Bernstein, who got little scraps of information from minor figures on the periphery of the scandal. Through persistence and imaginative questioning, the two reporters would piece together enough of a story to put a case before investigators or sources close to the investigation, who would either confirm or deny their findings. Occasionally such sources, like Deep Throat, would be of more help, but not often.[32]

It is generally fruitless to try to discover the source of a leak. Nevertheless, some presidents have tried. Stewart and Joseph Alsop, two of the most prominent columnists of their era, once wrote of the security investigations, phone tappings, questioning of friends, cutting off of information, and other harassments in which the Eisenhower administration engaged to punish those who published what they termed "trivial" classified information.[33] President Johnson was so upset by leaks that he had an aide keep a record of who on the White House staff talked to which reporters and for how long.[34] Reprisals, including withholding favors, criticism, complaints to editors, and FBI investigations, have been taken against reporters who print leaks. Subordinates have sometimes had critical notations placed in their personnel files, been subjected to lie detector tests, and received threatening memoranda.[35] None of these efforts have made much difference in the number or types of leaks from the executive branch.

As in so many other regards in relation to the press, Richard Nixon's reaction to leaks was extreme. According to aide Charles Colson the president told him in 1972: "I don't want excuses. I want results. I want it done, whatever the cost. . . . I don't give a damn how it is done, do whatever has to be done to stop these leaks and prevent further unauthorized disclosures. I don't want to be told it can't be done." Thus, government officials and reporters had their phones tapped. Even Nixon aide William Safire's phone was tapped because he had extensive contacts with the press. In virtually every instance, however, these and similar efforts failed to disclose the sources of leaks.[36]

The Reagan administration has added new sophistication to the effort to trace leakers. Reporters are required to make appointments when they visit top officials. These are logged into a computer. When the president's aides find an offending story based on an unidentified source, they can check the computer to learn which officials have been talking to the reporter.[37] Such measures, of course, cannot stop an official who desires to leak information from doing so and hiding his identify from the White House.

Summary

Leaks are an everyday occurrence in presidential politics. Most leaks are purposeful acts, and many emanate from the White House itself, some straight from the Oval Office. Although many leaks irritate the president and on occasion a leak may hinder national policy, there is little that can be done to stop them in a system as open as ours. The press, at least in this area, is largely an instrument of those who wish to reveal or disseminate information anonymously. The blame, if any is due, lies elsewhere.

SUPERFICIALITY

Early in this century Woodrow Wilson complained that most reporters were "interested in the personal and trivial rather than in principles and policies."[38] Things have not changed much in the ensuing generations. In this section we examine the questions of the superficiality of the coverage of the presidency and the reasons for it.

News Coverage: An Overview

A useful way to begin is with an overview of national news in general, starting with the electronic media, especially television.[39] Stories tend to be short, measured in seconds rather than minutes. Newscasters have only 22 minutes to present the network evening news, and radio stations typically devote only about 3 minutes to a news broadcast. The average White House story on radio runs about 45 seconds.[40] The amount of information verbally transmitted under such conditions is very limited. Indeed, the transcript for an entire network television evening news show would fit on one page of the *New York Times*. It is very difficult to communicate complex ideas in a few seconds and with a few words. According to CBS anchorman Dan Rather, "you simply cannot be a well-informed citizen by just watching the news on television."[41]

Even if the time allocated to the news were to expand, the length of individual stories would not necessarily increase. In 1963 CBS and NBC moved from 15 to 30 minutes of evening national news, yet it was the number of stories, not their length, that increased.

The networks do not want to bore viewers, who cannot choose to skip items on the screen as they can in the printed press. They are also concerned about not confusing their audience, because viewers cannot reread complex and detailed stories. Therefore, stories must be simple and short. They also must be fast-paced. Major stories are typically divided into short segments, and camera angles and film editing are employed to hold the audience's attention. As we can see, the marginal viewer has a major impact on the presentation of television news.[42]

A number of means besides shortening stories are used to simplify the news for the audience. A theme provides focus and a story line makes facts more intelligible. The facts illustrate the theme (a motorcade may be used to illustrate the "horse race" theme of a presidential election). On the other hand, simplified television themes are ill-equipped to deal with the ambiguities and uncertainties of most complex events and issues.[43]

A related method of simplifying the news is to employ symbols. Gas pumps, supermarket checkout lines, and school buses, for example, are shown to represent the issues of energy, inflation, and civil rights, respectively. Complex issues are presented in terms of human experience. Easily recognizable symbols encourage people to project themselves into the story, but they may not contribute toward edifying them.

At other times stories are personalized through using experts, spokesmen, or random representatives of groups (poor or unemployed persons, for example) to symbolize stories. Almost everyone readily recognizes the president, and as an individual he can personify issues. He serves as a symbol, and television exploits this by covering him more than it covers all 535 members of Congress.[44]

Most reporting in Washington is about events, about actions taken or words spoken by public figures.[45] Television is a visual medium, appealing primarily to sight. Coverage is given to dramatic and colorful events such as ceremonies, parades, disasters, and acts of violence more than it is to "talking heads" discussing ideas. Events are tangible and thus more amenable to film coverage than are ideas. They involve action and are thus more entertaining. The visual orientation emphasizes the immediate, making much of the news ahistorical and fragmentary. For the networks, however, this has the advantage of giving audiences coverage of "novel," and therefore more arguably "newsworthy," events.

To exploit the potential of film even further, television news producers often compress coverage of entire events into those portions with the most action. On our television screens we see hecklers at speeches, combat activity, and protest marchers, even though these actions may be atypical of the larger event and the film may therefore present a distorted picture. A study of the 1965 Dominican Republic crisis found that less than half of the film shown on network television contributed directly to reporting on the major events of the crisis.[46] The camera dramatizes stories, appealing to the emotions with vivid pictures, more than it adds to the audience's understanding of complex matters. Fact finding and contextual information receive much less attention than filmed action.

The networks place a particularly high value on conflict as audience-pleasing news, especially if it is between clearly identifiable antagonists and there is a tangible prize such as a public office or the passage of a bill. To simplify matters for viewers, multi-sided conflicts and complex relationships within and between coalitions and interests tend to be presented in simple pro-con terms. Thus the emphasis in coverage of a senator's reaction to a presidential statement is on the drama of conflicting personalities rather than on the issue at hand.

Finally, stories combining several elements from our previous discussion tend to receive substantial coverage. Human interest stories, especially those about the president and his family, are novel and easier for the public to relate to than are complex matters of public policy. They are always in high demand. Nancy Reagan's new White House china received more attention in the press than most issues. Scandals involving public persons of all kinds receive high priority coverage. Disasters and incidents of violence make for excellent film presentations, are novel, contain ample action, and are portrayed in easily understood terms. The intricacies of a presidential tax proposal are not so fortunate.

The focus of the preceding paragraphs has been on television, but the superficial coverage of the printed media has similar characteristics. As the chief White House correspondent for *Newsweek* said:

> Part of our problem is we are a mass circulation magazine and we tailor ourself to a mass audience, and sometimes more deserving stories go down the tube for that reason. . . . You can't afford to be boring, but some of the most boring stories are the best stories. That is a problem. . . . The stories with most news value are cabinet changes or scandal. The best stories are frequently without conflict or controversy.[47]

With a few exceptions, newspaper stories on the presidency and the president's programs follow the same outlines as those described for television.[48] Moreover, many newspapers have tried to be more visually interesting by changing their makeup, using larger headlines and photographs, more white space and fewer columns (meaning fewer words per page), and more dramatic language.

Newsmagazines rely heavily upon photographs and human interest angles to policy issues.[49] For example, on April 5, 1982, *Newsweek*'s cover story was entitled "Reagan's America: And the Poor Get Poorer." A little girl with a dirty face and dirty clothes was pictured on the cover. Inside, the story began with a full-page drawing of a polarized population and the next page was headed by "Reagan's Polarized America." The story followed the simplifying theme of rich versus poor yet provided no evidence of a polarized country. The headline, however, was dramatic.

About one-third of the three pages of this short article (not counting the full-page drawing) was devoted to two pictures, a cartoon, a drawing, and a graphic. Rather than deal with this topic in depth, the magazine eased the reader's burden by following this story with a six-page complementary story. It carried the human-interest title of "Life Below the Poverty Line," and half of it was composed of pictures of poor people and stories about poor families and individuals. This does not sound greatly different from television news, and when we consider that it only comes out once a week, the information provided the reader probably does not differ greatly from what television provides its viewers. Much of the rest of the magazine was composed of short articles on nonpolitical topics.

Coverage of the Presidency

Focusing more specifically on media coverage of the presidency, we now have a number of studies of newspaper, television, and newsmagazine coverage of presidential election campaigns, some of them quite extensive, stretching back to 1968.[50] The authors of these studies have found that the coverage is basically trivial, especially on television. Issue coverage is spotty. Most reference to issues on television news in the 1976 election campaign lasted less than 20 seconds![51]

The issue stands of candidates are usually old news to reporters who must suffer through hearing the same speech, with slight variations added for local audience appeal, again and again. The issue stands are not viewed as news. In general, substantive issues are reported in terms of their impact on the election rather than in terms of their merits.

Clear-cut issue differences between candidates have the potential for confrontation, even if the drama results from skillful tape editing, and these differences are emphasized within the space alloted to issue coverage. Such issues are not typical, however. Media coverage does not reflect the blend of issues advocated by the candidates. Moreover, the press generally ignores issues that the candidates neglect, even though they may be significant to the typical citizen.

What does receive extensive coverage is the "horse race," the campaign as opposed to what the campaign is ostensibly about. Stress is placed on who is ahead, the mechanics of campaigning, forecasts, candidates' action and reactions, and campaign trivia that feature action and color such as hecklers, crowds, motorcades, balloons, and rallies. Candidates' general personality traits, such as style of action, character, trustworthiness, and compassion, receive substantial attention, but their professional qualifications for the office of the presidency receive much less. Stories feature conflict, make brief points, are easily understood (often in either/or terms), and, especially on television, have film value.

Some examples from recent presidential campaigns will help to illustrate the media's emphasis on the trivial. In 1968, vice presidential candidate Spiro Agnew made a joking comment to a Japanese-American friend from his hometown (Baltimore) newspaper on his campaign plane, calling him a "fat Jap." This deserved no press attention whatsoever, but was widely presented as an ethnic slur.[52] In 1972 vice presidential candidate Sargent Shriver issued a 27-page report on how he would handle the economy if he were elected. It never was reported on television. But one day he rode a garbage truck and received television coverage for doing so.[53] This fit television's needs of color, action, symbolism, and simplicity.

In 1976, presidential candidate Jimmy Carter told a reporter during an interview that he did not see it as government's role to intervene to alter the "ethnic purity" of neighborhoods. The reporter did not consider the remark very important and placed it towards the end of his story. His editors buried that portion of the story on page 134 of the Sunday paper. A CBS television editor noticed it, however, and had a reporter ask Carter about it. Instantly the phrase, taken out of context, dominated the news. ABC correspondent Sam Donaldson even asked Carter if his comment was not "almost Hitlerian"! After a couple of days Carter apologized for his poor choice of words. Throughout the entire process the widely-shared view Carter was trying to express was lost in the flurry of attention given to the Georgian's particular phrasing.[54]

Even more sensational, and thus even more newsworthy, was an interview Carter gave to *Playboy*. In it he acknowledged that he had lusted in his heart for women to whom he was not married but had never acted on these emotions. Since no one seriously questioned the latter, and in the wake of Watergate and revelations about John Kennedy's sexual appetites, one might think that this admission of modest human imperfection was rather insignificant. The press viewed the matter differently, however, and turned it into a cause célèbre. If sex sells gothic novels and other modes of entertainment, why not use it to sell the news as well?

In the second debate between Gerald Ford and Jimmy Carter during the 1976 presidential campaign, Ford made a slip of the tongue and said that Eastern Europe was "free from Soviet domination." Everyone, including the president, knew that he had misspoken. Unfortunately for Ford, he refused to admit his error for several days while the press had a field day speculating about his basic understanding of world politics.[55]

President Ford's press secretary felt that the press presented issues in an oversimplified or trivial manner, when it presented them at all, and stressed the sensational over the substantive. Referring to television coverage of the election he wrote:

> the problem was that the networks thought things like Earl Butz [Secretary of Agriculture] jokes, juicy quotes from *Playboy*, mistakes, slips of the tongue, falls, Amy Carter's lemonade stand, Billy Carter's beer drinking,

Susan Ford's "affairs," et cetera, et cetera, made more interesting TV stories than where Ford and Carter stood on the issues.[56]

It is interesting that a comprehensive, systematic study of press coverage of the 1976 campaign found that the most intensely reported substantive topics were Ford's Eastern Europe gaffe, Carter's *Playboy* interview, and Earl Butz's racial joke and resignation.[57]

Superficial news coverage is not limited to elections. Most of the White House press's activity comes under the heading of what two leading authorities term the "body watch." In other words, reporters focus on the most visible layer of the president's personal and official activities and provide the public with a step-by-step account. They are interested in what the president is going to do, how his actions will affect others, how he views policies and individuals, how he presents himself, and whose stars are rising and falling, rather than in the substance of policies or the fundamental processes operating in the executive branch.[58]

Editors expect this type of coverage and reporters do not want to risk missing a story. As the Washington bureau chief of *Newsweek* said: "The worst thing in the world that could happen to you is for the President of the United States to choke on a piece of meat, and for you not to be there." The emphasis of news coverage is on short-run, "instant history." Perspective on the events of the day is secondary. Thus, embarrassing items such as blunders and contradictions made by the president and his staff are widely reported, especially if the president is low in the polls (providing a consistent theme).[59] Similarly, major presidential addresses are often reported in terms of how the president looked, how he spoke, and the number of times he received applause as much as in terms of what he had to say.

Gerald Ford's administration was especially plagued by the press's emphasis on the superficial. Coverage of trivial shortcomings, such as his skiing and golfing mishaps, his awkwardness on plane steps, his saying "Ohio State" instead of "Iowa State" in a speech, and his wearing ill-fitting pants when meeting Emperor Hirohito, regularly appeared on the front pages of America's newspapers and on its television screens. The substance of speeches or meetings were ignored or superficially covered in a few seconds or paragraphs. Similarly, Ford's television adviser once made a speech on the relationship between government and the broadcast industry, only to find that the most (and often the *only*) thing reported was his passing reference to "Police Woman" as the president's favorite television show. When Press Secretary Ron Nessen complained about such coverage, *that* also became news.[60]

The Ford White House was also frustrated in its attempts to encourage the press to pay attention to qualifiers, cautions, and explanations. Instead, the press often oversimplified, especially in headlines. The most famous example is probably the *New York Daily News*'s summary of a 45-minute presidential speech on New York's financial plight in the words "FORD TO N.Y.: DROP DEAD."[61]

The Carter administration also suffered from the media's focus on the dramatic and visually appealing rather than substantive issues. For example, an authority on mass media and politics reports that in March 1977

> the media focused on the terrorist activities of a Moslem sect in Washington. A remarkable presidential press conference occurring at the same time was all but swamped. In this conference, President Carter proposed a $1.5 billion youth employment bill, a Youth Conservation Corps, a new approach to peace in the Middle East, new procedures for the withdrawal of American troops from South Korea, and a new atomic weapons agreement with the Soviet Union.[62]

In a background briefing in 1979 the president complained to reporters that "I would really like for you all as people who relay Washington events to the world to take a look at the substantive questions I have to face as president and quit dealing almost exclusively with personalities."[63]

Presidential slips of the tongue or behavior are often blown out of all proportion. President Nixon once termed mass murderer Charles Manson as guilty before his trial had ended. Since almost everyone else in the country probably also felt Manson was guilty, the president's slip was not really extraordinary. Nevertheless, it was treated as such by the press. When he gave his press secretary, Ron Ziegler, a shove in New Orleans, speculation immediately began about the president's mental state.

At other times words are lifted out of context. When Richard Nixon described the persons "blowing up the campuses" as "bums," the press extended the adjective to all students, something the president had not meant.[64] The uproar following this "news" can well be imagined. Once Vice President Hubert Humphrey used the term "politics of joy" in a speech and was pummeled in the press for ignoring the misery of the world.[65] This was particularly ironic given Humphrey's long and distinguished career as a humanitarian.

In its constant search for "news," the press, especially the electronic media, is reluctant to devote repeated attention to an issue, although this might be necessary to explain it adequately to the public.[66] As a deputy press secretary in the Carter administration said: "We have to keep sending out our message if we expect people to understand. The Washington press corps will explain a policy once and then it will feature the politics of the issue." This is one incentive for the president to meet with the non-Washington press.[67] According to a high official in the Ford administration:

When a President goes to local papers, it is a great big thing to them and it is new. One of the things we learned is that the White House press corps gets tired of conveying the message. Repetition is necessary if the nation is going to understand it. But the White House press is sick and tired of it because they think they have heard nothing but it for weeks. The temptation is to think that they have conveyed a message to the nation because, by God, we reported a speech on this and an interview, and boy we really handled that one. Then we in the White House look at an opinion poll and find that two percent of the population has heard about the damn thing. But in the environment of the White House you have heard nothing else but this, and if you hear it one more time you are going to scream.[68]

Causes of Superficiality

One of the causes of superficial press coverage of the presidency is the demands of news organizations, which we discussed at the beginning of this section. According to the White House correspondent for a major newspaper chain: "it's a lot easier for me to get [my stories] into several newspapers in the chain with a story about Amy [President Carter's daughter] than with a story about an important policy decision. If they use both, the Amy story is likely to get on page one, while the policy story will be buried on page 29."[69] Similarly, as ABC White House correspondent Sam Donaldson commented, "A clip of a convalescent Reagan waving from his window at some circus elephants is going to push an analytical piece about tax cuts off the air every time."[70]

Given the emphasis on the short-run and the demand for details of the president's activities, reporters typically cover several stories each day and face continual deadlines. There is little time for reflection, analysis, or comprehensive coverage.[71]

A related factor contributing to the trivialization of the news is the great deal of money and manpower spent on covering the president, including following him around the globe and on vacations. Because of this investment and because of the public's interest in the president, reporters must come up with something every day. However, there is not always anything newsworthy happening every day. So reporters either emphasize the trivial or blow events out of proportion. For example, in December 1976 President Ford was vacationing at Vail, Colorado. During his vacation Senator Phillip Hart of Michigan died, and the president called his widow to offer his condolences. On her request he promised to take another look at amnesty for Vietnam draft evaders. The press reported this as a serious review of the issue with the potential for a change in policy. In reality, as any serious student of the president knew, it was merely a courtesy to Mrs. Hart. Similarly, the White House press often focuses on the exact wording of an announcement in an effort to detect a change in policy. Frequently they find significance where none really exists.

There are more than organizational imperatives at work in influencing coverage of the president, however. Reporters' backgrounds and personal interests also underlie the trivialization of the news. One recent study found that reporters are often ill at ease with abstractions and that when they talk to each other about politics, they emphasize the superficial aspects—who will be elected, what bills will pass, personalities, who has power.[72] Another scholar found that journalists' personal evaluations of candidates are generally not based on issues.[73]

The typical White House reporter lacks special background on the presidency and sees no need to have such background. Moreover, the White House press lacks policy expertise relevant to understanding the issues with which the president deals. Thus, its focus on politics and personalities rather than on issues is not surprising.[74]

To delve more deeply into the presidency and policy requires not only substantial expertise but also certain technical skills. Washington reporters in general and White House reporters in particular do little documentary research. They are trained to do interviews and transmit handouts from press secretaries and public information officials rather than to conduct research. Moreover, research requires a slow pace and some advance planning, and journalists tend to be comfortable with neither.[75]

The setting of the White House press also contributes to superficial coverage. White House correspondents work in an unusually controlled environment in which they are limited in whom they may interview, attend many formal or scheduled events, and generally suffer under the constraints of forced inactivity. They are very dependent upon the press office for arranging interviews, since they may not freely range the White House corridors, and a considerable proportion of their interviews are with press officials themselves. Reporters also rely heavily upon White House transcripts and news releases provided by the press office.[76] According to a former presidential press secretary: "The White House press corps is more stenographic than entrepreneurial in its approach to news gathering. Too many of them are sheep."[77] It is interesting that many journalists feel the best leads on stories on the president often come not from the White House but from Capitol Hill.[78]

Sometimes several factors influence coverage of the presidency at the same time. Despite the glamour attached to investigative reporting following the Watergate scandal, not much of it takes place. Most reporters are unwilling to accept the slower pace of in-depth investigative work and the necessity of coordinating with other reporters and news bureau staff. The ethic of journalism is to go it alone, and the incentives are generally to get news out fast. Similarly, the slowness of the process of using the Freedom of Information Act to force the release of documents inhibits its use. Using it may also antagonize officials whose cooperation is needed in the future. A final hindrance to investigative reporting is the reluctance of many editors to publish analyses sharply divergent from the president's position without some confirmation from what they consider to be an authoritative source.[79] Such sources are not always willing to go on the record in opposition to the president.

Missed Stories

Not only does the press provide superficial coverage of the stories it reports, but many important stories about the presidency are missed altogether as a result of this emphasis on the trivial. Implementation of policy, the predominant activity of the executive branch, is very poorly covered because it is not fast-breaking news, it takes place mostly in the field, away from reporters' natural territory, and it requires documentary analysis and interaction with civil servants who are neither famous nor experts at public relations.[80] Similarly, the White House press misses most of the flow of information and options to the president from the rest of the executive branch.[81]

Summary

Press coverage of the presidency is certainly superficial. Although television and especially radio may be worse than newspapers and large-circulation newsmagazines in this regard, no mass medium performs very well. Organizational influences, the need to appeal to a mass audience, the setting in which coverage of the presidency takes place, and the orientations of reporters themselves all influence the presentation of the news in the same direction: toward the trivial.

BIAS

Bias is the most politically charged issue in presidential-press relations. Ideally, we would evaluate bias in relation to a standard of its absence, but any such standard must be based on judgments about the nature of reality, knowledge, and truth and assumptions about the purpose of the news. Without launching an assault on these venerable issues, which would be far beyond the scope of this book, there is still a good deal that we can learn about bias in press coverage of the presidency.

Bias is an elusive concept with many dimensions. Although we typically envision bias as news coverage favoring identifiable persons, parties, or points of view, there are more subtle and more pervasive forms of bias that are not motivated by the goal of furthering careers or policies. Thus, we must broaden the scope of our discussion to include subtle as well as explicit bias.

Lack of Bias

A large number of studies covering topics such as presidential election campaigns, the war in Vietnam, and local news conclude that the news media are not biased *systematically* toward a particular person, party, or ideology, as measured in the amount or favorability of coverage. The bias found in such studies is inconsistent; the news is typically characterized by neutrality.[82] Even Richard Nixon's long-time media advisor, Herbert Klein, argues that the press was *not* unfair to Nixon in his 1962 campaign for governor of California, the loss of which provided the catalyst for Nixon's famous attack on the press in his "last press conference."[83] After a year in office President Reagan felt that on the whole the press had given him fair treatment.[84]

There are sometimes differences in the amount of coverage given to various individuals, but influences based on amount of coverage can be misleading. For example, in the 1972 presidential election campaign Richard Nixon received less coverage as a *candidate* than did his opponent, George McGovern. This resulted from the campaign strategies of the candidates, with McGovern campaigning hard across the country and Nixon remaining at home in the Rose Garden. Nixon, however, received more total attention in the media when coverage of his activities as president was added to his activities as a candidate.[85]

In a similar vein, the president is the most important continuing story in the news media, receiving coverage in virtually every news program, paper, and magazine.[86] Thus, the chief executive receives more coverage than any other political figure, including leaders of the opposition. Although this imbalance in news coverage may reflect a bias toward the presidency and the office's occupant, it is not a bias toward a particular person, party, or ideology.

Some may equate objectivity with passivity and feel that the press should do no more than report what others present to it. This is what occurs much of the time, and it is a fundamental reason for the superficiality of news coverage. Sometimes, however, reporters may feel the necessity of setting the story in a meaningful context. This may entail reporting what was *not* said as well as what was said, what had occurred before, and what political implications may be involved in a statement, policy, or event. All of this information is useful for citizens attempting to understand politics, and there are few substitutes for the press in providing it.

If the press is passive, it can be more easily manipulated, even passing lies along to the public. But it may refuse to play a passive role. For much of the 1976 presidential election campaign President Ford employed what is known as the "Rose Garden" strategy, in which the president remains in Washington acting "presidential." This includes holding impressive ceremonies in the White House Rose Garden dealing with consensual matters instead of campaigning across the country as his opponent is. The television networks responded by using "voiceovers" of reporters calling attention to the president's avoidance technique while showing a film of Ford's White House activities.[87] The reader can decide whether this is an example of bias.

Some authors have reached the conclusion that the media is biased, but they have not done so on the basis of systematic, scientific studies employing content analysis and validity and reliability checks of measurements.[88] Instead, they have written primarily political tracts to complain of coverage they oppose. Sometimes the media is criticized as being too conservative and at other times as being too liberal. Similarly, studies have shown that between one-third and one-fourth of the public feels that television news is biased, but there is no consensus on the direction of the bias.[89]

This discussion of the general neutrality of news coverage in the mass media pertains most directly to television, newspaper, and radio reporting. Columnists, commentators, and editorials usually cannot even pretend to be neutral. Newspaper endorsements for presidential candidates overwhelmingly favor Republicans. In 1972, 93% of the newspapers making endorsements supported Richard Nixon over George McGovern.[90] News magazines are sometimes less neutral than newspapers or television. In the 1940s, 1950s, and 1960s Henry Luce used *Time* to criticize Harry Truman, to campaign for his view of a China policy, to help elect Dwight Eisenhower as president, and to support the war in Vietnam, and the magazine has continued to favor Republican presidents.[91] Unfair but picturesque adjectives are often used in news magazines to liven up stories. So are cartoons and drawings, which are generally unflattering to the president.

Reasons for Neutrality

A number of factors help to explain why most mass media news coverage is not biased systematically toward a particular person, party, or ideology. The first is the characteristics of journalists. A growing number of studies paint a surprising portrait of the typical Washington journalist. Although self-described liberals considerably outnumber conservatives, the liberalism is superficial. Reporters generally are not personally partisan or ideological; nor are they politically aligned or holders of strong political beliefs. Journalists are typically not intellectuals or deeply concerned with public policy. Instead, they often feel themselves "above" issues and are not interested in politics apart from their work—getting stories. In fact, they often do not even vote in presidential elections, and are usually not close friends with newsmakers. Technicians, television producers, editors, and media executives are more moderate politically than are reporters, and they are even more detached from political loyalties.[92]

Journalists are not screened to fit a particular ideological mold but are hired for their professional skills, training, and experience. They rarely discuss each other's political values. On the other hand, the mass media consciously tries not to recruit ideologues, whom employers perceive as inflexible and biased. Ideologues whose reporting reflects bias that others cannot edit out will probably not last long.[93]

The organizational processes of story selection and editing provide opportunities for softening the judgments of reporters. The rotation of assignments and rewards for objective newsgathering, with which personal interest and political values can interfere, are further protections against bias.[94] Local television station owners and newspaper publishers are in a position to apply pressure regarding the presentation of the news, and, although they rarely do so,[95] their potential to act may restrain reporters.

Self-interest also plays a role in constraining bias. Individual reporters may earn a poor reputation if others view them as biased. The television networks, newspapers, news magazines, and the wire services, which provide most of the Washington news for newspapers, have a direct financial stake in attracting viewers and subscribers and do not want to lose their audience by appearing biased unless there is widespread consensus on one point of view.

Other factors that discourage bias include journalism's professional value of objectivity and the multiple versions of the same story available to major news outlets. Slander and libel laws; the Federal Communications Commission's "fairness doctrine," requiring electronic media news coverage of diverse points of view; and the "political attack" rule, providing those personally criticized on the electronic media with an opportunity to respond, are all formal limitations on bias.

Distortion

To conclude that the news contains little explicit partisan or ideological bias is not to argue that the news does not distort reality in its coverage. It does. Even under the best of conditions, some distortion is inevitable. All reporting involves fallible men and women who sometimes err[96] because of such factors as lack of careful checking of facts, the efforts of others to deceive them, and short deadlines.

In a very important sense values are pervasive in the news, and it is difficult to imagine how this could be otherwise. As members of our society, journalists are imbued with such values as democracy, capitalism, and individualism, and these unconsciously receive positive treatment in the media. Similarly, journalists have concepts of what is "new," "abnormal," and "wrong" and notions of how the world works (e.g., how power is distributed), and how to draw inferences that guide them in their efforts to gather and present the news.[97]

Journalism also contains a structural bias. Selecting, presenting, editing, and interpreting the news inevitably require judgments about what stories to cover and what to report about them, because there is simply not enough space for everything. Thus the news can never mirror reality. In addition, the particular ways in which the news is gathered and presented have consequences for distortion in news coverage.

We have already seen that the news is fundamentally superficial and oversimplified and is often overblown, all of which provides the public a distorted view of, among other things, presidential elections, statements, policies, and options. The emphasis on action and the deviant (and therefore "newsworthy" items) rather than on patterns of behavior and the implication that most stories represent more general themes of national significance contribute further to this distortion. Personalizing the news downplays structural and other impersonal factors that may be far more important in understanding the economy, for example, than individual political actors.

We have also seen that the press prefers to frame the news in themes, which both simplify complex events and provide continuity of persons, institutions, and issues. Once these themes are established, the press tends to maintain them in subsequent stories, even if they are inappropriate and therefore provide a distorted view of the world. In other words, because the themes determine what information is most relevant to news coverage and the context in which it is presented, the theme becomes "reality" and may influence how people perceive whoever and whatever is in the news.

Of necessity, themes emphasize some information at the expense of other information. This is perhaps most clear when the media changes the themes it employs, as network television did in 1968 regarding the war in Vietnam. Coverage had emphasized the combat aspect of the war until that time, but then began to focus on negotiations and U.S. withdrawal. Final U.S. withdrawal from a combat role did not occur until 1973, however, and combat activity was as heavy as ever when the changes in theme took place.[98]

Once a stereotype of President Ford as a "bumbler" was established, every stumble was magnified in coverage of him. He was repeatedly forced to defend his intelligence, and many of his acts and statements were reported as efforts to "act" presidential.[99] Once Ford was typecast, his image was repeatedly reinforced and was very difficult to overcome.

A prominent example of distorted coverage of an event was the press's performance on the 1968 North Vietnamese Tet offensive. The offensive had a tremendous political impact in the United States, and President Johnson announced his withdrawal from his efforts to gain reelection soon thereafter. The dominant theme of media coverage was defeat for the United States and its allies. In reality, however, Tet was not only an enormous political victory for the North Vietnamese but also a major military *setback* for them. The initial reaction of surprise and shock that the North could launch such a massive attack, due in large part to overly optimistic assessments by American officials of our success in the war, set the tone and supplied the theme the media applied for the entire period of the crisis. Little space was given to a few corrective stories that were prepared later in the fighting, providing little incentive for reporters to file more such reports.[100]

Sometimes themes are established by the press to attract an audience for coverage of an event. A well-known study of MacArthur Day in Chicago in 1951 illustrates this point. The media set expectations of a dramatic and approving welcome for the general, who had recently been relieved of his command in Korea by President Truman, and then presented the actual event in line with this theme. Its interpretation and camera shots were highly selective. Crowd size and reactions were greatly exaggerated (much of the wild cheering and enthusiasm shown on television were of people reacting to the camera rather than the parade). Ceremonies of the day were depicted as patriotic and unifying rather than as political and divisive. Although the crowds were attracted more by the prospect of a spectacle than by ideological support of MacArthur, the media emphasized the latter.[101]

This incident over thirty years ago was not unique. A study of television coverage of the 1972 Democratic National Convention found that, although they were neutral as to partisanship, the networks portrayed the convention as more disorderly and conflictual than it actually was. Television's requirements for themes and conflict encouraged reporters to focus on differences between delegates, and the techniques of switching from camera to camera gave the impression of rapidly shifting action.[102]

Reporters often fail to alert readers and viewers about the tentativeness of much of what the press reports. "Sources may be unreliable, motives obscure, facts disputed or confused, meanings unclear, yet the news [is] presented with a straight-forward clarity which denies, even belies, uncertainty."[103] Similarly, reporters often do not make it clear that they have made inferences in their reporting.[104]

All this enhances the credibility of journalists who present the news, but it provides the potential for distortion in the process. For example, in its coverage of the Tet offensive the press attempted to interpret and project events authoritatively, even though it lacked the competence and data to do so. The great bulk of its information was second- and third-hand and contained many gaps, and much of its commentary was speculative. Reporters did not warn their audience about these limitations, however.[105]

The use of the interview as the basic tool of journalism may produce biased coverage, although the bias is not necessarily related to party or ideology. Interviews favor articulate, magnetic speakers who make good copy. These are the people reporters desire to interview, but the interviewees will generally be more concerned with their own interests than with those of the public. To help the subjects of interviews appear more dignified and articulate, television reporters sometimes repeat questions to allow for sharpened answers, allow subjects to suggest questions, and even rephrase questions to better fit answers already given. All of this may give the impression of more intelligent arguments than are really at the root of many political differences.[106]

Negativism

Some observers feel that the press is biased against whoever holds office at the moment and that reporters want to expose them in the media.[107] Reporters hold disparaging views of most politicians and public officials, finding them self-serving, lacking in integrity and competence, hypocritical, and preoccupied with reelection. Thus it is not surprising that journalists see a need to expose and debunk them through general derogation.[108] One observer has characterized this orientation as neither liberal nor conservative, but "reformist."[109]

White House reporters are always looking to expose conflicts of interest and other shady behavior of public officials. Moreover, many of their inquiries revolve around the question, "Is he up to the job?"[110] One former presidential press secretary observes that reporters who are confined in the White House all day may attempt to make up for their lack of investigative reporting with sarcastic and accusatory questioning.[111] Another press secretary argues that the desire to keep the public interested and the need for continuous coverage create a subconscious bias in the press against the presidency that leads to critical stories.[112]

Studies of news coverage of Congress and the presidency have found an emphasis on the negative, while studies of presidential elections have produced mixed results, some finding primarily positive and others primarily negative portrayals of candidates.[113] One study found that in the 1980 election campaign the press portrayed President Carter as mean and Ronald Reagan as imprecise rather than Carter as precise and Reagan as nice. The emphasis, in other words, was on the candidates' negative qualities.[114] Findings of a negative tinge to the news are not surprising, given the attitudes of journalists towards politicians and public officials.

On the other hand, one could argue that the press is biased *towards* the White House. The general respect for the presidency is often transferred to individual presidents. Framed at a respectful distance by the television camera, the president is typically portrayed with an aura of dignity working in a context of rationality and coherence on activities benefitting the public. Word selection often reflects this orientation as well. For example, we hear of a president's "administration" instead of his "regime," the latter term carrying negative connotations for most people. In addition, journalists follow conventions that protect politicians and public officials from revelations of private misconduct.[115]

A large study of newspaper, magazine, and network news coverage of the president found that the White House enjoyed a consistent pattern of favorable coverage. The most favorable coverage comes in the first year of a president's term, before he has a record to criticize and critics for reporters to interview. Coverage focuses on human-interest stories of the president and his appointees and their personalities, goals, and plans. The president is pictured in a positive light as a policymaker dealing with problems. Controversies over solutions arise later. Newspaper headlines also favor the president,[116] and news of foreign affairs provides basic support for the policies and personalities of the administration.[117]

Video

A special word about video coverage of the news is appropriate because most of our discussion and most of the studies on which it is based focus on the printed or spoken word. The television camera is a flexible instrument and can film events in many different ways, including closeups, distance shots, a wide range of camera angles, cutaways, reaction shots, juxtapositions, and slow and fast motion. We experience some of this potential when we view candidates' advertisements during elections. These various techniques leave different impressions with viewers. Tight shots, for example, provide an image of warmth and intimacy while distance shots connote coldness and impersonality. Similarly, shots from below looking up to a person indicate power and dominance while shots from above looking down indicate weakness. A rapid change of images produces a feeling of excitement.

Fortunately, camera operators follow certain conventions in the interests of objectivity, such as filming a speaker from a medium distance and height, at normal film speed, and without simultaneous vertical and horizontal movement of the camera.[118] Thus, adding a video component to the news does not necessarily change the interpretation of the news people would give to audio alone.[119]

Nevertheless, studies have found that the video portion of television news does not necessarily parallel the verbal content,[120] as when crowd scenes are shown while a reporter discusses campaign issues.[121] Although we do not know the impact of such coverage, it is reasonable to argue that at the very least video can distract from or reinforce audio presentation of the news.

Since far more film is shot than can ever be shown on the news, it is possible that the inevitable editing of the film could produce distorted images. For example, one candidate could be shown mixing with voters and receiving warm greetings while another might be shown delivering forceful speeches, which is how vice presidential candidates Sargent Shriver and Spiro Agnew, respectively, were portrayed in 1972. These stereotypes fit the needs of the media,[122] but they were not necessarily accurate. We do not know how these different images affected viewers and we have little systematic data on the potential problem of bias in video presentation,[123] but video coverage might give a person or policy an advantage. Distortion, as in the example above, certainly takes place.

Summary

The media's coverage of public affairs is generally characterized by neutrality regarding persons, parties, and ideologies. Journalistic values and the process of gathering and presenting the news discourage bias. The media is not passive, however, and this may cause some to mistake a balanced presentation for bias. Moreover, the media's emphasis on action, conflict, authoritativeness, the deviant, personalities, and themes simplifies and screens information. Certain journalistic techniques, such as interviews and the use of short stories, affect how the news is covered and the persons and issues that are included in the news. All of these factors can distort the news. Biases against public officials and politicians and towards the White House may also be present. Moreover, widely-held values inevitably are reflected in news coverage and some errors are unavoidable.

MEDIA EFFECTS

The news often presents a superficial and distorted picture of the president and his environment. The most significant question about the substance of media coverage, of course, is about the impact it has, if any, on public opinion. Unfortunately, we know very little about this subject. Most studies on media effects have focused on attitude changes, especially in voting for presidential candidates, and have typically found little or no evidence of influence. Reinforcement of existing attitudes and opinions has been the strongest impact of the media.[124] As we shall see, however, there are other ways to look for media effects.

Limits on Impact

It is difficult to isolate the effects of the media on public opinion because the media are just one of many potential influences in the complex environment in which people live. We can reasonably argue, however, that certain characteristics of readers and viewers limit the potential impact of the press. These include short attention spans, lack of reading ability, distrust of the media, and selective perception. Related to this is the lack of exposure of citizens to the news media, their general disinterest in politics, and the limited attention many people pay to the media even when they are ostensibly exposed to it. On the average people watch television news only 55% of the time they have their sets tuned to it, about the same as for commercials.[125]

The nature of the news message also has a significant effect on the impact of the media. The great amount of information in the media, the limited time available to absorb it, especially for television viewers, the superficial coverage of people, events, and policies, the presentation of the news in disconnected snippets, and the lack of guidance through the complexities of politics all decrease the potential impact of the media on public opinion. In addition, the constant crisis atmosphere in which the media envelopes the news may leave users unimpressed by one more emergency situation.

The credibility of the media is a crucial factor in its impact on public opinion. The press receives a mixed rating overall on this dimension. For example, a 1981 poll found that 71% of the respondents felt that major news media were accurate all or most of the time on stories with which they had experience. On the other hand, 59% of the sample felt reporters include too much of their own opinions and not enough facts in their stories.[126]

Polls typically report that television has the most widely believed or credible news coverage. In a 1980 Roper Poll it received this rating from 51% of the sample, while newspapers, newsmagazines, and radio received 22%, 9%, and 8%, respectively.[127] Television's higher rating may be due to several factors, including the brevity of stories, which precludes detail that might be viewed as interpretation; the visual and often live coverage of events that hides from viewers the mediation of the news by human judgment; and the display of news personnel, which permits viewers to establish a "personal," and therefore more trusting, relationship with them.

Effects

This is not to argue that press coverage has no impact on public opinion. Selective perception may be a less powerful constraint on the influence of the media in affecting attitudes than we once thought. The public appears to be a fairly passive audience and usually does not do a great deal of perceptual screening of the news.[128] Repeated coverage of an issue or person by all the media and television's use of themes and simple story lines and the vividness of live coverage of visually exciting events can buttress the media's impact.

The media are more likely to influence perceptions than attitudes. The press can influence the perceptions of what public figures stand for, what their personalities are like, and what issues are important, and what is at stake.[129] By raising certain issues or personal characteristics to prominence, the salience of attitudes that people already hold may change and thus alter their evaluations of, say, presidential performance, without their attitudes themselves changing.[130]

Studies of press coverage of presidential elections have concluded that the public's information on and criteria for evaluating candidates parallels what is presented in the media: campaign performance, personality traits, mannerisms, and personal background rather than issue positions, ability to govern, and relevant experience.[131] Moreover, what the press emphasizes about elections (the horse race) is what the public says is important about them, what they discuss about them in private conversations, and what they remember about them.[132]

While it cannot be conclusively proven that media coverage contributes to the public's deemphasis of the professional capacities and policy plans of candidates, it is reasonable to speculate that the press's emphasis on the horse race and personality traits encourages the public to view campaigns in these terms. Thus, although the press may not directly influence voters to support a particular candidate, it probably amplifies the public's predispositions to view public affairs through personalities rather than more complex factors.

Earlier in this chapter we saw that the press gave substantial coverage to President Ford's misstatement about Soviet domination of Eastern Europe. This coverage had an impact on the public. Polls show that most people did not realize the president made an error until they were told so by the press. After that, pro-Ford evaluations of the debate declined noticeably[133] as voters' concerns for competence in foreign policy making became salient.

The press's impact on public perceptions of individuals and issues is probably greatest between election campaigns, when people are less likely to activate their partisan defenses. The prominent coverage of Gerald Ford's alleged physical clumsiness was naturally translated into suggestions of mental ineptitude. In the president's own words,

> every time I stumbled or bumped my head or fell in the snow, reporters zeroed in on that to the exclusion of almost everything else. The news coverage was harmful, but even more damaging was the fact that Johnny Carson and Chevy Chase used my "missteps" for their jokes. Their antics —and I'll admit that I laughed at them myself—helped create the public perception of me as a stumbler. And that wasn't funny.[134]

The gap between reality and images in the media is reflected in the comments of a congressional leader after attending a skillful and effective discussion of foreign policy by President Carter: "How can this guy be so Goddamned low in the polls and the object of so much ridicule when he's clearly in command and really quite impressive?"[135] Some astute observers of the Washington press corps believe that stories on Carter strongly reflected and amplified the opinions of Washington influentials who were disturbed by the president's lack of understanding of the nuances of Washington early in his term. Once such an image is established in the mass media, it is very difficult to change, even though Carter improved considerably after his first year in office. The press's penchant for stereotypes is difficult for a president to overcome as reporters continue to emphasize behavior that is consistent with their previously established themes.[136]

During the Iranian hostage crisis ABC originated a nightly program entitled "America Held Hostage," Walter Cronkite provided a "countdown" on the number of days of the crisis at the end of each evening's news on CBS, many feature stories on the hostages and their families were reported in all the media, and the press gave complete coverage to "demonstrations" in front of the U.S. embassy in Tehran. The latter were often artificially created for consumption by Americans. As we will see in Chapter 6, this crisis gave President Carter's approval rating a tremendous boost, at least for a while. Conversely, when the *Pueblo* was captured by North Korea, there were many more American captives, but there were also no television cameras and few reporters to cover the situation. Thus the incident played a much smaller role in American politics.

Those with only marginal concern for politics may be especially susceptible to the impact of the media because they have few alternative sources of information and less developed political allegiances. Thus, they have less cognitive dissonance to overcome. One study found that coverage of Watergate influenced attitudes toward President Nixon among those with low knowledge and low interest in politics.[137] Similarly, coverage of new issues that are removed from the experiences of people and their political convictions is more likely to influence public opinion than coverage of continuing issues.

Almost all citizens are basically ignorant of such areas of the world as Central America, Afghanistan, and Poland. The press plays a pivotal role in shaping perceptions of the personalities and issues involved in conflicts abroad (generally only conflicts receive coverage) and the U.S.'s stake in the outcomes of the disputes. In such situations we have seen that there is substantial potential for distortion. The public is heavily dependent on the media for information and has little basis for challenging what it reads and sees in the news. The illustrations of the conflict—scenes of combat or demonstrations, for example—may become the essence of the issue in the public's mind. The underlying problems, which the president must confront, may be largely ignored.

The president needs an understanding by the public of the difficulty of his job and the nature of the problems he faces. The role of the press here can be critical. Watching television news seems to do little to inform viewers about public affairs; reading the printed media is more useful.[138] This may be because reading requires more active cognitive processing of information than watching television, and there is more information presented in newspapers.

Given the poor performance of television in informing the public, one may find reports that the public relies heavily on it for information on public affairs disheartening. A 1980 Roper poll, in which respondents could give multiple responses, found that television was named as the major source of news by 64% of the sample, followed by newspapers (44%), radio (18%), and news magazines (5%).[139] This division has been about the same for the past decade.[140]

These figures are somewhat misleading, however. One study found that more than half the adult population does not watch the television news over a two-week period.[141] On an average day many more people turn to a newspaper for news than watch television for it[142] (although we do not know if they read the national news in the papers), and people perceive newspapers as providing more information than television.[143] Television, of course, still reaches millions of people who do not read newspapers. Very few people rely on the national news sections of news magazines.[144]

We have seen that press coverage of the president is superficial, oversimplified, and often overblown, providing the public a distorted picture of White House activities. This trivialization of the news drowns out coverage of more important matters, often leaving the public ill-informed about matters with which the president must deal, ranging from the renegotiation of the Panama Canal Treaty[145] to funding social security benefits. The preoccupation of the press with personality and the results of policies does little to help the public appreciate the complexity of presidential decision making, the trade-offs involved in policy choices, and the broad trends outside the president's control.

In Chapter 2 we saw that the president's access to the media is at least a potential advantage in influencing public opinion. The press's focus on the president has disadvantages as well. It inevitably leaves the impression that the president *is* the federal government and crucial to our prosperity and happiness. This naturally encourages the public to focus its expectations on the White House. When this is combined with the national frame of reference provided by a truly mass media and the press's penchant for linking its coverage of even small matters with responses from the president or presidential spokesmen, the pressures on him can be great.[146]

Moreover, the extraordinary attention the press devotes to the president magnifies his flaws and adds little to the glamour of the office. Even completely unsubstantiated charges against the president may make the news because of his prominence. Familiarity may not breed contempt, but it certainly may diminish the aura of grandeur around the chief executive.

The results of studies of the influence of commentary following presidential speeches and press conferences are mixed. Some have found no impact,[147] while others have concluded that a shift in attitudes takes place.[148] One experiment found that commentary influenced what viewers remembered about the speech, and, in general, viewers learned more when commentary was present.[149]

Although the negative impact of commentary on presidential addresses and press conferences is unclear, it is probably safe to argue that it is a constraint on the president's ability to lead public opinion. In the words of two observers,

> Critical instant analysis undermines presidential authority by transforming him from presentor to protagonist. The president's performance, if not the president, is laid out like a cadaver for dissection. Credible, familiar, apparently disinterested newsmen and -women, experts too, usually agreeing with each other, comment on the self-interested performance of a politician. Usually the president's rhetoric is deflated, the mood he has striven to create dissipated. Cadavers are rarely improved by dissection.[150]

Summary

The effects of superficiality and distortion in the news coverage of the presidency are difficult to determine. Characteristics of media users and the press itself limit its impact. Nevertheless, people's perceptions do seem to be affected by the content of the news. It may raise expectations of the president or magnify his flaws; it may raise certain issues to prominence at the expense of others; it may focus attention on the trivial and fail to develop an appreciation for the problems the president faces; and it may alter the president's role from statesman to partisan politician.

CASE STUDY

In this section we examine television news coverage of the president over the week of July 15, 1979. This was not a typical week. It was, instead, a dramatic one in which President Carter delivered what was perhaps his most important address to the nation, proposed a broad energy program, changed the occupants of several cabinet positions, and established a chief of staff in the White House. This case study is thus not intended to be a representative sampling of television news coverage of the presidency. It is designed only to illustrate some of the points we have made throughout this chapter on the nature of media coverage. Tapes of television news programs were obtained from the Television News Archives at Vanderbilt University.

July 15

On Sunday, July 15, President Carter returned from a lengthy period of consultation and reflection at Camp David and addressed the nation over television. His speech focused on the crisis of confidence he perceived in the country (discussed in greater detail in Chapter 1) and the energy crisis.

NBC devoted its "Prime Time Sunday" show to the president's speech and commentary on it. The show began with a journalist eliciting reactions to the speech from "an unscientific but instantaneous" sample of people who subscribed to the Warner Communications Cube System in Columbus, Ohio. Although viewers were told that the people in the sample overrepresented the middle and upper classes, the emphasis of this news segment was on the "fascinating" instant reaction to the president.

Almost all of the remainder of the show was composed of the reactions of three pairs of observers, two of whom were candidates for nomination for the presidency and who therefore were unlikely to be favorable towards the president, and two of whom were journalists introduced as "drama critics of American politics." Most of the commentary of these individuals was negative towards the president; only one person was supportive. The program ended with a cartoon drawn by Pat Oliphant for the occasion.

ABC provided more coverage of the president's energy proposals, pointing out possible pros and cons. But then one correspondent reported (instantly, of course) that economists would not like the president's proposals, and another concluded that the president had not helped himself politically. This was followed by interviews with two members of Congress, both of whom were positive towards the president's speech, and commentary by another reporter. To end its coverage, the network interviewed three couples from western Pennsylvania whom President Carter happened to talk to on a recent trip there. Why anyone should care about their reactions to the president's speech was left unclear.

CBS's coverage was basically neutral. It provided a brief summary of the president's speech and reactions from three correspondents, one of whom was introduced as an "expert in political standings."

What can we conclude from this overview of network television coverage of the president's speech? First, the coverage on ABC and CBS was neutral overall. The viewer was exposed to both positive and negative reactions, sometimes from the same person. NBC's commentary weighed in on the negative side, but the reactions of the sample of viewers in Columbus were generally favorable towards the president.

Second, the coverage was superficial, focusing on what the president did and how well others liked it. The way the president delivered his speech and its impact on his political standing and his image received emphasis. This provided reporters with an opportunity to examine the drama of the speech and conflicting reactions to it. To add a human-interest touch to the coverage, NBC and ABC elicited instant reactions from individuals. Unfortunately, these citizens could not be considered representative of the American public. The content of the president's speech received low priority on all the networks. Only ABC provided any real substantive coverage of the president's energy proposals, and none of the networks devoted much attention to the broad and potentially very significant issue of the crisis of confidence in America.

July 16

The remainder of this case study describes and evaluates coverage of the president and his energy policy proposals on the evening news over the rest of the week. On Monday, the day following his address to the nation, the president flew to Kansas City and then Detroit to speak on energy policy and the crisis of confidence. All three networks covered these speeches in summary fashion.

Each network also presented some of the details of the president's energy proposals, their cost, and reaction to them abroad. This was the only time during the week that any substantial coverage was allocated to policy matters. ABC and CBS also presented short background reports on related aspects of energy policy. Each network reported that the limits the president set on import quotas were higher than the country's present imports.

The networks also presented more of the ubiquitous reactions of public officials to the president's speeches. Then and throughout the week, senators were most likely to appear on the news. The interviews on ABC and CBS were critical of the president while those on NBC were neutral. The networks also noted that this was the day thermostats in public buildings were to be raised to 78°. Exploiting the human-interest potential of this story, each network featured warm people and elicited their reactions to the new policy.

NBC added other elements to its coverage. It inferred the absence of a vote of confidence in the president from the fact that the Dow Jones average of industrial stocks rose only a small amount during the day. It then turned to yet more human-interest reaction to the president, interviewing people at Frank and Marge's Tavern in Baltimore, farmers who gathered to watch the speech at a home in northern Illinois, and senior citizens at Williams Memorial Residence in New York City. One wonders how the other networks missed the opportunity to conduct these crucial interviews.

July 17

The next day saw the end of interest in policy. The networks together spent about three sentences on the substance of the president's energy proposals. They also reported that a congressional committee approved an earlier request for standby authority for the president to ration gasoline. Evidently the networks considered Monday's coverage of energy policy sufficient for the week.

The media's focus turned instead to other matters. All the networks led off with the news that members of the cabinet and top White House officials were told to offer their resignations to the president. Then they speculated as to whose resignations would be accepted. Both CBS and NBC presented yet further stories of public reaction to President Carter's Sunday night speech, this time with results from their own polling organizations.

Whereas on Monday the networks featured persons working in buildings with the temperature set at 78°, Tuesday they switched to the House of Representatives. One member of Congress came to the chamber without wearing a jacket, and each network decided this indiscretion warranted coverage of Speaker "Tip" O'Neill's reaction. After all, the story provided drama and conflict and personalized the issue of energy conservation. The fact that it was trivial did not weaken its appeal.

Not content with reporting reactions from Congress, bars, and polls, the networks turned to investors in gold. They all carried a story on the increase in the price of gold, and they displayed no inhibitions in providing definitive explanations for the increase. CBS reported that it marked "a dramatic loss of confidence in President Carter and the American economy." NBC declared, on the one hand, that "foreign uncertainty of what Mr. Carter is up to drove down the value of the dollar today," while, on the other hand, it concluded that "the United States' energy policies drove the price [of gold] to record levels." ABC asserted that the price increase was due to investors' predictions of the president failing to solve economic problems and the government "crisis." The bases for these inferences were never provided. Even the fact that the stock market remained unchanged was taken as evidence of a lack of investor confidence. Moreover, there was no discussion of why people should care about the views of speculators in gold. All this helped to create the impression that there *was* a crisis.

July 18

All the networks provided an overview of the ongoing personnel decisions in the White House and each discussed Hamilton Jordan's promotion to White House chief of staff. ABC continued to speculate about the other personnel changes and reported rumors about them. It and NBC carried both positive and negative comments about the president from prominent officials in Washington while CBS showed several senators criticizing the president and cited anonymous critics, including one claiming "the government is in chaos and disarray." All three networks commented upon the president's lack of a recent press conference.

CBS and NBC reported findings from an executive branch investigation that there was no evidence that oil companies deliberately withheld oil to increase their prices. NBC also presented more results from the poll on reactions to the president and noted delays in the Senate on his energy program. Finally, CBS alerted the public that the people in a town in Georgia with a population of 160 decided to invest in federal energy bonds when they were issued.

July 19

Today was the first day in which decisions about changes in the president's cabinet were announced, and the networks gave these prominent and generally neutral coverage. Each then turned to Congress for reactions, and most of those reported were negative. It is possible that this imbalance accurately reflected overt congressional reactions. Some of the statements that the networks reported could hardly be considered measured, however. Barry Goldwater appeared on ABC and proclaimed: "Well, I'd say something is really screwed up. A president asking for the

resignations of his cabinet members hasn't been done since in the 1840s."
(It had been done by Richard Nixon.) The first sentence of Goldwater's
statement was also shown on NBC.

Representative Charles Rangel appeared on CBS, declaring: "I just
can't perceive how a president can rely on staff people's decisions as
relates to cabinet positions. It is a process, to me, that is unheard of and
unbelievable, and I don't believe this. It cannot be happening." One is
tempted to conclude that the more outrageous the comments emanating
from Capitol Hill, the more likely the networks were to beam them to
the millions of people who watch the evening news. The emphasis was
on drama, not perspective.

While ABC claimed that Treasury secretary Michael Blumenthal's
firing and his replacement by Federal Reserve Board chairman G. William Miller "could mean a further world-wide decline in the dollar's
value," NBC asserted that "Miller is as respected as Blumenthal in financial circles for his conservative economic views." The basis for these
conclusions was not provided.

Both ABC and NBC ran stories on the White House's system of staff
evaluation, and each found an "expert" to say it was a poor idea. No one
from the White House who might defend it was shown. NBC aired an
interview with just-fired cabinet member Joseph Califano. The interviewer insisted on asking Califano the leading questions of whether the
president would no longer receive independent advice and whether he
felt "a sense of outrage" at being fired. The same interviewer then asked
a reporter if the president's action would "be perceived as *more* indecisive," implying that firing cabinet members is indecisive (!) and that there
had been previous indecision.

July 20

On Friday there were further changes in the cabinet, and the networks
continued their coverage of the shake-up. They also carried a story on the
dispute over what the president actually told Joseph Califano about the
reasons for his dismissal.

Each network carried a statement by Senator Ted Stevens that the
president must be suffering from "some sort of a breakdown." An ABC
interviewer said to White House Press Secretary Jody Powell: "Let me
ask you about the things people are saying on Capitol Hill and elsewhere.
They are actually questioning, as you know, whether the president has
taken leave of his senses." Just who these "people" were, aside from
Stevens, or why their views were significant, was never mentioned.

ABC then reported to Powell that it had called an unspecified number
of its affiliates and newspapers around the country and found negative
reaction to the president. What one should conclude from this small,

unrepresentative sampling of media outlets (owned primarily by Republicans) or even why anyone should care what they thought was never explained.

To its credit, CBS awarded only brief coverage to Senator Stevens's comment. It also provided the only contextual information of any of the networks on the week's events, pointing out that President Carter's cabinet had lasted intact longer than any in this century. In addition, it ran a story on the background of the president's speech on Sunday, including the results of White House polls of public attitudes and Carter's reading of philosophical and other literature relating to his concerns.

Not leaving well enough alone, however, CBS then aired a story on the president's wife, asserting, without any supporting evidence, that the president followed her advice. It also ran its story on the White House staff evaluation forms and added a segment on a humorous and critical form evaluating the White House staff that was circulating in congressional office buildings. NBC presented an interview with just-fired cabinet member Brock Adams.

July 21

Only CBS and NBC had evening news programs on Saturday. Both recapped the week and reported on an informal session the president held for reporters earlier in the day. NBC asserted that the cabinet members who were dismissed lost struggles with the White House staff, emphasizing conflict at the expense of other explanations such as their failing to support the president's policies. Both networks included two comments about the president from members of Congress. Only one, on NBC, was neutral. The other three were critical of the White House. CBS also ran a story on President Carter's nominee to head the Energy Department.

Week in Perspective

The week of July 15, 1979, was not typical. Network television news devoted more time than usual to coverage of the White House. Nevertheless, the total amount of time was small and the president's energy policy proposals received only a few minutes of air time on each network during the entire week. Actions and events—that is, what the president did, what he was going to do, why he did what he did, and what others thought of it—received the bulk of attention.

This discussion was kept on a superficial level and was composed of descriptions, speculations, cursory analyses, and, most of all, reactions. The network elicited reactions from national samples of the population, just-fired cabinet members, members of Congress, potential presidential nominees, people on the streets, network affiliates, anonymous sources, and seemingly anyone else they could find. These inevitably focused on conflict, and those that lacked a sense of proportion were particularly dramatic and therefore newsworthy.

The focus on reactions lent itself to an emphasis on the impact of events on the president's political standing, the equivalent of the horse race during election. It also provided the media an opportunity to personalize coverage and stress the human-interest angle of a situation. Interviews with "average" Americans after watching the president on television or experiencing 78° thermostat settings in the summer may make it easier for viewers to relate to events, but they do little to inform the public.

Overall, the coverage was more negative than positive, although much of it was neutral. One reason for this negativeness was the heavy reliance on reactions from others, especially members of Congress. The networks may have accurately reflected the balance of opinion in Congress at the time, but we have no way of knowing. It is reasonable to argue, however, that the coverage of critical comments about the president reflects the media's dependence on the initiatives of others. The statements of those who choose to hold press conferences often find their way onto the evening news. When a president is sitting low in the polls, as Jimmy Carter was in July 1979, more politicians are likely to exploit an opportunity to criticize him than are likely to jump publicly to his defense.

A related explanation is the networks' desire for conflict and drama. This influences the choices of both whom to interview and what stories to run. Critical comments and interviews with persons just dismissed by the president provide conflict and drama by their very nature, and the more sensational the commentary, the more it maintains viewer interest.

As the week went on and criticism of the president as reported on television grew more pronounced and more strident, the tone of the news also seemed to become more negative. Lacking a sense of context and perspective from which to view the events they were reporting and relying very heavily upon interviews, the networks appeared to adopt the tone of those they interviewed. Thus network television news not only provided an outlet for criticism of the president, but it also reflected it in its approach to coverage of the president.

Network news also presented a distorted picture of the week's events and their effects on others. As we have noted, inferences of causality flowed freely, typically without a hint of caveat. Moreover, unrepresentative and sometimes even anonymous individuals' and groups' opinions were broadcast with the clear implication that they were significant.

U.S. senators were interviewed much more often than any other group. One would be hard-pressed to argue, however, that senators are wiser or more knowledgeable than the hundreds of others whom one might imagine being interviewed. The networks do not seem to be very interested in these characteristics, however. Instead, they undoubtedly find that senators offer two advantages to them: they are accessible and they are frequently known to the viewers. Convenience and the need to simplify appear to dominate news gathering.

The themes the networks employed, apparently subconsciously, to simplify the news also contributed to distortion in coverage. Throughout the week references to the "small band of Georgians" surrounding the president appeared in the stories on changes in the White House's organization and personnel changes in the cabinet. The president's problems with some department heads were often articulated in terms of conflict between cabinet members and the White House staff. There was also heavy emphasis on the concept of loyalty. All of this plus the theme of the president's political standing placed events in a relatively shallow and even naive context. Although each of these considerations may have been relevant to understanding the president's actions, the media's focus on them crowded out broader concerns of policy and administration.

The projection of a crisis atmosphere also may have distorted the public's perception of what happened. There was no crisis or anything close to it. The treatment of change as disarray rather than as taking control, improving administration, or setting new directions helped foster this view, however. The notion of crisis was useful to the networks. It made what they were reporting seem more significant and more dramatic than it really was.

All the networks did not provide equally poor coverage each day. One would be less superficial and more neutral one day and then falter on the next. Nevertheless, given all the potential news stories they could cover, the networks displayed a striking similarity in their coverage, even down to the most trivial stories. This, of course, supports efforts to generalize about descriptions of and explanations for news coverage across networks.

CONCLUSION

Presidential-press relations pose many obstacles to the president's efforts to obtain and maintain public support. Although it is probably not true that press coverage of the White House is biased along partisan or ideological lines or towards or against a particular president, it frequently presents a distorted picture to the public and fails to impart a perspective from which to view complex events. Moreover, presidents are continuously harassed by leaks in the press and are faced with superficial, oversimplified coverage that devotes little attention to substantive discussion of policies and often focuses on trivial matters.

This type of reporting undoubtedly affects public perceptions of the president, usually in a negative way. It is no wonder that chief executives generally see the press as a hindrance to their efforts to develop appreciation for their performance and policies. As we will see later in the book, it is just these perceptions that are most important in the public's evaluations of the president.

Before leaving this chapter, however, it is important to put it in perspective. Numerous authors have eloquently established that Americans benefit greatly from a free press. We should not forget this as we examine the media's flaws. The same press that provides superficial coverage of the presidency also alerts us to abuses of authority and attempts to mislead public opinion. It is also much less biased than the heavily partisan newspapers that were typical early in our nation's history. The press is an essential pillar in the structure of a free society.

Moreover, perhaps the fundamental reason that the press's coverage is much less than its critics would like it to be is that it must appeal to the general public. When the public, or a sizeable segment of it, demands more of the mass media, it undoubtedly will receive it. In short, although mass media coverage of the presidency is often poor, it could be much worse and it is probably about what the public desires. The media reflects as well as influences American society.

NOTES

1. "What Secrets Are Safe?", *Newsweek*, March 14, 1977, p. 40.
2. "Silence Is Golden," *Newsweek*, September 26, 1977, p. 18.
3. "Operation Stifle," *Newsweek*, February 19, 1979, p. 34.
4. William Safire, *Before the Fall: An Inside View of the Pre-Watergate White House* (New York: Doubleday, 1975), p. 373; Henry Kissinger, *Years of Upheaval* (Boston: Little, Brown, 1981), p. 116.
5. See, for example, Herbert Y. Schandler, *The Unmaking of a President: Lyndon Johnson and Vietnam* (Princeton, N.J.: Princeton University Press, 1977), p. 253.
6. "Reagan Outburst on Leaks," *Newsweek*, January 18, 1982, p. 23; Walter S. Mossberg, "Reagan Prepares Curbs on U.S. Officials to Restrict News Leaks on Foreign Policy," *Wall Street Journal*, January 13, 1982, p. 7.
7. "Reagan Press Conference Text," *Congressional Quarterly Weekly Report*, January 23, 1982, p. 135.
8. See, for example, Herbert G. Klein, *Making It Perfectly Clear* (Garden City, N.Y.: Doubleday, 1980), pp. 435–36; George Christian, *The President Steps Down: A Personal Memoir of the Transfer of Power* (New York: Macmillan, 1970), p. 203.
9. Ron Nessen, "Poor Jody Powell," *Newsweek*, January 31, 1977, p. 9.
10. Klein, *Making It Perfectly Clear*, p. 435. See also Ron Nessen, *It Sure Looks Different from the Inside* (Chicago: Playboy Press, 1978), p. 58.

11. Christian, *The President Steps Down*, p. 203.
12. "The U.S. vs. William Colby," *Newsweek*, September 28, 1981, p. 30.
13. "The Tattletale White House," *Newsweek*, February 25, 1980, p. 21.
14. Michael Baruch Grossman and Martha Joynt Kumar, *Portraying the President: The White House and the Media* (Baltimore: Johns Hopkins University Press, 1981), p. 282. See also John Ehrlichman, *Witness to Power: The Nixon Years* (New York: Simon and Schuster, 1982), p. 275.
15. Robert T. Hartmann, *Palace Politics: An Inside Account of the Ford Years* (New York: McGraw-Hill, 1980), p. 38.
16. William J. Lanouette, "The Washington Press Corps—Is It All That Powerful?", *National Journal*, June 2, 1979, p. 898.
17. Grossman and Kumar, *Portraying the President*, pp. 173, 282.
18. *Ibid.*, pp. 172–4.
19. Kissinger, *Years of Upheaval*, p. 421.
20. Grossman and Kumar, *Portraying the President*, p. 279; Klein, *Making It Perfectly Clear*, p. 436; David Wise, *The Politics of Lying: Government Deception, Secrecy, and Power* (New York: Vintage, 1973), pp. 412–13, 417, 439–40; William E. Porter, *Assault on the Media: The Nixon Years* (Ann Arbor, Michigan: University of Michigan Press, 1976), pp. 139–42; Henry Kissinger, *White House Years* (Boston: Little, Brown, 1979), pp. 902, 919. For other examples, see Kissinger, p. 495; Kissinger, *Years of Upheaval*, pp. 119, 591.
21. Lanouette, "The Washington Press Corps," pp. 898–99.
22. Grossman and Kumar, *Portraying the President*, pp. 173–74; Lanouette, "The Washington Press Corps", p. 898; David Halberstam, *The Powers That Be* (New York: Knopf, 1979), pp. 542–43.
23. Grossman and Kumar, *Portraying the President*, p. 149; Klein, *Making It Perfectly Clear*, pp. 435–36; Hartmann, *Palace Politics*.
24. Kissinger, *White House Years*, pp. 1424, 1455.
25. In this case, however, the leak did not "take" very well. Wise, *The Politics of Lying*, chap. 6, pp. 484–92.
26. David L. Paletz and Robert M. Entman, *Media—Power—Politics* (New York: Free Press, 1981), p. 59.
27. Jack Anderson, "Nixon Leaks Too," *Houston Post*, June 26, 1974, section D., p. 19.
28. Wise, *The Politics of Lying*, pp. 406–11.
29. See, for example, Jeb Stuart Magruder, *An American Life: One Man's Road to Watergate* (New York: Pocket Books, 1975), pp. 196, 236.
30. Wise, *The Politics of Lying*, p. 412; John Herbers, *No Thank You, Mr. President* (New York: Norton, 1976), p. 42.
31. See, for example, Schandler, *The Unmaking of a President*, pp. 202–04; Grossman and Kumar, *Portraying the President*, p. 280.
32. Barry Sussman, *The Great Coverup: Nixon and the Scandal of Watergate* (New York: New American Library, 1974), p. 189.
33. William L. Rivers, *The Opinionmakers* (Boston: Beacon Press, 1967), pp. 30–31.
34. Grossman and Kumar, *Portraying the President*, pp. 281–82.
35. Leon V. Sigal, *Reporters and Officials: The Organization and Politics of Newsmaking* (Lexington, Mass.: D. C. Heath, 1973), p. 145.

36. Porter, *Assault on the Media*, pp. 93, 141–42, 179; Safire, *Before the Fall*, p. 345. See also Wise, *The Politics of Lying*, pp. 278–311.

37. "The Computer as Plumber," *Newsweek*, June 29, 1981, p. 17.

38. Quoted in William Small, *To Kill a Messenger: Television News and the Real World* (New York: Hastings, 1970), p. 221.

39. This discussion is based on the following: Edwards Jay Epstein, *News from Nowhere* (New York: Vintage, 1973); Herbert J. Gans, *Deciding What's News* (New York: Vintage, 1979); Grossman and Kumar, *Portraying the President*, pp. 186–87, 265–68; Doris A. Graber, *Mass Media and American Politics* (Washington, D.C.: Congressional Quarterly Press, 1980), chaps. 3 and 9; Stephen Hess, *The Washington Reporters* (Washington, D.C.: Brookings Institution, 1981), pp. 28–32, 121–27; Peter Braestrup, *Big Story* (Garden City, N.Y.: Anchor Books, 1978), pp. 514–15, 523–24; Edward Jay Epstein, "The Selection of Reality," in Elie Abel, ed., *What's News* (San Francisco: Institute for Contemporary Studies, 1981), pp. 119–132; William A. Henry III, "News as Entertainment: The Search for Dramatic Unity," in Abel, ed., *What's News*, pp. 133–58.

40. Grossman and Kumar, *Portraying the President*, pp. 50, 270, 272.

41. Hoyt Purvis, ed., *The Presidency and the Press* (Austin, Tex.: Lyndon B. Johnson School of Public Affairs, 1976), p. 56. See also Hess, *The Washington Reporters*, pp. 6, 142–43; Grossman and Kumar, *Portraying the President*, p. 218, on the White House press's views of the shortness of their stories.

42. On this, see Gans, *Deciding What's News*, p. 239.

43. On this point, see Braestrup for his discussion of coverage of the 1968 Tet offensive, especially p. 511.

44. Hess, *The Washington Reporters*, p. 98.

45. *Ibid.*, pp. 15, 124.

46. Russell F. Harney and Vernon A. Stone, "Television and Newspaper Front Page Coverage of a Major News Story," *Journal of Broadcasting* 13 (Spring 1969), pp. 181–88. See also Braestrup, *Big Story*, pp. 523–24.

47. Grossman and Kumar, *Portraying the President*, p. 65.

48. On the absence of analysis and interpretation in newspapers, see *ibid.*, p. 265–68; Hess, *The Washington Reporters*, p. 16.

49. See Grossman and Kumar, *Portraying the President*, pp. 265–68, 272.

50. Thomas E. Patterson and Robert D. McClure, *The Unseeing Eye: The Myth of Television Power in National Politics* (New York: G. P. Putnam's Sons, 1976); Thomas E. Patterson, *The Mass Media Election: How Americans Choose Their President* (New York: Praeger, 1980); Graber, *Mass Media and American Politics*, pp. 167–69, 259–61; Richard C. Hofstetter, *Bias in the News: Network Television Coverage of the 1972 Election Campaign* (Columbus, Ohio: Ohio State University Press, 1976); Robert L. Stevenson, Richard A. Eisinger, Barry M. Feinberg, and Alan B. Kotok, "Untwisting *The News Twisters*: A Replication of Efron's Study," *Journalism Quarterly* 50 (Summer 1973), pp. 211–19; David H. Weaver, Doris A. Graber, Maxwell E. McCombs, and Chaim H. Eyal, *Media Agenda-Setting in a Presidential Election* (New York: Praeger, 1981), p. 201; Douglas Lowenstein, "Covering the Primaries," *Washington Journalism Review*, September 1980, pp. 38–42; Michael Robinson with Nancy Conover and Margaret Sheehan, "The Media at Mid-Year:

A Bad Year for McLuhanites?", *Public Opinion*, June–July 1980, pp. 41–45; John Foley, Dennis A. Britton, and Eugene B. Everett, Jr., *Nominating a President: The Process and the Press* (New York: Praeger, 1980); C. Anthony Broh, "Horse-Race Journalism: Reporting the Polls in the 1976 Presidential Election," *Public Opinion Quarterly* 44 (Winter 1980), pp. 514–29. But see John M. Russonella and Frank Wolf, "Newspaper Coverage of the 1976 and 1968 Presidential Campaigns," *Journalism Quarterly* 56 (Summer 1979), pp. 360–64, 432.

51. Patterson, *The Unseeing Eye*, pp. 34, 157–59.
52. See Klein, *Making It Perfectly Clear*, pp. 160–61.
53. Purvis, ed., *The Presidency and the Press*, p. 93.
54. Jules Witcover, *Marathon: The Pursuit of the Presidency, 1972–1976* (New York: New American Library, 1977), pp. 320–26.
55. See, for example, Nessen, *It Sure Looks Different*, pp. 268–77.
56. *Ibid.*, pp. 302, 354–55; Nessen, "Poor Jody Powell."
57. Patterson, *The Mass Media Election*, pp. 99–100.
58. See Grossman and Kumar, *Portraying the President*, pp. 35, 43–45, 168–69, 179; Hess, *The Washington Reporters*, pp. 15–16, 60; Michael Baruch Grossman and Martha Joynt Kumar, "Carter, Reagan, and the Media: Have the Rules Really Changed or the Poles of the Spectrum of Success?" (paper presented at the Annual Meeting of the American Political Science Association, New York, September 1981), p. 11; Kissinger, *White House Years*, pp. 159, 1053; Kissinger, *Years of Upheaval*, pp. 160, 1021.
59. Grossman and Kumar, *Portraying the President*, pp. 35, 43–45.
60. Nessen, *It Sure Looks Different*, pp. 29–30, 45, 53, 138, 163–78, 190, 307, 332, 341, 353; Nessen, "Poor Jody Powell"; Gerald R. Ford, *A Time to Heal* (New York: Harper and Row, 1979), pp. 289, 343–44. See also Herbers, *No Thank You, Mr. President*, p. 182.
61. Nessen, "Poor Jody Powell."
62. Graber, *Mass Media and American Politics*, p. 75.
63. Quoted in Grossman and Kumar, "Carter, Reagan, and the Media," p. 8. See also Dick Kirschten, "A Little Humor, a Little Humility Help Powell Weather Stormy Seas," *National Journal*, July 26, 1980, p. 1228.
64. James Keogh, *President Nixon and the Press* (New York: Funk and Wagnalls, 1972), pp. 56–57.
65. Hubert H. Humphrey, *The Education of a Public Man: My Life and Politics* (Garden City, N.Y.: Doubleday, 1976), p. 370.
66. Gans, *Deciding What's News*, p. 169; Weaver, et al., *Media Agenda-Setting*, p. 205; Henry, "News as Entertainment," pp. 144–45.
67. Grossman and Kumar, *Portraying the President*, p. 26.
68. *Ibid.*, p. 90.
69. *Ibid.*, p. 231.
70. Quoted in "Washington Press Corps," *Newsweek*, May 25, 1981, p. 90.
71. Grossman and Kumar, *Portraying the President*, p. 50; Purvis, ed., *The Presidency and the Press*, p. 96.
72. Hess, *The Washington Reporters*, p. 124. See also Gans, *Deciding What's News*, pp. 206–07.
73. Epstein, *News from Nowhere*, pp. 212–13, 224.

74. Nessen, *It Sure Looks Different,* p. 353; Grossman and Kumar, *Portraying the President,* pp. 33–34, 183.

75. Grossman and Kumar, *Portraying the President,* p. 45; Epstein, *News from Nowhere,* p. 154; Hess, *The Washington Reporters,* pp. 18–19, 125.

76. Hess, *The Washington Reporters,* p. 60; Grossman and Kumar, *Portraying the President,* pp. 37–38, 45.

77. Quoted in Paletz and Entman, *Media—Power—Politics,* p. 55.

78. Hess, *The Washington Reporters,* p. 99; Grossman and Kumar, *Portraying the President,* p. 216.

79. Grossman and Kumar, *Portraying the President,* p. 45; Sigal, *Reporters and Officials,* p. 52; Michael Baruch Grossman and Francis E. Rourke, "The Media and the Presidency: An Exchange Analysis," *Political Science Quarterly* 91 (Fall 1976), pp. 464–66.

80. On this, see Hess, *The Washington Reporters,* p. 127. See also Nessen, *It Sure Looks Different,* pp. 29–30, 72–73.

81. See, for example, Grossman and Kumar, *Portraying the President,* pp. 294–95.

82. George Comstock, *Television in America* (Beverly Hills, Calif.: Sage, 1980), p. 52; Robert S. Frank, *Message Dimensions of Television News* (Lexington, Mass.: D. C. Heath, 1973); Graber, *Mass Media and American Politics,* pp. 165–68, 171–76; Frank Russo, "A Study of Bias in TV Coverage of the Vietnam War: 1969 and 1970," *Public Opinion Quarterly* 35 (Winter 1971–72), pp. 539–43; Hofstetter, *Bias in the News;* Terry F. Buss and C. Richard Hofstetter, "The Logic of Televised News Coverage of Political Campaign Information," *Journalism Quarterly* 54 (Summer 1977), pp. 341–49; David L. Altheide, *Creating Reality: How TV News Distorts Events* (Beverly Hills, Calif.: Sage, 1976); Michael J. Robinson and Karen A. McPherson, "Television News Before the 1976 New Hampshire Primary: The Focus of Network Journalism," *Journal of Broadcasting* 21 (Spring 1977), pp. 177–86; Robinson, et al., "The Media at Mid-Year"; Michael Jay Robinson, "A Statesman Is a Dead Politician: Candidate Images on Network News," in Abel, ed., *What's News,* pp. 159–86; Stevenson, et al., "Untwisting *The News Twisters*"; Gans, *Deciding What's News,* pp. 197–98; David L. Paletz and Martha Elson, "Television Coverage of Presidential Conventions: Now You See It, Now You Don't," *Political Science Quarterly* 91 (Spring 1976), pp. 109–31; Robert G. Meadow, "Cross-Media Comparisons of Coverage of the 1972 Presidential Campaign," *Journalism Quarterly* 50 (Autumn 1973), pp. 482–88; Michael J. Robinson and Kevin R. Appel, "Network News Coverage of Congress," *Political Science Quarterly* 94 (Fall 1979), p. 412; Dennis T. Lowry, "Agnew and the Network TV News: A Before/After Content Analysis," *Journalism Quarterly* 48 (Summer 1971), pp. 205–10; George Bailey, "Interpretive Reporting of the Vietnam War by Anchormen," *Journalism Quarterly* 53 (Summer 1976), pp. 319–24; Dru Evarts and Guido H. Stempel III, "Coverage of the 1972 Campaign by TV, News Magazines, and Major Newspapers," *Journalism Quarterly* 51 (Winter 1974), pp. 645–48; Lawrence W. Lichty and George A. Bailey, "Reading the Wind: Reflections on Content Analysis of Broadcast News," in William Adams and Fay Schreibman, eds., *Television Network News: Issues in Content Research* (Washington, D.C.: School of Public and International Affairs, George Washington University, 1978), pp. 125, 127; C. Richard Hof-

stetter, "Perception of News Bias in the 1972 Presidential Campaign," *Journalism Quarterly* 56 (Summer 1979), pp. 370–74; C. Richard Hofstetter, "News Bias in the 1972 Campaign: A Cross-Media Comparison," *Journalism Monographs* 1978, No. 58; Howard S. Friedman, Timothy I. Mertz, and M. Robin DiMatteo, "Perceived Bias in the Facial Expressions of Television News Broadcasters," *Journal of Communication* 30 (Autumn 1980), pp. 103–11.

83. See Klein, *Making It Perfectly Clear,* chap. 4, especially pp. 58–59, 63–64. See also pp. 65, 197.

84. Danforth W. Austin, "Media Get High Rating for Fairness, Less for Quality, in Covering Slump," *Wall Street Journal,* April 26, 1982, p. 29; Dom Bonafede, "The Washington Press—Competing for Power with the Federal Government," *National Journal,* April 17, 1982, p. 673; "Meeting the Press: A Conversation with David Gergen and Jody Powell," *Public Opinion,* December–January 1982, p. 57.

85. Meadow, "Cross-Media Comparison of Coverage of the 1972 Presidential Campaign." See also Donald E. Repass and Steven H. Chaffee, "Administrative vs. Campaign Coverage of Two Presidents in Eight Partisan Dailies," *Journalism Quarterly* 45 (Autumn 1968), pp. 528–31.

86. Grossman and Kumar, *Portraying the President,* pp. 258–59, 265. See also Gans, *Deciding What's News,* p. 147.

87. On this point, see Grossman and Kumar, *Portraying the President,* p. 48; Nessen, *It Sure Looks Different,* pp. 256–58.

88. See, for example, the criticism of Edith Efron, *The News Twisters* (Los Angeles: Nash, 1971) in Epstein, *News from Nowhere,* pp. 235–36; Paul H. Weaver, "Is Television News Biased?", *Public Interest* 26 (Winter 1972), pp. 57–74; Stevenson, et al., "Untwisting *The News Twisters.*"

89. Comstock, *Television in America,* p. 50 and sources cited therein.

90. John P. Robinson, "The Press as King-Maker: What Surveys from Last Five Campaigns Show," *Journalism Quarterly* 51 (Winter 1974), pp. 587–94, 606.

91. On this see Halberstam, *The Powers That Be,* chaps. 2, 17; John C. Merrill, "How *Time* Stereotyped Three U.S. Presidents," *Journalism Quarterly* 42 (Autumn 1965), pp. 563–570; Fred Fedler, Mike Meeske, and Joe Hall, "*Time* Magazine, Revisited: Presidential Stereotypes Persist," *Journalism Quarterly* 56 (Summer 1979), pp. 353–359.

92. Epstein, *News from Nowhere,* chap. 7; Grossman and Kumar, *Portraying the President,* p. 316; Hess, *The Washington Reporters,* pp. 87, 89; Gans, *Deciding What's News,* pp. 184–85, 190–91, 195, 203, 211–12; Graber, *Mass Media and American Politics,* pp. 148–50, 249; John Johnstone, *The Newspeople* (Urbana, Ill.: University of Illinois Press, 1976), pp. 225–26; S. Robert Lichter and Stanley Rothman, "Media and Business Elites," *Public Opinion,* October–November 1981, pp. 42–46, 59–60.

93. Gans, *Deciding What's News,* pp. 191–92.

94. *Ibid.,* pp. 194–95.

95. Hess, *The Washington Reporters,* pp. 5, 136; Klein, *Making It Perfectly Clear,* p. 417; Grossman and Kumar, *Portraying the President,* p. 258.

96. See, for example, Keogh, *President Nixon and the Press,* chaps. 4, 6.

97. See Gans, *Deciding What's News,* pp. 41–42, 194, 201.

98. Epstein, *News from Nowhere,* pp. 17–18.

99. Nessen, *It Sure Looks Different*, pp. 163, 165, 170. See also Grossman and Kumar, *Portraying the President*, p. 317.

100. Braestrup, *Big Story*. For another example of distortion, see Todd Gitlin, *The Whole World Is Watching: Mass Media in the Making and Unmaking of the New Left* (Berkeley, Calif.: University of California Press, 1980).

101. Kurt Lang and Gladys Engel Lang, *Politics and Television* (Chicago: Quadrangle Books, 1968), chap. 2.

102. Paletz and Elson, "Television Coverage of Presidential Conventions."

103. David L. Paletz and Roberta E. Pearson, " 'The Way You Look Tonight': A Critique of Television News Criticism," in Adams and Schreibman, eds., *Television Network News*, p. 80.

104. Lowry, "Agnew and the Network TV News."

105. Braestrup, *Big Story*, pp. 515–16, 519–20, 524.

106. Hess, *The Washington Reporters*, p. 88; Epstein, *News from Nowhere*, pp. 154–59.

107. Hess, *The Washington Reporters*, p. 88.

108. See, for example, Gans, *Deciding What's News*, p. 187; Epstein, *News from Nowhere*, pp. 215–20.

109. Gans, *Deciding What's News*, pp. 68–69.

110. Grossman and Kumar, *Portraying the President*, pp. 319, 321.

111. Nessen, *It Sure Looks Different*, p. 32.

112. "Meeting the Press," p. 10.

113. Robinson, "A Statesman Is a Dead Politician"; Robinson and Appel, "Network News Coverage of Congress"; Richard A. Pride and Daniel H. Clarke, "Race Relations in Television News: A Content Analysis of the Networks," *Journalism Quarterly* 50 (Summer 1973), pp. 326–28; Graber, *Mass Media and American Politics*, pp. 170–71, 173–76; Hofstetter, *Bias in the News*; Arthur H. Miller, Edie H. Goldenberg, and Lutz Erbring, "Type-Set Politics: Impact of Newspaper on Public Confidence," *American Political Science Review* 73 (March 1979), pp. 67–84; Doris A. Graber, "Press and TV as Opinion Resources in Presidential Campaigns," *Public Opinion Quarterly* 40 (Fall 1976), pp. 285–303; Richard A. Pride and Barbara Richards, "Denigration of Authority? Television News Coverage of the Student Movement," *Journal of Politics* 36 (August 1974), pp. 646–47; Stevenson, et al., "Untwisting *The News Twisters*." See also Klein, *Making It Perfectly Clear*, p. 284; Dennis T. Lowry, "Gresham's Law and Network TV News Selection," *Journal of Broadcasting* 15 (Fall 1971), pp. 397–408.

114. Robinson, "A Statesman Is a Dead Politician," pp. 178–82.

115. Paletz and Entman, *Media—Power—Politics*, p. 163; Graber, *Mass Media and American Politics*, pp. 81–82.

116. Grossman and Kumar, *Portraying the President*, pp. 255–59; 270–71, 274–79; Grossman and Kumar, "Carter, Reagan, and the Media," p. 13; Hess, *The Washington Reporters*, p. 98.

117. Graber, *Mass Media and American Politics*, p. 260 and sources cited therein.

118. Gaye Tuchman, "The Technology of Objectivity: Doing 'Objective' TV News Film," *Urban Life and Culture* 2 (April 1973), pp. 3–26.

119. See Richard A. Pride and Gary L. Wamsley, "Symbol Analysis of Network Coverage of the Laos Incursion," *Journalism Quarterly* 49 (Winter 1972), pp. 635–40, 647.

120. Frank, *Message Dimensions of Television News*, p. 47; Harney and Stone, "Television and Newspaper Front Page Coverage of a Major News Story."
121. Hofstetter, *Bias in the News*, pp. 92–93.
122. Frank, *Message Dimensions of Television News*, pp. 45–47.
123. For a unique study see Friedman, et al., "Perceived Bias in the Facial Expressions of Television News Broadcasters."
124. For an overview, see Cliff Zukin, "Mass Communication and Public Opinion," in Dan D. Nimmo and Keith R. Sanders, eds., *Handbook of Political Communication* (Beverly Hills, Calif.: Sage, 1981), pp. 359–90.
125. George Comstock, Steven Chaffee, Nathan Katzman, Maxwell McCombs, and Donald Roberts, *Television and Human Behavior* (New York: Columbia University Press, 1978), pp. 143–47. See also Mark R. Levy, "The Audience Experience with Television News," *Journalism Monographs*, No. 55, 1978; Robert L. Stevenson and Katheryn P. White, "The Cumulative Audience of Television Network News," *Journalism Quarterly* 57 (Autumn 1980), pp. 477–81.
126. "Stay Tuned for the News," *Public Opinion*, October–November 1981, p. 36.
127. *Ibid.*
128. See Patterson, *The Mass Media Election*, chap. 8.
129. See *ibid.*, pp. 95–96; Weaver, et al., *Media Agenda-Setting*; Maxwell E. McCombs, "The Agenda-Setting Approach," in Nimmo and Sanders, eds., *Handbook of Political Communication*, pp. 121–40; William Thomas Gormley, Jr., "Newspaper Agendas and Political Elites," *Journalism Quarterly* 52 (Summer 1975), pp. 304–8; Michael Bruce MacKuen and Steven Lane Coombs, *More Than News: Media Power in Public Affairs* (Beverly Hills, Calif.: Sage, 1981), pp. 1–144; and sources cited therein. But we must be cautious about media agenda-setting during elections. See Frank, *Message Dimensions of Television News*, pp. 61–65; Robert G. Meadow, "Issue Emphasis and Public Opinion: The Media During the 1972 Presidential Campaign," *American Politics Quarterly* 4 (April 1976), pp. 177–92; Shanto Iyengar, "Television News and Issue Salience: A Reexamination of the Agenda-Setting Hypothesis," *American Politics Quarterly* 7 (October 1979), pp. 395–416; Lutz Erbring, Edie H. Goldenberg, and Arthur H. Miller, "Front-Page News and Real World Cues: A New Look at Agenda-Setting by the Media," *American Journal of Political Science* 24 (February 1980), pp. 16–49; L. Edward Mullins, "Agenda-Setting and the Young Voter," in Donald L. Shaw and Maxwell E. McCombs, eds., *The Emergence of American Political Issues: The Agenda-Setting Function of the Press* (St. Paul: West, 1977), pp. 133–48. See also the views of John Ehrlichman in *Witness to Power*, p. 332.
130. See Herbert E. Krugman, "The Impact of Television Advertising: Learning Without Involvement," *Public Opinion Quarterly* 29 (Fall 1965), pp. 349–56.
131. Patterson, *The Mass Media Election*, chap. 12; Doris A. Graber, "Personal Qualities in Presidential Images: The Contribution of the Press," *Midwest Journal of Political Science* 16 (February 1972), pp. 29–45; Graber, *Mass Media and American Politics*, pp. 184–85.
132. Patterson, *The Mass Media Election*, pp. 84–86, 98–100, 105.
133. *Ibid.*, pp. 123–25; Frederick T. Steeper, "Public Response to Gerald Ford's Statements on Eastern Europe in the Second Debate," in George F. Bishop,

Robert G. Meadow, and Marilyn Jackson-Beeck, eds., *The Presidential Debates: Media, Electoral, and Public Perspectives* (New York: Praeger, 1978), pp. 81–101; David O. Sears and Steven H. Chaffee, "Uses and Effects of the 1976 Debates: An Overview of Empirical Studies," in Sidney Kraus, ed., *The Great Debates: Carter vs. Ford, 1976* (Bloomington, Ind.: Indiana University Press, 1979), pp. 239–40.

134. Ford, *A Time to Heal*, p. 289. See also pp. 343–44.

135. Quoted in Haynes Johnson, *In the Absence of Power: Governing America* (New York: Viking, 1980), p. 256.

136. Grossman and Kumar, *Portraying the President*, pp. 316–17; Grossman and Kumar, "Carter, Reagan, and the Media," pp. 9, 24; Richard E. Neustadt, *Presidential Power: The Politics of Leadership from FDR to Carter* (New York: Wiley, 1980), pp. 229–30, 237.

137. Thomas A. Kazee, "Television Exposure and Attitude Change: The Impact of Political Interest," *Public Opinion Quarterly* 45 (Winter 1981), pp. 507–18.

138. Patterson and McClure, *The Unseeing Eye*, chap. 2; Peter Clarke and Eric Fredin, "Newspaper, Television and Political Reasoning," *Public Opinion Quarterly* 42 (Summer 1978), pp. 143–60; Patterson, *The Mass Media Election*, pp. 62–64, chap. 13; John Kessel, *Presidential Campaign Politics: Coalition Strategies and Citizen Response* (Homewood, Ill.: Dorsey, 1980), pp. 185–88; Serena Wade and William Schramm, "The Mass Media as Sources of Public Affairs, Science, and Health Knowledge," *Public Opinion Quarterly* 33 (Summer 1969), pp. 197–209; David H. Weaver and Judith M. Buddenbaum, "Newspapers and Television: A Review of Research on Uses and Effects," in G. Cleveland Wilhoit, ed., *Mass Communication Review Yearbook, Volume I* (Beverly Hills, Calif.: Sage, 1980), pp. 376–77; and sources cited therein. See Patterson and McClure, *The Unseeing Eye*, pp. 125–28, on the impact of commercials in informing the poorly informed. See Patterson, *The Mass Media Election*, pp. 69–73, on television's role in affecting interest in politics. Special television coverage of political events such as documentaries or coverage of the Watergate hearings does seem to inform those who watch them. See Michael J. Robinson, "The Impact of the Televised Watergate Hearings," *Journal of Communication* 24 (Spring 1974), pp. 17–30; Stephen J. Fitzsimmons and Hobart G. Osburn, "The Impact of Public Affairs Television Documentaries," *Public Opinion Quarterly* 32 (Fall 1968), pp. 379–98.

139. "Stay Tuned for the News," p. 36.

140. See "And That's the Way It Is Today," *Public Opinion*, August–September 1979, pp. 30–31. For similar results see Kessel, *Presidential Campaign Politics*, pp. 185, 188; Comstock, et al., *Television and Human Behavior*, pp. 135–39 and sources cited therein.

141. Robinson, "The Audience for National TV News Programs."

142. Patterson, *The Mass Media Election*, pp. 59–60; Comstock, *Television in America*, p. 48.

143. See, for example, Peter Clarke and Lee Ruggels, "Preference Among News Media for Coverage of Public Affairs," *Journalism Quarterly* 47 (Autumn 1970), pp. 464–71.

144. Patterson, *The Mass Media Election*, p. 64.

145. On foreign policy, see Graber, *Mass Media and American Politics*, pp. 255, 261–62.
146. See Richard L. Rubin, *Press, Party, and Presidency* (New York: Norton, 1981), pp. 151–60, 213–14.
147. Dwight F. Davis, Lynda Lee Kaid, and Donald Singleton, "Information Effects of Political Commentary," *Experimental Study of Politics* 6 (June 1977), pp. 45–68; Lynda Lee Kaid, Donald L. Singleton, and Dwight Davis, "Instant Analysis of Televised Political Addresses: The Speaker versus the Commentator," in Brent D. Ruben, ed., *Communication Yearbook I* (New Brunswick, N.J.: Transition Books, 1977), pp. 453–64; John Havick, "The Impact of a Televised State of the Union Message and the Instant Analysis: An Experiment," unpublished paper, Georgia Institute of Technology, 1980.
148. David L. Paletz and Richard J. Vinegar, "Presidents on Television: The Effects of Instant Analysis," *Public Opinion Quarterly* 41 (Winter 1977–1978), pp. 488–97; Michael Jay Robinson, "The Impact of 'Instant Analysis,'" *Journal of Communication* 27 (Spring 1977), pp. 17–23.
149. Davis, et al., "Political Effects of Political Commentary"; Kaid, et al., "Instant Analyses of Televised Political Addresses."
150. Paletz and Entman, *Media—Power—Politics*, p. 70.

PUBLIC EXPECTATIONS OF THE PRESIDENT

When a new president assumes his responsibilities as chief executive, he enters into a set of relationships, the contours of which are largely beyond his control. The nations with which he will negotiate, the Congress he must persuade, and the bureaucracy he is to manage, for example, have existed long before he arrives in the White House. They have well-established routines and boundaries within which they function. These set the context of the president's relationships with them.

Public evaluations of the president also occur within an established environment: public expectations. The public has demanding expectations of what the president should be, how he should act, and what his policies should accomplish. It is up to him to live up to these expectations. Although some presidents may succeed in educating the public to alter their expectations over time, the public's views change slowly and usually the changes that take place only create additional burdens for the president. In addition, the static nature of the president's personal characteristics and leadership style and the constraints on his power and capacity to choose the most effective policies that are inherent in governing in the American political system limit his ability to meet the public's expectations. Frustration on the part of both the president and the public is inevitable in such a situation.

In this chapter we examine the nature and causes of the public's expectations of the president, the severe limitations the president faces in trying to meet these expectations, especially those focused on policy performance, and the consequences of these limitations for the president's standing with the public.

EXPECTATIONS

The public's expectations of the president's public and private behavior, his style of leadership, and his policy performance are high and appear to be climbing. Promises made on the campaign trail and once in office, the president's prominence, political socialization focused on great former presidents, faulty memories of past chief executives, the public's penchant for personalizing complex issues, and its lack of understanding of the president's power all serve to maintain and increase expectations of the president.

Expectations of the president are not only high but often contradictory as well. Among the characteristics the public wants in its president is leadership yet responsiveness, flexibility yet firmness, statesmanship yet political skill, openness yet control, and empathy for the common man yet uniqueness. In other words, the president is expected to be all things to all people.

The fact that its expectations of the president are high and contradictory is not entirely lost upon the public, but it holds the expectations anyway. And the greater the expectations of the president, the more potential exists for disappointment. In this section we explore these dimensions of expectations with the aid of a specially commissioned Gallup poll taken in the fall of 1979.[1]

High Expectations

The public's expectations of the president in the area of policy are substantial and include his insuring peace, prosperity, and security. Table 5.1 shows the results of polls taken in December 1976 and 1980 following the elections of Presidents Carter and Reagan. Performance expectations of each president are quite high and cover a broad range of policy areas. As President Carter told a group of visiting journalists in 1979, "The President is naturally held to be responsible for the state of the economy . . . [and] for the inconveniences, or disappointments, or the concerns of the American people."[2] We want the good life, and we look to the president to provide it.

Later in this chapter we will see that the president's influence on economic conditions and, more broadly, public policy and its consequences, is quite limited most of the time. Nevertheless, as Table 5.2 indicates, the public holds the president responsible for them anyway. To quote President Carter again: "When things go bad you [the president] get entirely too much blame. And I have to admit that when things go good, you get entirely too much credit."[3] Since conditions emphasized in the press seem to be bad more often than good, it is usually blame that presidents receive.

In addition to expecting successful policies from the White House, Americans expect their presidents to be extraordinary individuals. (This, of course, buttresses the public's policy expectations.) As Table 5.3 shows, the public expects the president to be intelligent, cool in a crisis, competent, highly ethical, and possessing a sense of humor. Substantial percentages also want him to have imagination and charisma. Obviously, it is not easy to meet these expectations, and, as we have seen, presidents are watched very carefully to see whether they do.

The public has not only high expectations for the president's official

TABLE 5.1   EARLY EXPECTATIONS OF PRESIDENTS CARTER AND REAGAN

| | % Feel Can Expect | |
Policy	Carter	Reagan
Reduce unemployment	72	69
Reduce inflation	*	66
Reduce cost of government	59	70
Increase government efficiency	81	89
Deal effectively with foreign policy	79	77
Strengthen national defense	81	76

*Not available.
SOURCE: "Early Expectations: Comparing Chief Executives," *Public Opinion*, February–March 1981, p. 39.

TABLE 5.2   POLICY EXPECTATIONS OF THE PRESIDENT

President Carter at Least Partly to Blame for:	% Agreeing
Continued inflation	78
High energy prices	68
Gasoline shortage	61

SOURCE: NBC–AP Poll, Summer 1979, cited in Thomas E. Cronin, "Looking for Leadership, 1980," *Public Opinion*, February–March 1980, p. 15.

TABLE 5.3 PUBLIC EXPECTATIONS OF THE PERSONAL
CHARACTERISTICS OF PRESIDENTS

Characteristic	% Feel Important
Intelligence	82
Sound judgment in a crisis	81
Competence, ability to get job done	74
High ethical standards	66
Sense of humor	50
Imagination	42
Personal charm, style, charisma	33

SOURCE: Gallup Poll, Fall 1979.

TABLE 5.4 PUBLIC EXPECTATIONS OF THE PRIVATE BEHAVIOR OF
PRESIDENTS

Behavior	% Would Strongly Object
If he smoked marijuana occasionally	70
If he told ethnic or racial jokes in private	43
If he were not a member of a church	38
If he used tranquilizers occasionally	36
If he used profane language in private	33
If he had seen a psychiatrist	30
If he wore blue jeans occasionally in the Oval Office	21
If he were divorced	17
If he had a cocktail before dinner each night	14

SOURCE: Gallup Poll, Fall 1979.

performance, but also lofty expectations for his *private* behavior. Table 5.4 provides the results of asking poll respondents if they would *strongly* object if the president acted in certain ways. As we can see, substantial percentages of the population would not merely object, but would strongly object, if the president engaged in behavior that is very common in American society. For example, when the Watergate tapes revealed that President Nixon frequently used profane and obscene language in his private conversations, many Americans were outraged. Many people were probably more upset by the president's language than by the sub-

TABLE 5.5   CHANGING PERCEPTIONS OF THE DIFFICULTY OF BEING
PRESIDENT

Perceptions Compared to the Past	% Agreeing
The public's expectations of the president are higher.	73
Congress is more difficult to deal with.	75
The problems the president must solve are more difficult.	77
The press is more critical of the president.	76

SOURCE: Gallup Poll, Fall 1979.

stance of his statements. We demand that the president's public and
private life be exemplary.[4]

It is interesting that the public seems to be aware of both the increasing difficulty of being president and its own rising expectations of his
performance. The public overwhelmingly believes that the president's
job is more difficult than in the past and that he is likely to receive more
criticism in the press (see Table 5.5). Moreover, it believes that expectations of the president are higher than in the past. Nevertheless, when we
correlate people's perceptions of the difficulty of being president with
their approval of his performance, controlling for party, we find that
there is no statistically significant relationship. Those who feel the president's tasks are more challenging than in the past do not take this into
consideration when they evaluate him.

In addition, there is a substantial gap between the expectations the
public has of what the president should accomplish (and for which it will
hold him accountable) and the degree of success the public expects the
president to have in meeting its expectations. For example, when Jimmy
Carter took office 63% of the people felt he could not stop inflation and
50% believed he could not balance the budget.[5] The fact that the juxtapo-
sition of these views might be unfair to the president does not seem to
disturb many of his constituents. Under such conditions we should not
be surprised that recent presidents have often been low in the polls.

Reasons for High Expectations

What is perhaps more surprising is the fact that expectations of the
president remain high despite the disappointment in their presidents
many Americans have experienced over the past generation. The tenacity
with which Americans maintain high expectations of the president may
be due in large part to the encouragement they receive from presidential
candidates to do so. The extremely lengthy process by which we select
our presidents lends itself to political hyperbole. For one year out of
every four we are enticed to expect more from our president than we are
currently receiving. Evidently we take this rhetoric to heart and hold our

presidents to ever higher standards, independent of the reasonableness of these expectations.

High expectations of presidents are also supported by our political socialization; we are often taught American history organized by presidential eras. Implicit in much of this teaching is the view that great presidents were largely responsible for the freedom and prosperity Americans enjoy. From such lessons it is a short step to our presuming that contemporary presidents can be wise and effective leaders and, therefore, that we should expect them to be so.

Those most attentive to the presidency and politics are as susceptible to the influence of a "remembered" past in their expectations as are other citizens. Richard Neustadt's comments about reactions in Washington to Jimmy Carter are especially insightful on this.

> Almost from the outset of his term, and savagely at intervals since his first summer, press commentators and congressional critics have deplored Carter's deficiencies in ways suggestive of a markedly higher standard, apparently compounded out of pieces of performance by the Presidents *since* Truman, as Washingtonians recall them.
>
> To characterize these briefly, one is Johnson's skills with Congress, especially in 1965 (sometimes the press looks back as far as Franklin Roosevelt's Hundred Days of 1933). Another is Dwight Eisenhower's popularity, hence credibility. . . . A third is Nixon's strategic sense as manifested by the opening to Peking, the so-called detente with Moscow, and in politics by his plan to back John Connally for 1976. Add, fourth, John Kennedy's performance on TV, which had become by 1963 a masterful affair, of "star" quality, unfailingly of interest, hence always entertaining on an entertainment medium. Finally, fifth, is an implicit Golden Age when White House aides were under tight control, truly anonymous and deferential to their seniors in the great departments. Carter himself contributed to this with early talk of "Cabinet government." But Ford and Nixon do not qualify, nor LBJ, nor Kennedy; few critics can remember farther back, so this is vague . . .
>
> The standard raised by Carter's critics seems to me too high, higher than realism counsels or necessity compels.
>
> Too much is expected of a President in Carter's shoes. . . . Washingtonians, like less attentive publics, tend to project on the Presidency expectations far exceeding anyone's assured capacity to carry through. Objectively, 1977 had little in common with 1965; still, as Carter started out the LBJ analogy filled many minds, some of them in his own entourage. Whatever were they thinking of? Ignorance is bliss.[6]

Yet another factor encouraging high expectations of the White House is the prominence of the president. He is our national spokesman, the personification of our nation—the closest thing we have to a royal sovereign. Upon his election he and his family dominate the news in America, as we have seen. The president's great visibility naturally induces us to focus our attention and thus our demands and expectations upon him.

Related to the president's prominence is our tendency to personalize. Issues of public policy are often extremely complex. To simplify them we tend to think of issues in terms of personalities, especially the president's. It is easier to blame a specific person for our personal and societal problems than it is to analyze and comprehend the complicated mix of factors that really cause these problems. Similarly, it is easier to project our frustrations onto a single individual than it is to deal with the contradictions and selfishness in our own policy demands. At the midpoint of his term in office President Carter reflected: "I can see why it is difficult for a President to serve two terms. You are the personification of problems and when you address a problem even successfully you become identified with it."[7]

Part of the explanation for the public's high expectations of the president probably lies in its lack of understanding of the context in which the president functions. We shall see below in some detail that the president's basic power situation in our constitutional system is one of weakness rather than strength. Yet this is widely misperceived by the public. In 1979, for example, only 36% of the people felt the president had too little power. Forty-nine percent felt his power was "just right."[8] Twenty years earlier, following five years of divided rule in which a Republican occupied the White House and Democrats dominated Congress, only 35% of the public felt it was disadvantageous for the presidency and Congress to be controlled by different political parties.[9]

Impact of High Expectations

Do high expectations of the president affect the public's evaluations of his performance? Although we lack sufficient data to reach a definitive conclusion, there is reason to believe that they do. One author found that presidents of whom the public had the highest initial expectations, Johnson and Nixon, suffered the most marked declines in support.[10]

For additional support for the conclusion that high expectations are detrimental to public approval of the president, we can turn to Table 5.6, in which June 1979 job ratings for President Carter among Democrats are presented, controlling for expectations in inflation and energy policy. As we can see, Carter received higher approval ratings among those who felt that no president could successfully deal with these policies, especially for energy policy. What is perhaps even more striking is that the levels of *disapproval* of the president were considerably lower among those who had low expectations of presidents handling inflation and energy policy.

TABLE 5.6 CARTER JOB RATING BY EXPECTATIONS

	Carter Job Rating Among Democrats			
	Could Any President Control Inflation?		Could Any President Handle the Energy Problem?	
	Yes	No	Yes	No
Approve	37%	40%	33%	48%
Disapprove	47	39	50	30
No Opinion	16	21	17	22

SOURCE: CBS News/*The New York Times* Poll, June 1979, reprinted in Warren J. Mitofsky and Kathleen A. Frankovic, "Don't Count Jimmy Carter Out," *Public Opinion,* August–September 1979, p. 8.

Sometimes the negative impact of high expectations in the public's support for the president is of the chief executive's own making. Jimmy Carter provides a good example of a president who is his own worst enemy in this regard. Both before and after taking office he set very high standards for himself and his administration, and he assured us that he *would* live up to them.[11] Unfortunately, he was unable to keep many of his promises such as balancing the budget and keeping his administration free from scandal.

In a strong statement to the State Department he declared unequivocally:

> I am determined that every single appointment that I ever make . . . is on the basis of merit and nothing else. And I want to root out once and for all the cheap political appointments that sometimes in the past have been an embarrassment to our own country and sometimes an insult to the nations to which we send diplomatic officers to represent us.[12]

But he appointed two wealthy Atlantans without diplomatic experience as ambassadors, and the press lost no time in reminding its readers of the president's promises about meritorious appointments.[13]

When he gave large pay increases to top White House aides shortly after taking office, the press did not hesitate to report the disparity between this action and his campaign theme of frugality. He pledged to present a complete reform of the welfare system by the first of May of his first year in office, but he had to change his plans when he found the task more difficult than he had anticipated, opening himself up to criticisms once again.[14] And he raised the public's expectations when he announced that there would be a change in the status quo regarding a

Soviet army brigade in Cuba. When this failed to happen, many people were naturally disappointed.

We have, of course, no way to calculate precisely the influence of these episodes on the president's standing with the public, and none of them alone were probably of much significance. Yet their collective impact was undoubtedly to depress Carter's approval ratings because they helped to undermine the aura of statesmanship and competence that attracted support in his election campaign. Perhaps presidents should follow Richard Neustadt's advice and lower expectations, especially at the beginning of their terms, so they will not mortgage their reputation and prestige to nuances of governing they have not yet learned.[15]

Contradictory Expectations

The contradictions in the public's expectations of the president present an additional obstacle to presidents in their efforts to gain public support.[16] With contradictory expectations it is very difficult for them to escape criticism and loss of approval—no matter what they do.

Contradictory expectations of the president deal with either the content of policy or his style of performance. Our expectations of policy are confused and seemingly unlimited. We want taxes and the cost of government to decrease, yet we do not want a decrease in public services. We desire plentiful gasoline, but not at a higher price. We wish inflation to be controlled, but not at the expense of higher unemployment or interest rates. We yearn for a clean environment, yet we are anxious to have economic growth.

Despite the contradictions inherent in such expectations, we have little hesitation in holding our presidents accountable for meeting them. When they fail to do so, as they inevitably must, we have little capacity to understand their dilemma and make allowances for it. Instead, we tend to accept no excuses for failure and withdraw our support.

It is true, of course, that the public is not entirely to blame for holding these contradictory expectations. Presidential candidates often enthusiastically encourage voters to believe that they will produce the proverbial situation in which everyone can have their cake and eat it, too. In the 1980 presidential campaign Ronald Reagan promised, among other things, to slash government expenditures, substantially reduce taxes, increase military spending, balance the budget, and maintain government services. Nevertheless, as we saw in Chapter 1, the public has little concern for the consistency of its views, and any encouragement it receives to hold contradictory views falls on receptive ears.

Expectations of the president's leadership style are also crucial in the public's evaluation of the president. Table 5.7 lists some of the performance expectations the American people had of the president in 1979. These figures will serve as part of the basis of the discussion that follows in which we examine some of the contradictory expectations Americans hold of presidential leadership.

Leadership vs. Responsiveness. We expect the president to be a leader, an independent figure who speaks out and takes stands on the issues even if his views are unpopular.[17] We also expect the president to preempt problems by anticipating them before they arise. Similarly, we count on the president to provide novel solutions to the country's problems. To meet these expectations the president must be ahead of public opinion, acting on problems that may be obscure to the general populace and contributing ideas that are different from those currently in vogue in discussions of policy.

In sharp contrast to our expectations for presidential leadership are our expectations that the chief executive be *responsive* to public opinion and that he be constrained by majority rule as represented in Congress. We now have a substantial number of polls taken over more than four decades that show that the public overwhelmingly desires Congress to have final authority in policy disagreements with the president, and it does not want the president to be able to act against majority opinion.[18]

Even in the area of national security, the public is not necessarily deferential to the president. It had more confidence in the judgment of Congress than in that of the president on the question of entry into World

TABLE 5.7 PUBLIC EXPECTATIONS OF THE PRESIDENT'S LEADERSHIP STYLE

Characteristic	% Feel Important
Placing country's interest ahead of politics	83
Taking firm stand on issues	75
Compassion, concern for little man/average citizen	70
Ability to anticipate the nation's needs	68
Saying what one believes, even if unpopular	64
Ability to inspire confidence	63
Forcefulness, decisiveness	59
Having consistent positions on issues	52
Flexibility, willingness to compromise	52
Political savvy, know-how	51
Having modern, up-to-date ideas and solutions	51
Loyalty to one's party	30

SOURCE: Gallup Poll, Fall 1979.

War II and on reorganization of the Defense Department in the 1950s—even when the president was former General of the Army Dwight Eisenhower.[19]

An exception to this deference may be the president's committing troops into hostile actions. For example, by a 47% to 45% plurality the public supported President Nixon's ordering the invasion of Cambodia in 1970 without consulting Congress. Yet opinion may have changed, in large part due to our experiences with the war in Vietnam. One month after the poll on Cambodia reported above, 62% of the public felt that the president should be *required* to obtain approval by Congress before sending troops back into Cambodia.[20] By 1973, 80% of the people supported a requirement that the president obtain the approval of Congress before sending U.S. armed forces into action outside the U.S.[21] That year Congress passed the War Powers Act over the president's veto. This law substantially limited the president's flexibility to continue the use of U.S. forces in hostile actions without the approval of Congress.

The contradictory expectations of leadership versus responsiveness place the president in a no-win situation. If he attempts to lead, he may be criticized for losing contact with his constituents and being unrepresentative. Conversely, if he tries to reflect the views of the populace, he may be reproached for failing to lead and for not solving the country's problems.

Flexibility vs. Firmness. We expect our presidents to be open-minded politicians in the American tradition and thus exhibit flexibility and willingness to compromise on policy differences. At the same time we also expect the president to be decisive and to take firm and consistent stands on the issues. These expectations are clearly incompatible, and presidents can expect to be criticized for being rigid and inflexible when they are standing firm on an issue. Ronald Reagan suffered such a fate in 1982 when he refused to yield on defense spending in the face of massive deficits. Presidents will also be disparaged for being weak and indecisive when they do compromise.

Statesman vs. Politician. A large majority of the public wants the president to be a statesman, to place the country's interests ahead of politics. Yet a majority of the same public also desires their president to be a skilled politician and a substantial minority favors the president exercising loyalty to his political party. If the president acts statesmanlike, he may be criticized for being too far above the political fray, for being an ineffective idealist and insufficiently solicitous of his party supporters. Jimmy Carter began his term on such a note when he attempted to cut back on "pork barrel" water projects. If he emphasizes a party program, however, the president may be criticized for being a crass politician, without concern for the broader national interest.

Openness vs. Control. Americans like their presidents to run open administrations. We desire a free flow of ideas within the governing circles in Washington, and we want the workings of government to be visible to us and not sheltered behind closed doors. At the same time we want to feel that the president is in control of things and that the government is not sailing rudderless. If a president allows internal dissent in White House decision making and does not try to hide or succeed in hiding this dissent from the public, he will inevitably be reproached for not being in control of his own aides. But if he should attempt to either stifle dissent or conceal it from the public, he will be accused of being isolated, undemocratic, and unable to accept criticism and of attempting to muzzle opposition.

Empathy vs. Uniqueness. Finally, Americans want their presidents to be able to relate to the average person in order to inspire confidence in the White House and to have compassion and concern for the typical citizen. Yet, as we have seen throughout our discussion of expectations, the public also expects the president to possess characteristics far different from its own and to act in ways that are beyond the capabilities of most people. To confuse the matter further, we also expect the president to act with a special dignity befitting the leader of our country and the free world and to live and entertain in splendor. In other words, presidents are not supposed to closely resemble the common man at all.

If a president seems too common, he may be disparaged for being just that—"common." One only has to think of the political cartoons of Harry Truman and Gerald Ford, implying that they were really not up to the job of president. On the other hand, if a president seems too different, appears too cerebral, or engages in too much pomp, he will likely be denounced as snobbish and isolated from the people and as being too regal for Americans' tastes. Again, one has to think back only to the Nixon White House to recall such criticisms.

Expectations in Perspective

The public's expectations of the president are neither modest nor consistent. As House Majority Leader Jim Wright declared in 1979, no president could live up to the "superhuman expectations" of the American people.[22] Yet we do not hesitate to hold the president accountable for meeting our highest hopes. It is within the confines of these expectations that the president struggles to gain and maintain enough public support to enable him to govern effectively.

MEETING POLICY EXPECTATIONS

We have seen what the public expects of the president. The question naturally arises of whether the president can satisfy these expectations. A president's personal characteristics and leadership style are largely set by the time he takes office.[23] Aside from cosmetic changes in appearance and behavior, there is little a president can do to alter these central features of his identity. Moreover, contradictory expectations are by definition impossible to meet. All a president can do is rely on rhetoric and symbols to obscure perceptions enough to be all things to all people.

At least theoretically, the president has the greatest flexibility for action and the most opportunities to affect his constituents' lives in the area of policy. Here he can work to gain their support. His policy performance provides the foundation for the public's evaluation of his personal characteristics and leadership style.

But what are the chances of the president meeting the public's policy expectations? In Chapter 2 we discussed the difficulties any president faces in trying to influence the economy. There are many factors that hinder the president in achieving his goals, and a complete analysis of them would be an enormous task well beyond the scope of this book. What follows is a brief overview highlighting some of the basic features of politics and policymaking that present formidable obstacles to programmatic success for the White House. These impediments include Congress, the courts, our party system, the executive branch, and limits on rational decision making.

Congress

Our constitutional system of separation of powers is really a system of shared powers. The president usually finds it difficult to act without the acquiescence of Congress. The president spends money, but Congress must first authorize and appropriate it. The president proposes laws, but Congress must approve them. The president nominates people to serve in official positions, but the Senate must confirm them. If the president vetoes a bill that has been passed by Congress, the latter may override the veto.

Even in national security policy, where the president has more leeway because he is the sole organ of the United States government representing the nation abroad, he must rely on Congress to exercise his power effectively. Although the president may negotiate treaties, the Senate must ratify them. Although the president is commander-in-chief of the armed forces, Congress decides if and when there will be a draft, how much soldiers and sailors will be paid, the rules governing the armed forces, and whether or not the United States will declare war. The War Powers Resolution of 1974 buttresses Congress's power to limit the chief executive as commander-in-chief by severely restricting his authority to engage in sustained combat without explicit congressional approval.

As a result of the dependence of presidents on Congress, they often fail to get what they want. This has many implications, but the important one for our purposes is that difficulty in bringing about change is inherent in our system of government. This may frustrate a public that does not understand why a president cannot deliver on his promises to enact new policies.

Table 5.8 shows the boxscore of presidential proposals submitted to Congress over a twenty-three-year period. The last column provides clear evidence that presidents often fail to get their way in Congress. In most cases the percentage of presidential requests approved by Congress in a given year falls below 50%. In 1963, 1971, and 1975 (under three different presidents) the boxscore was below 30%. In general, presidents had greater success when their party controlled Congress (which occurred in 1953–1954 and 1961–1968). Nevertheless, each president had many failures, and the scores vary considerably both within and between the terms of presidents.

The boxscore has a number of limitations. All requests are weighted equally; a request is counted as approved only if it passes in the same calendar year during which it was submitted (although most important legislation takes two or more years to pass after its introduction); no compensation is made for the fact that some presidents send complex legislation to Congress as one bill while others divide it into several parts, and that some anticipate congressional opposition and therefore do not send particular bills to the Hill; and no information is given about how individual members of Congress voted. Nevertheless, the boxscore alerts us to the very real problems that all presidents have in obtaining support for their policies in Congress.

The Courts

Presidents generally do not require positive action from the courts in order to make policy, so they are frustrated in their policy efforts less often by the judiciary than by Congress. Nevertheless, the courts do sometimes hinder presidents by denying them the right to take certain actions. President Nixon, for example, lost in the courts on his efforts to impound funds appropriated by Congress, exercise pocket vetoes when Congress was recessed but not adjourned, and withhold Watergate-

TABLE 5.8 PRESIDENTIAL BOXSCORE ON PROPOSALS SUBMITTED TO CONGRESS

Year	No. Submitted	No. Approved	% Approved
1953*	44	32	73
1954	232	150	65
1955	207	96	46
1956	225	103	46
1957	206	76	37
1958	234	110	47
1959	228	93	41
1960	183	56	31
1961	355	172	48
1962	298	132	44
1963	401	109	27
1964	217	125	58
1965	469	323	69
1966	371	207	56
1967	431	205	48
1968	414	231	56
1969	171	55	32
1970	210	97	46
1971	202	40	20
1972	116	51	44
1973	183	57	31
1974 (Nixon)	97	33	34
1974 (Ford)	64	23	36
1975	156	45	29

*The 1953 figures are not comparable to those of later years.
SOURCE: George C. Edwards III, *Presidential Influence in Congress* (San Francisco: W. H. Freeman, 1980), p. 14.

related tape recordings from the courts under a claim of executive privilege.

Judges not only veto presidential actions, but they also create obligations for him, obligations he may wish to avoid. If a court orders the executive branch to strictly enforce the law prohibiting federal aid to segregated school districts, the president is obligated to comply with the decision. If he delays or slackens on enforcement, he will alienate those who support the court's position. If he vigorously enforces the ruling, on the other hand, he risks angering opponents of the court's policy. This is an imposed, no-win situation for the president. Public support is a scarce commodity and if the president must risk losing the approval of a substantial number of people, he usually prefers to do so over issues of his own choosing.

Party System

The president operates within a highly decentralized party system. Lacking a crucial role in electoral politics, party leaders (including the president, who is the nominal head of his party) have no mechanisms to control the behavior of elected officials. They lack effective sanctions over officeholders because the latter win office largely independent of them. In addition, unlike parliamentary systems, the president as head of the executive branch remains in office even after losing important votes in the legislature. This further reduces the costs to members of Congress of failing to support a president of their party.

Nor do presidents control their party's machinery in Congress. Committee chairpersons and ranking minority members have traditionally been determined by seniority, and the chairpersons always come from the majority party in the chamber, which often is not the president's. The few exceptions to the seniority rule in recent years were not in any way inspired by the White House (which was controlled by Republicans while both houses of Congress were controlled by Democrats). For all practical purposes, the president plays no role at all in determining the holders of these important positions.

Congressional party leaders, who at least theoretically serve as liaisons with the president, are not always dependable supporters. They certainly are not simple extensions of the White House. As one presidential aide said of Senate Majority Leader Robert Byrd in 1977: "God, is he independent. He ain't our man—he's the Senate's man."[24] Presidents do not lobby for candidates for congressional party leadership positions and virtually always remain neutral during the selection process. They have no desire to alienate important members of Congress, whose support they will need. What sanctions leaders might apply on behalf of party loyalty, such as poor committee assignments, are rarely used because legislators are very hesitant to set precedents that could be used against themselves.

Yet other problems confront a president trying to mobilize his party in Congress. If it has just won the presidency, his party will have to adjust from its past stance as the opposition. This is not always easily done. Moreover, when a new party gains control of the White House, committee and party leaders, if they are of that party, will be less influential because they will be expected to take their lead on major issues from the White House. This may also make party discipline more difficult. In addition, there is a lack of consensus within the parties on many issues.

As a result of the decentralized nature of American parties, the president is not in a position to impose a position on elected officials of his party. Table 5.9 shows the average support of members of Congress by

TABLE 5.9   AVERAGE SUPPORT FOR PRESIDENTS BY PARTY,
1953–1981

	% Support	
	Democratic Presidents	Republican Presidents
House Democrats	68	46
House Republicans	40	64
Senate Democrats	63	44
Senate Republicans	45	67

party for presidents of each party. The basis for these figures are Congressional Quarterly's Presidential Support Scores, which measure the level of support of each member of Congress on votes on which the president has taken a stand. While it is clear that members of the president's party provide him more support than do members of the opposition party, it is equally clear that there is a great deal of slippage within the president's party in terms of party loyalty. As President Kennedy said in 1962: "Party loyalty or responsibility means damn little. They've got to take care of themselves first. They [House members] all have to run this year —I don't and I couldn't hurt most of them if I wanted to . . . and there's little the National Committee can do to help them."[25] Typically, a president can depend on the support of no more than two-thirds of his fellow party members on a given vote—dramatic evidence of the weakness of party control in Congress.[26]

The Executive Branch

Another aspect of the structure of American politics that often frustrates presidents in their efforts to achieve their goals and satisfy the public is the nature of the executive branch. This branch implements most of the policies of the national government, and the president is therefore highly dependent upon its performance. The bureaucracy is not always a reliable partner, however.[27]

One of the safest predictions about a new presidential administration is that the president will often find the federal bureaucracy unresponsive to his desires. In a study of President Nixon's orders, commands, requests, and directives to the executive branch in 1969 and 1970, political scientist Raymond Chambers found noncompliance with more than half of them.[28] Nixon's White House chief of staff, H. R. Haldeman, later wrote that by 1971 the president "realized that he was virtually powerless to deal with the bureaucracy in every department of government. It was no contest."[29]

President Jimmy Carter was also frustrated by the federal bureaucracy:

> Before I became president, I realized and I was warned that dealing with the federal bureaucracy would be one of the worst problems I would have to face. It has been even worse than I had anticipated.[30]

The experiences of recent presidents in implementation are summarized by Richard Cheney, President Ford's White House chief of staff:

> There is a tendency before you get to the White House or when you're just observing it from the outside to say, "Gee, that's a powerful position that person has." The fact of the matter is that while you're here trying to do things, you are far more aware of the constraints than you are of the power. You spend most of your time trying to overcome obstacles getting what the President wants done.[31]

Factors deeply imbedded in the bureaucracy and largely beyond the president's control, especially in the length of a term in office, cause slippage in the translation of policies on paper into functioning programs. This not only disappoints advocates of the programs that are not implemented effectively, but also may alienate those concerned generally about inefficiency, waste, and hindrances to policy implementation.

The president has limited resources with which to implement policies. The bureaucracy, quite contrary to popular rhetoric, often lacks staff of the proper size and with the necessary expertise; relevant and adequate information on how to implement policies and the compliance of others involved in implementation; authority to ensure that policies are carried out as they are intended; and facilities (including buildings, equipment, and supplies) in which or with which to provide services. Insufficient resources increase the probabilities that laws will not be enforced, services will not be provided, and reasonable regulations will not be developed, all of which will disappoint at least some people.

As a result of parochialism in the bureaucracy, executive branch officials will often be unfavorably disposed towards enthusiastic implementation of policies established by higher officials. Moreover, those implementing policy tend to see the health of their organizations as a high priority. Inevitably, there are differences in policy viewpoints among top decision makers and between bureaucratic units, and efforts are made to serve narrow organizational interests. These dispositions often hinder policy implementation as bureaucrats exercise their considerable discretion in interpreting the generally vague decisions and orders of the president and other high officials. They may ignore or selectively carry out their instructions, refuse to cooperate with their cohorts managing other programs and agencies, allocate resources on the basis of their own narrow priorities, and waste scarce resources fighting for program responsibility and autonomy. Replacing existing personnel with those more responsive to the president's policies or providing incentives for responsiveness is more useful to him in theory than in practice.

The structure of the bureaucracy also has a significant influence on the president's ability to implement policy. Organizational fragmentation may hinder the coordination necessary to implement successfully a complex policy requiring the cooperation of many people, and it may also waste scarce resources, inhibit change, create confusion, lead to policies working at cross-purposes, and result in important functions being overlooked. Standard operating procedures (SOPs) designed for ongoing policies are often inappropriate for new policies and may cause resistance to change, delay, waste, or unwanted actions. Lengthy chains of communication from the White House to the field create opportunities for distortion, as personnel at each rung of the bureaucratic ladder exercise judgment in expanding orders from above.

Decision Making

Presidents, and all other public officials, are burdened with the necessity of making choices on policies in order to please their constituents. At the same time, they are severely constrained in meeting the expectations of the public by their inevitable inability to make rational decisions.[32]

Rational decision making in the White House should begin with identifying and measuring the extent of problems that require the president's attention. Yet, there is often disagreement over whether or not problems even exist. Does the minimum wage cause unemployment among black teenagers, for example? To make matters worse, we generally have poor measurements of the extent of such problems as crime, pollution, inflation, unemployment, illegal aliens, or hundreds of others. Thus, even at this early stage of policymaking the president is severely limited in his ability to engage in rational decision making.

After identifying problems deserving of attention, the rational decision maker should clarify and rank his goals in order to provide a basis for evaluating competing demands on the government's time, energy, and resources. The goals of public policies are rarely clear, however. It is unusual for there to be consensus on direction, what policies are heading toward. Instead, we have vague statements of avoidance, what we want to move away from, such as poverty, war, and inefficiency. There is little agreement on what efficiency in government, equality, national security, and many other general policy goals mean in operational terms. Moreover, there is often disagreement over the proper role of the federal government (or, sometimes, any government) in alleviating problems that most observers agree exist. Naturally, if there is disagreement over whether problems exist or the nature of those problems, there is unlikely to be agreement over the goals of policies designed to alleviate these problems.

Ranking goals is just as problematic as clarifying them. We have no way to assign scalar values to various goals. There is no agreement in our society on either the criteria to employ in ranking goals or how to define possible criteria such as "equity," "justice," and the "public interest." To complicate matters further, there are hundreds or perhaps thousands of potential goals for national programs, and many of these goals, as we have seen, are quite vague. The intellectual task involved in ranking vague goals is truly staggering. Moreover, consensus is unlikely to occur because of the differences in the preferences of officials and their constituencies. Some are more concerned with unemployment than inflation, for example, and others have just the opposite priority.

The next step in rational decision making after establishing goals is to list the alternative policies for accomplishing these goals and gather all the relevant information available on them. The president relies heavily upon the executive branch bureaucracy to supply him with these options and their supporting data. Attempts to protect organizational and personal interests and to gain organizational and personal influence may distort the process of generating options and gathering information. So may the many layers through which communications usually flow to the White House, and SOPs may delay the president's recognition of critical information. He is also plagued by limited time to consider options and information, an enormous mass of communications from which to choose, and staffs that sometimes compete for his favor and attempt to shield him from unpleasant news.

A president's personal traits may be extraordinary, but they may still not be appropriate to effective decision making. The chief executive may not be sufficiently sensitive to the potential limitations on rational decision making and may not attempt to compensate for them; nor may he be able to cope with the conflict inherent in the advocacy of diverse points of view. All presidents need to simplify the complex and uncertain environments in which they operate and to maintain their self-esteem. These and other inherent psychological needs plus beliefs and values developed over a lifetime inevitably limit the president's ability to consider a wide range of options in a logical, detached manner.

Once options are listed and information on them gathered, the next step in rational decision making is to assess each option's potential for maximizing the president's goals. This involves predicting the consequences of each policy alternative, which is extremely difficult to do. What is the impact of a tax cut on the federal deficit? We simply do not know enough to make such predictions with much confidence, even for ongoing policies. Tests of proposed policies on a small scale are rarely politically, administratively, or morally feasible. Thus errors and unfortunate unintended consequences are common.

In this context of uncertainty, it is difficult to match the goals of policies with the alternatives best suited to meet them, especially if the goals are unclear or if there are several goals associated with a policy. In the words of Joseph Califano, a former White House advisor and cabinet member, "the basis of recommendations by an American cabinet officer . . . nearly resembles the intuitive judgment of a benevolent tribal chief in remote Africa."[33]

After predicting the consequences of various policy alternatives, a president attempting to engage in rational decision making will try to measure these consequences in some common units so that he can systematically compare them to each other. Perhaps the most common criterion for comparison of policies is efficiency. Using this criterion policymakers attempt to maximize the potential for achieving their goals at the least possible cost. A second common criterion is equity, which is concerned with the distribution of the benefits and costs of policies. We have great trouble measuring units of policies in these terms, however. What is the value of a human life, for example, or of national defense? Sometimes we even disagree on what are benefits and what are costs. Naturally, the less reliable our predictions of the consequences of alternatives, the less reliable will be our conclusions as to their costs and benefits. Many of these same problems hinder the calculation of equity. We lack a unit of measurement, a consensus on what is "equitable," and information on the distribution of the costs and benefits of policies. Yet another dilemma arises when we have to make trade-offs between criteria such as efficiency and equity. Since we have no common units of measurement with which to calculate these values and since we have no consensus on which is more important, we are unable to resolve conflicts between the two objectively.

Meeting Expectations in Perspective

Although the president is the dominant figure in American politics and the focus of our expectations for public policies, he is not in a strong position to satisfy his constituents. His power to make and implement policies is limited by the decentralized nature of government and politics in America and characteristics inherent in the federal bureaucracy. Moreover, decision making about public policies is a very complex enterprise and rife with uncertainties. As a result of the incongruity between the public's expectations for policy outcomes and the likelihood of the president satisfying these demands, a gap between expectations and performance is inevitable.

The nature of the constraints on the president vary somewhat according to his goals. If he is basically concerned with limiting government, as in the case of Ronald Reagan, he requires less positive action from Congress and the bureaucracy. Nevertheless, such a president is still dependent on Congress to pass the taxing and spending measures he desires and on the bureaucracy not to act contrary to his wishes (that is, too aggressively). The president also has the responsibility for providing a program for prosperity at home and peace and security abroad. The courts may still provide unwanted obligations and limitations on his power. Thus, the impact of the nature of politics and policymaking in the United States cannot be avoided.

CONCLUSION

In his search for public support the president finds himself confronted by more than just the press, the public's general inattentiveness to politics and policy, and the public's frequent resistance to his efforts at influencing it. An additional obstacle to the chief executive obtaining and maintaining public support is citizens' expectations. These expectations are wide-ranging and include the president's private behavior, personal characteristics, leadership style, and policy performance. What is worse, the public's expectations are high and sometimes contradictory, making them very difficult to meet. Moreover, since a president's personality, personal characteristics, and leadership style are largely set by the time he takes office, it is in the area of policy in which he has the most flexibility to act to satisfy the public. However, limits on policymaking inherent in the American political system severely constrain the president's ability to achieve his programmatic goals.

This is the context of the public's evaluations of the president, and it is not a particularly favorable one for the White House. Tension between public expectations and presidential performance is inevitable, and it is likely to lower his support in the country. The president enters his relationship with the public fighting an uphill battle. In the final chapter we examine factors that may directly influence the public's evaluations of the president's performance throughout his tenure.

NOTES

1. The survey consisted of a national sample of 1,520 adults who were interviewed during the period September 28–October 6, 1979.
2. Office of the White House Press Secretary, *Remarks of the President at a Meeting with Non-Washington Editors and Broadcasters*, September 21, 1979, p. 12.

3. Quoted in Godfrey Hodgson, *All Things to All Men: The False Promise of the Modern American Presidency* (New York: Simon and Schuster, 1980), p. 25.
4. See also Roberta S. Sigel, "Image of the American Presidency: Part II of an Exploration into Popular Views of Presidential Power," *Midwest Journal of Political Science* 10 (February 1966), p. 131.
5. "The Reagan Presidency—Same Old Expectations," *CBS News/The New York Times Poll*, January 1981, p. 2.
6. Richard E. Neustadt, *Presidential Power: The Politics of Leadership from FDR to Carter* (New York: Wiley, 1980), pp. 210–12.
7. "Carter Interview," *Congressional Quarterly Weekly Report*, November 25, 1978, p. 3354.
8. Gallup Poll, *Attitudes Toward the Presidency*, January 1980, p. 21. See also Jack Dennis, "Dimensions of Public Support for the Presidency" (paper presented at the Annual Meeting of the Midwest Political Science Association, Chicago, 1975), Tables 3, 5.
9. George H. Gallup, *The Gallup Poll: Public Opinion 1935–1971, Vol. III* (New York: Random House, 1972), pp. 1624–25.
10. James A. Stimson, "On Disillusion with the Expectation/Disillusion Theory: A Rejoinder," *Public Opinion Quarterly* 40 (Winter 1976–77), pp. 541–43.
11. Haynes Johnson, *In the Absence of Power: Governing America* (New York: Viking Press, 1980), p. 153.
12. Quoted in *Ibid.*, p. 154.
13. *Ibid.*, p. 173.
14. *Ibid.*
15. Neustadt, *Presidential Power*, p. 232.
16. For an insightful essay on this topic see Thomas E. Cronin, "The Presidency and Its Paradoxes," in Thomas E. Cronin and Rexford G. Tugwell, eds. *The Presidency Reappraised*, 2nd ed. (New York: Praeger, 1977), pp. 69–85.
17. See Sigel, "Image of the American Presidency," pp. 125, 130; Eric B. Herzik and Mary L. Dodson, "The President and Public Expectations: A Research Note," *Presidential Studies Quarterly* 12 (Spring 1982), p. 172.
18. Dennis, "Dimensions of Public Support," Tables 4, 8; Hazel Erskine, "The Polls: Presidential Power," *Public Opinion Quarterly* 37 (Fall 1973), pp. 492, 495. An exception is Sigel, "Image of the American Presidency," p. 125, who found more people favoring the president leading Congress and the people rather than following what the people and Congress decided. Perhaps this is due to the survey taking place in 1966 and the sample being limited to Detroit, a population highly favorable toward the president at the time.
19. Erskine, "The Polls," pp. 499–500.
20. *Ibid.*, pp. 500–501. See also Sigel, "Image of the American Presidency," p. 125.
21. George H. Gallup, *The Gallup Poll: Public Opinion 1972–1977, Vol. I* (Wilmington, Delaware: Scholarly Resources, 1978), pp. 210–11.
22. "Presidents Doomed by Super Expectations," *The Bryan–College Station Eagle*, September 12, 1979, p. 8A.
23. On this point see, for example, James David Barber, *The Presidential Character: Predicting Performance in the White House*, 2nd ed. (Englewood Cliffs, N.J.: Prentice-Hall, 1977).

24. "Jimmy's Oracle," *Newsweek*, October 3, 1977, p. 27.
25. Theodore Sorenson, *Kennedy* (New York: Bantam Books, 1966), p. 387.
26. See George C. Edwards III, *Presidential Influence in Congress* (San Francisco: W. H. Freeman, 1980), pp. 71–81.
27. This section relies on George C. Edwards III, *Implementing Public Policy* (Washington, D.C.: Congressional Quarterly Press, 1980).
28. Raymond L. Chambers, "The Executive Power: A Preliminary Study of the Concept of the Efficacy of Presidential Directives," *Presidential Studies Quarterly* 7 (Winter 1977), pp. 21–37.
29. H. R. Haldeman, *The Ends of Power* (New York: Times Books, 1978), p. 149.
30. G. Calvin Mackenzie, "Personal Appointment Strategies in Post-War Presidential Administrations" (paper presented at the Annual Meeting of the Midwest Political Science Association, Chicago, 1980), introductory page.
31. Stephen J. Wayne, "Working in the White House: Psychological Dimensions of the Job" (paper presented at the Annual Meeting of the Southern Political Science Association, New Orleans, 1977), p. 10.
32. See George C. Edwards III, *The Policy Predicament* (San Francisco: W. H. Freeman, 1978), chaps. 4–6.
33. Quoted in Daniel P. Moynihan, *The Politics of a Guaranteed Income* (New York: Vintage, 1973), p. 240.

PUBLIC APPROVAL
OF THE
PRESIDENT

The most visible and significant aspect of the president's relations with the public is his level of approval. The president's efforts to understand and lead public opinion and his efforts to influence the press's portrayal of him are aimed at achieving public support. This support is related to his success in dealing with others, especially the Congress. The higher the public's level of approval of the president, the more support his programs receive.[1]

Whether they are based on perceptions encouraged by the White House, the press, or other political actors, or based on detached and careful study, Americans hold opinions about the president and his policies. People are also affected, sometimes quite directly, by the impact of foreign and domestic policies. In this chapter we examine the economy, war, foreign policy, issue stands, the president's personality and personal characteristics, and international events as possible explanations for presidential approval. Regarding specific policies, we are concerned with whether evaluations of the president's performance, the success of the president's policies, or people's personal experiences of those policies are most influential in determining presidential approval.

In addition, there are certain less dynamic factors in the form of predispositions that citizens hold, such as political party identification and the positivity bias, that may strongly influence citizens' evaluations of the president. Party in particular not only directly affects opinions of the president, but also mediates the impact of other variables. Thus it is important that we examine predispositions as well as more specific opinions about the president and his policies.

The basic measure of public approval of the president that we use is the Gallup Poll question, "Do you approve or disapprove of the way [name of president] is handling his job as President?" There are a number of advantages to this measure, and they are elaborated in Appendix A at the end of this chapter. For our analysis of presidential approval we rely on 450 Gallup polls containing responses to the approval question from national samples in the 1953–1980 period. In addition, we analyze in considerable detail the biannual national election studies of the Center for Political Studies at the University of Michigan from 1968 through 1980. The 1972–1980 studies include the Gallup approval question, while the 1968 and 1970 studies include related questions, which are also discussed in Appendix A.

PREDISPOSITIONS

Research focused on explaining the president's level of approval in the public generally attempts to explain shifts in presidential approval by correlating it with variables representing possible influences such as the economy, war, and international crises. (This research is discussed in Appendix B.) All of these factors are potentially important influences on presidential approval, of course, but focusing exclusively on variables that are subject to change in the short run leads us to overlook factors that explain much of the public's level of approval of the president. In this section we examine the impact of predispositions in the public on its support for the president.

Party Identification

The political party identification of Americans exercises a strong influence on their political attitudes. A large body of research has shown that people have a need for cognitive balance, for consistency in their views.[2] Another large body of literature has shown that most Americans develop psychological attachments to one of the major political parties by the time they reach adulthood.[3] This partisan identification affects how individuals view what the president stands for and how well he is performing his job.

Those of the president's party tend to attribute their policy positions to him[4] or to change their issue stands to bring them in line with his.[5] In addition, these partisans tend to view his performance in a favorable light. Citizens of the opposition party have less need to perceive consistency between their own views and those of the president and have a tendency to evaluate his performance less favorably.[6]

An interesting example of the impact of partisan attachments on the evaluation of political leaders comes from a study of changes in the popular image of Dwight Eisenhower, one of the world's most popular men, after he publicly declared himself a Republican. The authors concluded:

> There is no reason to believe that admiration for him had followed any lines of political or social cleavage. Therefore it is noteworthy that our first measurements of public response to Eisenhower drawn after his commitment to the Republican Party showed a popular image quite strongly correlated with the individual's own partisan attachment. The stronger the loyalty the voter felt for the Republican Party, the more unconditional his respect for Eisenhower. Democrats were much less enthusiastic, and where sense of identification with the Democratic Party was strong enough, evaluated Eisenhower negatively . . .
>
> . . . Had Eisenhower chosen instead the Democratic Party, we may assume the relationship would have rotated in the opposing direction: strong Republicans would have decided they disliked Eisenhower.[7]

Thus, evaluations of the president's performance reflect the underlying partisan loyalties of the public. Members of the president's party are predisposed to approve of his performance and members of the opposition party are predisposed to be less approving. Independents, those without explicit partisan attachments, should fall between the Democrats and Republicans in their levels of approval of the president.

Our data bear this out. Democrats, Republicans, and Independents evaluate presidents differently. Table 6.1 shows the average level of approval of the president for each of these groups in the 1953–1980 period.[8] The average absolute difference in support between Democrats and Republicans is 35 percentage points, a very substantial figure. Independents fall in between, averaging 17 percentage points difference from Democrats and 18 percentage points from Republicans.

The impact of partisanship on evaluations of the president can also be seen by examining presidential approval at a cross section of time. In July of 1974, shortly before he resigned, Richard Nixon's overall support stood at 25%. Approval among Democrats had diminished to a meager

TABLE 6.1   AVERAGE YEARLY PRESIDENTIAL APPROVAL BY PARTISAN GROUPS, 1953–1980

Year	Party of President	Partisan Group % Approval		
		Democrats	Republicans	Independents
1953	R	56	87	67
1954	R	49	87	69
1955	R	56	91	74
1956	R	56	93	75
1957	R	47	86	66
1958	R	36	82	56
1959	R	48	88	66
1960	R	44	87	64
1961	D	87	58	72
1962	D	86	49	69
1963	D	79	44	62
1964	D	84	62	69
1965	D	79	49	59
1966	D	65	31	44
1967	D	59	27	38
1968	D	58	27	36
1969	R	50	83	61
1970	R	42	83	57
1971	R	36	79	49
1972	R	41	86	58
1973	R	26	71	43
1974	R	24	60	35
1975	R	33	66	45
1976	R	36	71	51
1977	D	73	46	60
1978	D	56	28	42
1979	D	47	25	35
1980	D	54	26	36

SOURCE: Gallup Poll.
R = Republican
D = Democrat

13%, and among Independents he received only a 23% approval rating. Yet even at the height of the Watergate crisis, 52% of Republicans gave the president their approval.

Five years later, at the end of July 1979, Jimmy Carter, a Democratic president, saw his approval fall to an overall 29%. Republican approval stood at only 18%. Democrats, on the other hand, were more than twice as likely to support Carter, giving him 37% approval. Independents were in the middle at 27%.

Not only do the absolute levels of presidential approval differ for each group of partisans, but they also may shift by different magnitudes or in opposite directions. In other words, Democrats, Republicans, and Independents do not always react the same to the president or to the events and conditions by which they evaluate him. What Democrats see as positive, Republicans may view as quite negative and vice versa.

We can get a better feel for these relationships by examining Table 6.2, which shows levels of public approval of the president by Democrats and Republicans from June 1977 through June 1978. In the first three polls Democratic support is completely stable while Republican support varies substantially. We find a similar stability in Democratic support from the late-October poll through the end of 1977, and instability in Republican approval levels. In January Republican support remains stable while Democratic approval decreases 5%. In each of the last five polls in the table, Democratic and Republican support move in the opposite direction. Finally, even when support shifts in the same direction for both Democrats and Republicans, the shift is often of differing percentages, indicating differing reactions of partisans to the same conditions and events in their environment.

Party identification, then, is an important determinant of presidential approval. In recent years the percentage of the population affiliating with one of the two major parties has been decreasing. The impact of part of this change has been more apparent than real because many Independents really lean towards one of the parties and act as partisans do. Nevertheless, the relative size of the Independent category has grown, and the percentage of strong partisans in the population has decreased.[9] Thus, a somewhat smaller percentage of the population is strongly predisposed to support or withhold support from the president because of party affiliation. As a result, presidential approval should be more variable, a prediction supported by the increased volatility of the polls in the 1970s.

Although party identification is a significant influence on presidential approval, it is far from the only one. Changes in the party identification of individuals are made slowly, if at all. Yet sharp changes in presidential approval can occur between polls taken two weeks apart. Obviously, other factors must account for these changes. After examining other predispositional factors, we shall turn to an examination of these influences on public opinion, always remembering that partisan identification affects how people perceive and react to the president and the events and conditions by which they evaluate him.

Positivity Bias

We have seen that party identification is an important predisposing influence on public approval of the president. Another predisposing factor is

TABLE 6.2 PRESIDENTIAL APPROVAL AMONG PARTY GROUPS, JUNE 1977–JUNE 1978

Date	% Approval	
	Democrats	Republicans
June 3–6, 1977	73	44
June 17–20, 1977	73	52
July 8–11, 1977	73	43
July 22–25, 1977	77	47
August 5–8, 1977	69	46
August 19–22, 1977	76	52
September 9–12, 1977	64	37
September 30–October 3, 1977	69	41
October 14–17, 1977	64	36
October 21–24, 1977	66	35
October 28–31, 1977	65	33
November 4–7, 1977	66	43
November 18–21, 1977	69	35
December 9–12, 1977	67	43
January 6–9, 1978	65	34
January 20–23, 1978	60	34
February 10–13, 1978	55	28
February 24–27, 1978	63	32
March 3–6, 1978	64	32
March 10–13, 1978	62	31
March 31–April 3, 1978	59	31
April 14–17, 1978	51	25
April 28–May 1, 1978	56	21
May 5–8, 1978	51	27
May 19–22, 1978	55	25
June 2–5, 1978	54	28
June 16–19, 1978	56	23

SOURCE: Gallup Poll.

the "positivity bias," which David Sears defines as the tendency "to show evaluation of public figures and institutions in a generally positive direction."[10] Americans have a general disposition to prefer, to learn, and to expect positive relationships more than negative relationships and to perceive stimuli as positive rather than negative. They tend to have favorable opinions of people.

The causes of the positivity bias are not well known,[11] but it seems to have the greatest potential for influence in ambiguous situations, such as the beginning of a president's term. New occupants of the White House are unknown to the public as chief executives and therefore may receive the benefit of the doubt in the public's evaluation of them.

Although positivity should encourage presidential approval throughout a president's tenure, it should be especially important at the beginning of a new president's term, when he lacks a track record. One way to see the impact of positivity bias is to compare the electoral percentages by which presidents first won election and their approval in the first Gallup poll taken after their election. Such a comparison is made in Table 6.3 (President Ford is excluded because he never won an election for the presidency). The figures clearly show that, with the exception of Ronald Reagan, a substantially larger percentage of the people are willing to give new presidents their approval at the beginning of their terms than were willing to vote for them two months earlier. Obviously, favoring another candidate is not the same as being opposed to the person who wins the election.

When presidents win election the second time, they do not necessarily receive the same boost from the positivity bias that they benefited from in their first election. After four years they are no longer ambiguous stimuli to the public. Only two men have won two presidential elections in recent history, Dwight Eisenhower and Richard Nixon, so we must exercise caution in reaching generalizations. Eisenhower received 57% of the popular vote in his reelection in 1956 and began his second term with a 74% approval rating. Even supporters of Adlai Stevenson liked Ike. Conversely, Richard Nixon won 61% of the vote in 1972 but began his second term with only a 52% approval rating, a drop of 9%.

Additional evidence in support of both the ambiguity surrounding new presidents and the benefits a new president receives from this is shown in Table 6.4. Although Ronald Reagan was one of the best-known persons in the country in 1981, had run for the Republican nomination for president three times, and had just finished a year-long election campaign, 43% of the people did not feel they knew enough about him to have an opinion about him, favorable or unfavorable (a broader question

TABLE 6.3 COMPARISON OF ELECTORAL PERCENTAGES AND POSTINAUGURAL APPROVAL

President	% of Popular Vote in First Election	% Approval in First Postinaugural Poll
Eisenhower	55	69
Kennedy	50	72
Johnson	61	71
Nixon	43	60
Carter	50	66
Reagan	51	51

SOURCE: Gallup Poll.

than the Gallup presidential approval question). This percentage steadily *increased* over the previous year when only 20% of the people had no opinion. It appears that the public in January 1981 was waiting to evaluate him on new criteria. It is especially significant that Reagan benefited from this increased ambiguity. As the table shows, the percentage of people holding an opinion of him as "not favorable" steadily decreased to a mere 11% at the time of his inauguration. Moving people from negative to neutral opinions increases the prospects of their eventually supporting the president.

As presidents perform their duties, they become better known to citizens, who have more bases for judgments about them. Moreover, the public may begin to perceive more implications of presidential policies for their own lives as time passes. If these are viewed unfavorably, people may be more open to, and pay more attention to, negative information about the president.[12]

Other Factors

A related factor may be at work in affecting presidents' approval in the public early in their terms. As the people have little basis on which to evaluate the president, they may turn to others for cues. A new chief executive is generally treated favorably in the press. Moreover, there is excitement and symbolism inherent in the peaceful transfer of power, inaugural festivities, and "new beginnings." All of this creates a very positive environment in which initial evaluations of elected presidents take place and buttresses any tendency toward the positivity bias.

Several studies have found evidence of what some authors term a *fait accompli* or bandwagon effect. In other words, after an election people, especially those voting for the loser, tend to view the winner more favorably than they did before the election. The depolarization of politics following an election and the positivity bias itself probably help to create an environment conducive to attitude change.[13]

TABLE 6.4 FAVORABILITY OF OPINION ON RONALD REAGAN, JANUARY 1980–JANUARY 1981

Opinion of Reagan	January 1981	November 1980	August 1980	January 1980
Favorable	46%	41%	46%	42%
Unfavorable	11	21	27	38
No Opinion	43	38	27	20

SOURCE: CBS News/*The New York Times* Poll, February 2, 1981, p. 2.

The Persistence of Approval

We have seen, then, that presidents begin their initial terms with the benefit of substantial support in the public. But how long does this honeymoon last? Conventional wisdom seems to indicate that soon presidents will have to begin making hard choices that will inevitably alienate segments of the population. This is the essence of the "coalition of minorities" variable introduced by John Mueller in his seminal study of presidential approval.[14]

Support for this view comes from a revealing response of President Carter in 1979 to a reporter's question concerning whether it was reasonable to expect the president to rate very highly with the American people. The president answered:

> In this present political environment, it is almost impossible. There are times of euphoria that sweep the nation immediately after an election or after an inauguration day or maybe after a notable success, like the Camp David Accords, when there is a surge of popularity for a President. But most of the decisions that have to be made by a President are inherently not popular ones. They are contentious. There is not a single vote to be derived from the evolution of a national energy policy. It is down all the way because the highly motivated consumer groups, for instance, or environmentalists, and so forth, can never be satisfied with any acceptable proposal that has a chance to be approved by the Congress, and the oil companies, and all those who are from producing states can never be satisfied with a compromise that's acceptable to Congress and is able to be passed.
>
> And for the President to espouse a balanced program naturally arouses the condemnation, certainly the opposition, criticism at least, of those highly-motivated opinion-shapers.
>
> In addition, there are times when you have to take a stand that you know is unpopular. A typical case that comes to my mind as I sit here is the Panama Canal Treaties. When we got to the conclusion of the Panama Canal negotiations after 14 years of negotiating, knowing that this is in the best interest of our country, there was a public opinion poll run . . . that showed only 8 percent of the American people favored a new Panama Canal Treaty. But my predecessors, ever since President Johnson, all the knowledgeable people in the State Department, mine and the previous Administrations, knew that we had to have a new Panama Canal Treaty. And for me to espouse that, to work with a great deal of commitment to get two-thirds vote in the Senate, was patently a losing political proposition. . . .
>
> And you are constantly involved in contention and debate.[15]

Despite the reasonableness of these expectations, presidential honeymoons are not always short-lived. President Eisenhower began his tenure with a 69% approval rating. A year later it had risen to 71%, in January

1955 it was back to 69%, and in January 1956, after 3 years in office, Eisenhower had a 76% approval rating. In December 1956 he was even higher at 79%. In other words, he ended his first term with a 10% *higher* approval rating than he began it. The second term showed more slippage, ending at 59%. Nevertheless, a 10% decrease in popularity over eight years is not very substantial and provides weak support for the argument that hard choices induce disapproval.

Of course, for reasons to be discussed below, Eisenhower might simply be an exception. So let us turn from the elderly, conservative Republican war hero to the young, dynamic leader of the New Frontier, John Kennedy. He began his term with 72% approval and saw it rise to 79% a year later. In January 1963 at 74% he was still 2 percentage points higher than when he took office. Between that time and his assassination in November his approval fell to 59%, still a comfortable majority and only 13 percentage points below where he began.

Lyndon Johnson's experience was different. He began his administration with a 78% approval rating in the wake of the death of John Kennedy, and this rose to 80% in February 1964. At his inauguration in 1965 his approval still stood at 71%, but it gradually deteriorated throughout the rest of his term. We shall return to the causes of this deterioration later.

President Nixon's approval rating did not vary greatly early in his first term. He began at 60%; this rose to 67% in March 1969, and stood at 65% in January 1970. A year later, in the middle of his first term, he had a 57% approval rating, only 3 percentage points below where he began. His approval at the beginning of his second term was only 52%, however, and it fell steadily until his resignation in August 1974.

Like Lyndon Johnson, Gerald Ford took office with the goodwill of the American people following a tragedy. His first approval rating was 73%. His public support plummeted 22 points in September, however, following his pardon of Richard Nixon. Nevertheless, by August 1975 he had lost only 4 additional points, and he finished his term at 53%, two points above his September 1974 figure.

The first Gallup poll following Jimmy Carter's inauguration showed him with a 66% approval rating. This rose to 75% six weeks later, but he had fallen to 55% after a year in office and 50% at the mid-point of his term. By September 1980 his approval was only 38%.

What these shifts in presidents' approval ratings show is that declines certainly do take place, but they are neither inevitable nor swift. Eisenhower maintained his standing in the public very well for two complete terms. Kennedy and Nixon held their public support for two years, as did Ford, once he suffered his sharp initial decline. Johnson's and Carter's approval losses were steeper, although Johnson's initial ratings were inflated due to the unique emotional climate at the time he assumed office. The same was true, of course, for Ford.

Thus, honeymoons are not necessarily fleeting phenomena in which new occupants of the White House receive a breathing period from the public. Instead, the president's constituents seem to be willing to give a new chief executive the benefit of the doubt for some time. In January 1982 over 70% of the public felt it would not be fair to judge President Reagan's economic program, passed in mid-1981, until at least the end of 1982.[16] It is up to each president to exploit this goodwill and build solid support for his administration in the public.

Long–Term Decline

In addition to examining approval levels within presidential terms, we also need to look for trends in public support across presidents. As we can see in Table 6.5, from 1953 through 1965 at least 60% of the public approved the president on the average, with the single exception of 1958. Support of two out of three Americans was not unusual. Starting in 1966, approval levels changed dramatically. Since that time support from even half the public has been the exception rather than the rule.

What happened? We cannot provide a definitive answer to this question, but it seems reasonable to argue that the war in Vietnam, a highly divisive policy following an era of peace, had a destructive effect on President Johnson's approval levels. Although Richard Nixon rebounded somewhat from his predecessor's low standing in the polls in 1966–1968, he did not rise back to pre-1966 levels, and Watergate sent his approval levels to new lows.

Just how much residual effect the factors of Vietnam and Watergate have had on the approval levels of the presidents that followed is impossible to determine with certainty. We do know that President Ford's pardon of Nixon tied Ford irrevocably to Watergate and that his public support plummeted immediately following his announcement. Moreover, a 1974 survey of Wisconsin residents found that 55% of the respondents agreed that Watergate had reduced their confidence in the office of the president.[17]

We also know that Presidents Carter and Reagan have not enjoyed high levels of approval. Ronald Reagan, as we saw in Table 6.3, began his term with less public approval than any president in our study. Like his predecessor, he was below the 50% level by his second year in office. Although it is possible that the generally low levels of support for recent presidents is purely a product of their individual actions and characteristics, it is difficult not to conclude that the events of the late 1960s and early 1970s have weakened the predispositions of many Americans to support the president.

TABLE 6.5   AVERAGE YEARLY PRESIDENTIAL APPROVAL, 1953–1980

Year	% Approval
1953	68
1954	66
1955	71
1956	73
1957	64
1958	54
1959	64
1960	61
1961	76
1962	71
1963	65
1964	75
1965	66
1966	50
1967	44
1968	43
1969	63
1970	58
1971	51
1972	58
1973	43
1974	36
1975	44
1976	49
1977	63
1978	45
1979	38
1980	42

SOURCE: Gallup Poll.

PERSONALITY OR POLICY?

Political party identification and the tendency towards a positivity bias predispose many members of the public to approve of the president's performance. Yet presidential approval may shift rapidly while these two factors remain largely unchanged. What accounts for these alterations in the president's standing in the public?

One factor that we commonly associate with someone's approval is personality. When focusing on presidents or other public figures, there may be a tendency to evaluate them more on style than substance. The fact, as we saw in Chapter 1, that Americans pay relatively little detailed attention to politics and policy adds further support for the view that the president's personality plays a large role in his approval.

Dwight Eisenhower was unique among modern presidents in that his public standing developed previous to and independent of his involvement in partisan politics. He was a likeable war hero who had been a principal leader in the highly consensual policy of defeating Germany in World War II. His image following the war was so apolitical that *both* parties approached him about running for president under their labels.

Some observers have argued that as president, Eisenhower was able to keep his public support largely on a personal level,[18] and there is some evidence to support this view. When the University of Michigan's Survey Research Center asked voters why they would vote for Eisenhower in 1952 and 1956, the voters were as likely to cite personal characteristics such as his integrity, ideals, personality, sincerity, and patriotism as his more job-specific qualifications such as experience, leadership, independence, decisiveness, or administrative abilities.[19] Unfortunately, the nature of the questions asked and the schemes used to code the responses of voters in future elections are sufficiently different from the 1952 and 1956 surveys that we cannot reasonably compare the bases of Eisenhower's public standing with those of other presidents.

Not only was Eisenhower said to be popular for his personal qualities, but he was also often viewed as a nonpartisan figure, above petty politics and narrow ideologies. For example, in June 1955, 57% of the public said that Ike was neither a Democrat *nor* a Republican but was "somewhere in between." Two months later 65% of those who characterized themselves as liberals viewed Eisenhower as a liberal and 61% of those who identified themselves as conservatives viewed the president as a conservative.[20] Moreover, unlike the case for the more actively partisan Franklin D. Roosevelt, Eisenhower's popularity did not move voters to switch their allegiance to the Republican party.[21]

On the other hand, as we saw in Table 6.1, Eisenhower was *evaluated* by the public as a partisan figure. Republicans were much more likely to approve his handling of the presidency than were Democrats. Moreover, the differences between the approval levels of the two groups of party identifiers are typical of those for other presidents. Thus, the personal component of Eisenhower's public support may have kept his overall level of approval high, but it did not protect him from evaluations as a partisan figure or from fluctuations in approval related to other conditions and events in the public's environment.

As Richard Neustadt pointed out in his famous treatise on presidential power, personality may buttress presidential approval, but it is not a dynamic factor. In other words, it cannot explain shifts in the president's standing with the public. Sharp changes in approval have occurred for presidents whose public manners have remained unaltered.[22]

Although impressions the public holds of the president's personality form early and change slowly, what the public feels ought to be and the way people evaluate what they see can change more rapidly. "Cleverness" can soon be viewed as "deceit," "reaching down for details" as "a penchant for the trivial," "evaluating all the alternatives" as "indecisiveness," "charm" as "commonness" or, even worse, "vulgarity," "staying above politics" as "naiveté."[23] The contradictory expectations the people hold of the president, which we examined in the last chapter, help to set the scene for these changing interpretations of presidential behavior, allowing the public to switch emphasis in what it looks for in a president and how it evaluates what it sees.

In addition, the public may "like" presidents, but still disapprove of the way they are handling their jobs. As we saw in Appendix A, a poll near the middle of President Carter's term found that almost twice as many people liked the president as approved of the manner in which he was handling the presidency. In November 1981 a Gallup poll found that 74% of the public approved of President Reagan as a person, but only 49% approved of his performance as president.[24]

Thus, although we cannot specify the contribution of personality to presidential approval, we do know that policy matters play a large role in evaluations of presidents.[25] In several articles with a series of coauthors, Richard Brody has found that presidential approval increases when the news is good and decreases when the news is bad.[26] More specifically, these researchers have done content analyses of the most important story in each day's news and calculated the balance of negative and positive news occurring between each presidential approval poll. The news stories were evaluated on the basis of whether they reflected results that were good, bad, or neutral from the perspective of the president's policy aims.

The ratio of good results compared to all results in the news forms the basis by which current news is evaluated. Shifts in presidential approval correlate with the discrepancy between how positive the news has been since the last poll and the cumulative ratio to that point. The greater the discrepancy between current news and past news, the more presidential approval shifts in the direction of the discrepancy. Each typical new item has less impact than the previous one because the denominator (the total number of news items) of the measure constantly increases.

We do not know whether it is the ratio of good news to bad news per se that explains levels and shifts of presidential approval, or whether it is the more specific events and conditions occurring in the country and the world that are reported in the news that have this influence. Nevertheless, the work of Brody et al. shows that changes in presidential approval are in large part a response to what people see happening in the world and not merely a reaction to a particular personality. It is the president's actions and the consequences of policies that are reported in the news. And, as we should expect in light of the findings in the previous chapter, the president's approval is affected whether or not he is responsible for these policy outcomes.

CROSS-SECTIONAL ANALYSES

In the remainder of this chapter we analyze several additional potential influences on presidential approval, including the economy, war, issue differences with the president, personal characteristics, and rally events. We will do this using the 1968, 1970, 1972, 1974, 1976, 1978, and 1980 surveys from the Center for Political Studies at the University of Michigan. Naturally, this involves employing cross-sectional analysis.

The reader should understand a few general points regarding the analysis that follows. First, the sheer volume of results is enormous. Space limitations and concern for the reader's tolerance induce me to broadly summarize some of the results, especially where relationships are weak or statistically insignificant and where the addition of control variables has no significant impact on the primary relationships.

Second, standard tests of statistical significance were computed for every potential relationship we tested. If a measure of association is not statistically significant at the .01 level, we declare it statistically insignificant. For those unaccustomed to statistical analysis, the .01 level of significance means that such relationships should occur by chance only 1% of the time. This conservative level of significance testing was selected because of the large samples contained in the surveys. With large samples even very weak relationships turn out to be statistically "significant," although they really do not represent relationships with substantive or theoretical importance.

The figures in Tables 6.6–6.15 and 6.18 are *tau-bs*. This statistic is commonly used to test for relationships in cross-tabulations, and it is more appropriate than *tau-c* for the model of the relationships we are testing.[27] It is also important to employ the same statistic when making comparisons between independent variables. Because of the potential distortion in *tau-b* when marginal distributions are greatly imbalanced,[28] Somer's *D* was also calculated for each relationship. Major differences in results seldom appeared, however.

It is also important to note that the surveys we will be analyzing were not taken with this study or even a study of presidential approval in mind. Thus the questions vary over time. In some years, for example, there are more questions on the economy and on particular types of economic circumstances (unemployment, inflation, financial condition) than in other years. Potentially useful control variables appear in one election study, are absent in the next one, and then reappear in the next. This lack of uniformity is often frustrating, but there is no alternative to using the data at hand. We cannot survey the past. As a consequence, we focus on finding relevant data to answer our questions rather than focusing on comparing data over time periods. At the same time we must keep in mind that ideally we would have comparable data for each survey.

Earlier in this chapter we saw the great importance of party identification as an influence on the public's evaluation of the president. We must take this into account in our analysis of the possible impact of other factors on presidential approval. Running a regression analysis of either time-series or cross-sectional data and including a control for party are insufficient. Relying on such methods will not allow us to discover the different relationships that may exist for each group of partisan identifiers. Instead, such an approach may mask relationships. We need to disaggregate our sample into Democrats, Republicans, and Independents and do separate analyses for each group.

An additional advantage of our approach is that it allows us to divide the public along lines relevant to the thinking of elected officials. As I have shown elsewhere,[29] Democrats in Congress are responsive to Democrats in the public, and Republicans in Congress are responsive to Republicans in the public. Since one of the principal reasons that we care about presidential approval is that its level affects the president's influence, it is useful to determine the influences on those to whom officials respond.

THE ECONOMY

The state of the economy has a pervasive influence on our lives. Our sense of income security, self-esteem, social status, and hope for the future are often related to the economy. So are the opportunities for our children and our life styles. It is no wonder, then, that the economy is the factor most often studied as an influence on the public's approval of the president.

The conventional view is that people's evaluations of the president are affected strongly by their personal economic circumstances. That is, people are more likely to approve of the president if they feel they are prospering personally than if they feel they are not. According to Richard Neustadt, "The moving factor in [presidential] prestige is what men outside Washington see happening to *themselves*."[30] Lyndon Johnson believed that "the family pocketbook was the root-and-branch crucial connection to all his plans and hopes for the future."[31]

Yet, as two authors who have studied the subject extensively have argued, "Pocketbook politics, in the guise of economic self-interest, narrowly defined, figures heavily—and rather uncritically—in social science thinking about politics."[32] Thus, recently some scholars have articulated a different view of presidential approval, arguing that citizens evaluate the president on the basis of broader views of the economy than just their narrow self-interests. In other words, rather than asking what the president has done for them lately, citizens ask what the president has done for the *nation*.[33]

There is plenty of reason to be skeptical of the role of self-interest in presidential approval. On issues including busing, the war in Vietnam, energy, law and order, unemployment, and national health insurance, scholars have found little relationship between the self-interest of respondents and their policy preferences or presidential voting behavior.[34] Many studies have focused on the question of the impact of economically self-interested behavior in voting for Congress or the presidency, and, although the results have been quite mixed,[35] there is substantial support for the assertion that general evaluations of the economy are more important influences on voting than are the narrow self-interests of voters.

Additional support for the view that personal economic circumstances do not dominate evaluations of the president comes from Brody and Sniderman, who have found that most people do not politicize their personal problems and most of those concerned about personal economic problems do not believe the government should come to their assistance.[36] These general findings are supported by the detailed study by Schlozman and Verba of personal experiences with unemployment.[37] If people perceive that their economic problems are due to their own failings or those of their immediate environment, then their personal experiences should not necessarily lead to discontent with national political figures or institutions.

Moreover, people differentiate their own circumstances from those of the country as a whole. In January 1981 the Gallup poll found that although 81% of the public was dissatisfied with the way things were going in the country, 83% were satisfied with the way things were going in their personal lives.[38] Another recent study found that people's personal economic circumstances have little impact on their evaluations of government economic performance.[39]

This argument does not imply that the public does not evaluate the president in terms of the economy, only that when it does so it looks beyond narrow self-interest and personal problems. People may evaluate the president in terms of the state of the economy as a whole, rather than its effect on them personally. Moreover, it does not necessarily follow that the public bases its evaluations directly on the overall performance of the economy. People may simply evaluate how well the president is handling economic policy, regardless of the short-term impact of his actions. The public may approve of a president who is struggling with a difficult situation even if he is not meeting with great tangible success. Franklin Roosevelt in 1933 and 1934 may have been such a case.

Furthermore, we do not argue that the public is peculiarly altruistic in its evaluations. People may be quite self-interested but perceive that what is best for the nation as a whole is also best for them. Or they may feel that the president is handling a situation as well as he can.

The reasoning regarding the public's evaluation of the president advanced in the preceding paragraphs also applies to other factors, which we examine below as possible influences on the public's approval of the president. The war in Vietnam may have influenced citizens' evaluations of the president because of how they viewed it as a general policy rather than how it affected them personally. Jimmy Carter's standing in the public may have benefited from favorable public perceptions of his handling of the Iranian hostage crisis, despite the fact that the hostages were not released for over 14 months.

Personal Economic Circumstances

Financial Conditions. There have been two general questions asked regarding personal economic circumstances in each of the seven surveys we are using: "Would you say that you (and your family living here) are better off or worse off financially than you were a year ago?" and "Do you think that a year from now you (and your family living here) will be better off financially, or worse off, or just about the same as now?" Table 6.6 shows the results of crosstabulating these questions with presidential approval. The findings are quite mixed. Twenty-two of 42, or 52%, of the coefficients are statistically significant, but none represent strong relationships.

It is possible that stronger relationships are being masked by our level of aggregation and that further controls are needed. In the 1974, 1976, and 1978 surveys respondents were asked to place themselves on a scale ranging from the view that the federal government is responsible for every person's having a good job and a good standard of living to the view that the government should let each person get ahead on his own. Although this variable does not focus exclusively on the president's responsibility for the economy, it is a useful indicator of the level of responsibility people see the federal government as having for their economic well-being. Perhaps those who view the government as having responsibility tie their evaluations of their own financial condition more closely to their evaluations of the president than those who see government as having little or no such responsibility.

For 1974 and 1976, employing the control does not produce stronger positive significant coefficients for those who believe in greater govern-

TABLE 6.6   CORRELATIONS BETWEEN EVALUATIONS OF PERSONAL
FINANCIAL SITUATIONS AND PRESIDENTIAL APPROVAL

Year	Financially Better Off Than Last Year		
	Democrats	Independents	Republicans
1968	.10*	.19*	.07
1970	.10	.12	−.00
1972	.17*	.11	.07
1974	.15*	.13*	.06
1976	.16*	.10*	.16*
1978	.12*	.09*	.07
1980	.05	.09	.15*

Year	Financially Better Off Next Year		
	Democrats	Independents	Republicans
1968	−.04	−.00	.03
1970	.08	.09	−.09
1972	.14*	.13	.11
1974	.06	.17*	.13*
1976	.09*	.08*	.13*
1978	.11*	.16*	.16*
1980	.11*	.09	.14*

*significant at ≤ .01
All figures are tau-b's.

ment responsibility to maintain their financial condition than for those who feel the opposite. The same is true for both Democrats and Republicans in 1978. But Independents are a different story. Significant coefficients of respectable size appear for comparisons with the past year (.26) and with the coming year (.29).

There is one more point to raise before we move on to more specific indicators of citizens' personal economic circumstances. Some authors have recently raised a question about the relative impact of retrospective and prospective evaluations.[40] In other words, they have been concerned with whether citizens evaluate officials or candidates on the basis of what they have experienced already or what they anticipate will occur in the future. At least for our data here, there seems to be no difference. Overall, the coefficients in the top and bottom halves of Table 6.6 are very similar. Thus, we cannot reach a conclusion about the relative importance of prospective and retrospective evaluations. We must not forget, however, that the relationships are generally weak throughout the table.

Unemployment. Unemployment is certainly one of the most personally devastating economic conditions. If personal economic circumstances affect presidential approval, it should show up there. Each of the seven surveys contain questions that allow us to determine whether (a) the respondent and (b) the family head were unemployed at the time of the survey or in the recent past (defined as the past year or the past two years). We would expect that if unemployment influences evaluations of the president, those who have experienced it personally or in their family would evaluate the president more negatively than those who have not. As Table 6.7 shows, however, in no instance do significant relationships in the hypothesized direction occur. Controlling for respondents' views on the role of government in guaranteeing jobs and standards of living for 1974, 1976, and 1978 does not alter this finding of the lack of significant relationships.

It is possible that persons directly affected by unemployment would be more likely to blame (i.e., disapprove of) the president if they felt unemployment was a problem that could be dealt with than if they felt

TABLE 6.7   CORRELATIONS BETWEEN UNEMPLOYMENT EXPERIENCE AND PRESIDENTIAL APPROVAL

| | Respondent Unemployed | | |
Year	Democrats	Independents	Republicans
1968	−.07	.01	−.03
1970	.01	.02	.15
1972	.10	.07	.07
1974	.06	−.01	.01
1976	−.03	.08	−.00
1978	−.04	−.10	−.09
1980	−.06	−.02	.05

| | Family Head Unemployed | | |
Year	Democrats	Independents	Republicans
1968	−.05	.02	−.03
1970	.05	.04	.11
1972	.08	.13	.05
1974	−.02	.01	.13
1976	−.04	.14*	.04
1978	−.07	−.08	−.09
1980	−.02	−.08	.05

*significant at $\leq$ .01
All figures are tau-b's.
Signs have been standardized.

it was unsolvable. Employing this control variable, which was available only in the 1980 survey, we find that it has an impact only for Democrats in the respondent question, raising the coefficient to a statistically significant but still weak −.11 for those who felt unemployment could be dealt with. There was no impact for the family head question.

A somewhat related control is available in 1978, a control for the locus of responsibility for handling the problem of unemployment. Those who perceive the president as having the greatest say in handling unemployment may be more likely to disapprove of him if they are affected by unemployment. However, controlling for this factor does not produce significant relationships. Controlling for the responsibility of the federal government to provide everyone with a good job and a good standard of living also fails to produce significant relationships for those who view the government as having more responsibility.

Personal experience with unemployment does not seem to strongly influence evaluations of the president. This may be due to the fact that people look beyond their own personal economic circumstances, as we hypothesized above, or that the impact of unemployment has been softened, as we argue in Appendix B, or a combination of these factors.

Inflation. The economic condition with the most widespread impact is inflation, affecting virtually everyone in the country. We might reasonably expect inflation, at least as it is perceived by survey respondents, to affect presidential approval if people evaluate the president at least partially in terms of their personal economic circumstances. The only survey in which we have data on the personal impact of inflation is that for 1980. A question was asked regarding the degree to which respondents were affected by inflation. The results for members of each party are weak, −.08, −.08, and −.07 for Democrats, Independents, and Republicans, respectively, and not statistically significant. Controlling for whether the respondent felt inflation could be dealt with had no effect on these results.

Summary. Personal economic circumstances, then, at least as we have measured them, have neither a strong nor a systematic influence on presidential approval. It is also important to note that other research has found that personal economic circumstances do not affect partisan identification, and thus do not affect presidential approval indirectly through party affiliation.[41]

Broader Views of the Economy

Rather than being responsive to their personal economic circumstances, citizens may employ a broader view of the state of the economy when they evaluate the president. Tables 6.8 and 6.9 show the results of correlating evaluations of business conditions and other aspects of the economy with presidential approval. Overall the results are not impressive. None of the coefficients represent a strong relationship. Thus, general evaluations of the economy do no better than perceptions of personal economic circumstances in predicting presidential approval.

On the issue of retrospective versus prospective evaluations, there are

TABLE 6.8 CORRELATIONS BETWEEN EVALUATIONS OF BUSINESS CONDITIONS AND PRESIDENTIAL APPROVAL

	Business Conditions Better Than Last Year		
Year	Democrats	Independents	Republicans
1976	.23*	.20*	.20*
1978	.17*	.16*	.15*
1980	.14*	.21*	.21*

	Business Conditions Better Next Year		
Year	Democrats	Independents	Republicans
1976	.06	.10*	.14*
1978	.14*	.19*	.10
1980	−.16	−.06	−.13

*significant at $\leq$ .01
All figures are tau-b's.

TABLE 6.9 CORRELATIONS BETWEEN EVALUATIONS OF THE NATION'S ECONOMY AND PRESIDENTIAL APPROVAL

Year	Question	Democrats	Independents	Republicans
1972	Expect prices to decrease next year	−.25*	−.13*	−.09
1976	Expect unemployment to increase next year	−.07	−.10*	−.22*
1980	How serious a national problem is inflation?	.10*	.16*	.02
1980	How serious a national problem is unemployment?	.03	−.03	−.05
1980	Nation's economy better than last year	.14*	.21*	.16*
1980	Nation's economy better next year	.11*	.07	.10

*significant at $\leq$ .01
All figures are tau-b's.

small but consistent differences in favor of the retrospective position in the tables, but once again we are unable to give clear support to one side or the other.

Policy Performance

Finally, we turn to the public's evaluation of the performance of the government in general and presidents in particular in handling the economy. Table 6.10 provides the results when the independent variable is the public's evaluation of the "government's" performance on the economy in general, or its handling of unemployment or inflation. As a group the coefficients show noticeably stronger relationships than we have seen before in our study of the economy and presidential approval. Evidently, the public evaluates the president more on the basis of how it thinks the government is performing on economic policy than how it thinks the economy itself is performing.

We employed the control for the government's responsibility for people's jobs and standard of living on each of the relationships in 1974,

TABLE 6.10 CORRELATIONS BETWEEN EVALUATIONS OF THE GOVERNMENT'S ECONOMIC POLICY PERFORMANCE AND PRESIDENTIAL APPROVAL

Year	Question	Demo-crats	Indepen-dents	Repub-licans
1972	Government will decrease unemployment	.20*	.24*	.15
1972	Government will decrease inflation	.21*	.25*	.15*
1972	Government's job on the economy	.40*	.34*	.24*
1974	Government's job on the economy	.38*	.31*	.29*
1976	Government's job on the economy	.29*	.30*	.16*
1976	Government's job on unemployment	.35*	.35*	.20*
1976	Government's job on inflation	.45*	.36*	.27*
1978	Government's job on unemployment	.27*	.21*	.17*
1978	Government's job on inflation	.30*	.29*	.31*

*significant at ≤ .01
All figures are tau-b's.

1976, and 1978, to see if those who felt the government had such a responsibility were more likely to tie their evaluations of the government's economic performance to their evaluations of the president. The hypothesized relationships exist only for Independents on the 1978 inflation question.

We also employed the control for who has the greatest say in handling unemployment and inflation issues in the 1978 inflation and unemployment questions to see if those who felt the president did were more likely to tie their evaluations of the government's economic performance to their evaluations of the president. The hypothesized relationships occurred only for Independents on the 1978 inflation question.

Although these controls bring interesting refinements to our analysis, we must not lose sight of the most crucial point: even where the controls worked as hypothesized, there were significant relationships in all the cells of the crosstabulations. In other words, the basic relationships between perceptions of the government's economic performance and presidential approval exist for all categories of the control variables. They were merely stronger in some categories than in others.

The results in Table 6.11 are even more impressive than those in the previous table and show that when we focus directly on people's perceptions of the president's performance in economic policy, we find the strongest relationships with their approval of the president.

Here, and in some of the tables that follow, the questions asked respondents in 1976 and 1980 sometimes contain the word "would" before asking about the policy performance or other behavior of the president.

TABLE 6.11 CORRELATIONS BETWEEN EVALUATIONS OF PRESIDENT'S HANDLING OF ECONOMIC POLICY AND PRESIDENTIAL APPROVAL

Year	Question	Demo-crats	Indepen-dents	Repub-licans
1976	Ford would reduce unemployment	.46*	.41*	.29*
1976	Ford would reduce inflation	.45*	.41*	.29*
1980	Carter handling of unemployment	.41*	.37*	.47*
1980	Carter handling of inflation	.46*	.50*	.47*
1980	Carter would solve economic problems	.45*	.49*	.34*

*significant at $\leq .01$
All figures are tau-b's.

This occurs because in the surveys the questions were asked about a range of candidates for president, including Presidents Ford and Carter. One could argue, therefore, that these are evaluations of future rather than of current performance. Since respondents normally would have no other basis for evaluating the incumbent president's future performance than his current performance, we treat these questions as evaluations of the president's current performance.

The only controls available for Table 6.11 are for the questions dealing with the public's views on President Carter's performance on unemployment and inflation. We first controlled for how serious as national problems people viewed unemployment and inflation, hypothesizing that those who considered them more serious would tie their evaluations of Carter's economic performance more closely to their overall evaluations of him. This occurred only for Republicans on the inflation question.

We then controlled for whether people felt unemployment and inflation could be dealt with, hypothesizing that those who felt it could be would tie their evaluations of Carter's economic performance more closely to their overall evaluations of him. In light of our findings in Chapter 5, we should not be surprised that these relationships occurred only for Republicans in the inflation question and Democrats in the unemployment question. Once again, the imposition of these controls does not alter the fact that the basic relationships between evaluations of Carter's performance on economic matters and his overall approval exist in all categories of the central variables.

Indirect Influence

Before leaving the topic of the economy, we must consider one other possibility regarding personal economic circumstances. It is possible that in addition to their weak or nonexistent direct influence on presidential approval, personal economic circumstances affect it indirectly through their influence on evaluations of the president's handling of economic issues such as inflation and unemployment. These latter attitudes, as we have seen, influence overall evaluations of the president's job performance.

Our most relevant data for investigating this question appear in the 1980 election study. When we correlate personal economic circumstances with evaluations of President Carter's handling of economic issues, however, we find that the relationships are no higher than the direct relationships with overall presidential approval. Thus, even if we add the indirect to the direct influence of personal economic circumstances on presidential approval, the total impact is small.

Summary

In sum, economic factors affect the president's standing in the public, but not in the manner we might expect. Neither personal economic circumstances nor general evaluations of the economy exercise strong influence on the public's evaluations of the president. However, when we examine the public's perceptions of how well the government, particularly the president, is performing on economic policy, we find a different pattern. Here the relationships are substantial. The public evaluates the president's role in the economy more on the basis of his performance than on its view of the state of the economy.

WAR

War is a factor that is frequently discussed as having impact on presidential approval. The reasons for this attention are obvious: wars disrupt and sometimes polarize society and are very costly in terms of lives and money. The president, moreover, in his role as commander-in-chief, is inevitably closely identified with war policy. Unlike the economy, war, fortunately, is not always with us. The war in Vietnam took place during part of the period covered by our study, and the 1968, 1970, and 1972 polls include a few questions useful for our purposes.

In 1968 respondents were asked if a member of their immediate family had served in the armed services due to the Vietnam war. They were then asked whether an immediate family member had served in the armed forces in Vietnam. The same questions were repeated for close friends or relatives.[42] If people evaluated the president to some degree in terms of the immediate impact of the Vietnam war on their lives, it ought to show up here. The results were quite different, however. In no case was a relationship significant, as we can see in Table 6.12. As in the case of the impact of the economy on presidential approval, the personal circumstances of individuals do not seem to affect their evaluations of the president.

In the three surveys each respondent was asked where he or she fit on a scale of possible policies in Vietnam, ranging from immediate withdrawal to complete military victory. Respondents were then asked to place the president on the same scale. We then computed the differences between the two and tested whether policy differences with the president on Vietnam were related to presidential approval. As we can see in the table, all the coefficients are significant, although they vary widely in strength. The relationships for Democrats and Independents in 1972 are substantial. Controlling for the importance of the Vietnam issue to respondents (1968) did not systematically affect the relationships.

A 1968 question on whether the U.S. did the right thing in getting

TABLE 6.12 CORRELATIONS BETWEEN VIETNAM EXPERIENCE AND ATTITUDES AND PRESIDENTIAL APPROVAL

Year	Question	Demo-crats	Indepen-dents	Repub-licans
1968	Immediate family member in armed forces due to Vietnam	−.03	.08	.02
1968	Immediate family member served in Vietnam	.03	−.03	−.00
1968	Close friend or relative in armed forces due to Vietnam	.04	−.01	.08
1968	Close friend or relative served in Vietnam	−.01	−.00	−.03
1968	Vietnam policy	.14*	.15*	.23*
1970	Vietnam policy	.18*	.24*	.20*
1972	Vietnam policy	.35*	.46*	.16*
1968	U.S. did right thing in getting into Vietnam	.18*	.20*	.25*
1972	Nixon would bring peace in Vietnam	.47*	.52*	.26*

*significant at $\leq$ .01
All figures are tau-b's.

into the war produced significant but modest relationships, but a 1972 question on whether President Nixon would bring peace in Vietnam revealed strong relationships for both Democrats and Independents. Republican opinion is dominated by partisanship.

These findings, in sum, are much like those for the economy. People did not evaluate presidents in terms of their personal experiences with the war in Vietnam, at least as we have measured them here. Their responses to broad policy considerations produced significant relationships of varying strength. The strongest relationships of all, for those not of the president's party, were revealed when respondents were asked to specifically focus on the president's handling of the war.

OTHER ISSUES

There are many issues besides the economy and war, of course, and in this section we look at how the public's evaluations of the president's stands and performance on a range of issues influence its approval of him.

Issue Stands

In each of the seven surveys respondents were asked to place both themselves and the president on a scale for each of a variety of issues. From these we compute issue-proximity scores by calculating the absolute differences between the respondent and the president on each issue. This is a measure of agreement with the president's issue stands. We then correlate these with presidential approval. The results are reported in Table 6.13.

Almost all of the coefficients are statistically significant, and they vary widely in strength. The relationships for Republicans are generally modest, especially when a Republican occupies the White House. Republicans typically saw little difference between their views and those of Presidents Nixon and Ford. The coefficients for Democrats weaken noticeably when a Democrat is president, but they generally are noteworthy.

It is possible that the relationships in Table 6.13 would be strengthened for those for whom the issues were most salient (important for their presidential vote). Those who cared most about the issues may be more likely to evaluate the president in terms of them. Unfortunately, there were no such controls in 1972, 1974, 1976, and 1978. Moreover, the distribution of responses for possible controls in 1970 and 1980 were too skewed to employ here. They lacked variance because very few people did not care about the issues.

For the one issue in the table for 1968, however, the question of salience was well distributed over a four-point scale. In this case those who found the issue most salient were especially likely to tie their issue stand to their overall evaluation of the president. Nevertheless, the significant relationship between the proximity score on the issue and presidential approval remained for almost all categories of respondents.

Policy Performance

Table 6.14 lists a range of policy performance questions and shows the results of correlating citizens' evaluations of the president's performance on them with their summary approval of the president. Overall, all the coefficients are statistically significant and most of them are quite respectable in size. Although there is some evidence of the normal impact of party affiliation, it is less systematic, especially for the Democrats, than we have seen it in earlier tables. The coefficients for each party show greater stability across administrations.

Summary

The findings in this section are consistent with those in the sections on the economy and war. The public's views regarding a broad range of issues are related to its level of approval of the president, especially when we focus directly on perceptions of the president's policy performance.

PERSONAL CHARACTERISTICS

Much of the commentary on the president in the press and in other forums focuses on his personal characteristics, especially integrity, intelligence, and leadership abilities. Table 6.15 lists questions asked in our surveys that evaluate the president on a range of personal characteristics. The questions about "personality" explicitly ask whether Nixon and Ford have the proper personalities *to be president*, not if they are "nice," etc. Thus, these are job-related characteristics.

As we can see, all but one of the coefficients in the table are statistically significant, and the relationships they represent range in strength from very strong to modest. Most of the relationships are of quite respectable strength, providing substantial evidence that the public's evaluations of the president's personal characteristics influence their approval of his performance in office.

We can see the importance of party affiliation by comparing the coefficients for the "trust" question in 1972, 1976, and 1978. Relationships are strong for Republicans only when a Democrat is chief executive. At the same time, the coefficients for Republicans are typically modest and lower than those for Democrats and Independents, even when we control for the party of the president. This may be partially due to the fact that by 1980 only about one out of six or seven Republicans approved of Carter. Thus there was little variation in the dependent variable. Moreover, few Republicans found fault with the characteristics of Republican presidents.

RALLY EVENTS

To this point we have examined factors that may affect presidential approval systematically over time, but sometimes public opinion takes sudden jumps. One popular explanation for these surges of support are "rally events." John Mueller, in his seminal definition of the concept, defined a rally event as one that is international, directly involves the U.S. and particularly the president, and is specific, dramatic, and sharply

TABLE 6.13 CORRELATIONS BETWEEN ISSUE PROXIMITY TO THE
PRESIDENT AND PRESIDENTIAL APPROVAL

Year	Issue	Democrats	Independents	Republicans
1968	Dealing with urban unrest	.22*	.18*	.21*
1970	Dealing with urban unrest	.30*	.29*	.13*
1970	Dealing with student disturbances	.23*	.25*	.11*
1970	Federal aid to minorities	.25*	.20*	.06
1970	Government action against inflation	.23*	.25*	.15*
1970	Protection of rights of accused	.23*	.18*	.15*
1970	Government regulation of pollution	.18*	.27*	.17*
1970	National health insurance	.20*	.16*	.15*
1972	Federally guaranteed jobs and standard of living	.33*	.40*	.11
1972	Progressivity of taxes	.28*	.30*	.09
1972	Legalization of marijuana	.32*	.28*	.21*
1972	Busing for integration	.24*	.24*	.18*
1972	National health insurance	.30*	.26*	.16*
1972	Women's rights	.20*	.33*	.16*
1972	Government action against inflation	.36*	.25*	.16*
1972	Protection of rights of accused	.26*	.36*	.09
1972	Federal aid to minorities	.22*	.26*	.10
1972	Ideology	.40*	.42*	.06
1974	Federally guaranteed jobs and standard of living	.36*	.37*	.13*
1974	Dealing with urban unrest	.33*	.28*	.23*
1974	Protection of rights of accused	.29*	.34*	.21*
1974	Busing for integration	.26*	.09	.09

TABLE 6.13 (continued)

Year	Issue	Democrats	Independents	Republicans
1974	Federal aid to minorities	.26*	.36*	.07
1974	Ideology	.28*	.30*	.08
1976	Federally guaranteed jobs and standard of living	.34*	.21*	.14*
1976	Protection of rights of accused	.18*	.22*	.11*
1976	Busing for integration	.20*	.25*	.14*
1976	Federal aid to minorities	.30*	.24*	.20*
1976	National health insurance	.36*	.24*	.18*
1976	Ideology	.38*	.30*	.15*
1976	Dealing with urban unrest	.33*	.37*	.13*
1976	Legalization of marijuana	.12*	.18*	.13*
1976	Progressivity of taxes	.22*	.09	.21*
1976	Women's rights	.20*	.16*	.16*
1978	Federally guaranteed jobs and standard of living	.09*	.25*	.27*
1978	Protection of rights of accused	.17*	.23*	.19*
1978	Federal aid to minorities	.24*	.19*	.33*
1978	National health insurance	.12*	.18*	.18*
1978	Women's rights	.09*	.15*	.04
1978	Ideology	.16*	.24*	.31*
1980	Ideology	.26*	.27*	.22*
1980	Defense spending	.24*	.22*	.15*
1980	Services vs. spending reductions	.24*	.27*	.17*
1980	Unemployment vs. inflation	.23*	.25*	.17*
1980	Freedom of abortion	.14*	.21*	.16*
1980	Tax cut	.28*	.25*	.16*
1980	Federal aid to minorities	.11*	.16*	.27*
1980	Relations with Russia	.15*	.20*	.19*

TABLE 6.13 (continued)

Year	Issue	Democrats	Independents	Republicans
1980	Women's rights	.18*	.04	.05
1980	Federally guaranteed jobs and standard of living	.07	.20*	.27*

*significant ≤ .01
All figures are tau-b's.

TABLE 6.14 CORRELATIONS BETWEEN EVALUATIONS OF PRESIDENTIAL POLICY PERFORMANCE AND PRESIDENTIAL APPROVAL

Year	Question	Demo-crats	Indepen-dents	Repub-licans
1972	Nixon would control crime	.39*	.37*	.18*
1974	Ford's pardon of Nixon	.38*	.36*	.28*
1976	Ford's pardon of Nixon	.41*	.32*	.22*
1976	Ford would reduce size and power of government	.31*	.36*	.27*
1976	Ford would increase efficiency of government	.54*	.49*	.36*
1980	Carter's handling of Iranian hostage crisis	.43*	.37*	.37*
1980	Carter's handling of Afghanistan crisis	.11*	.25*	.21*
1980	Carter's handling of energy situation	.39*	.33*	.40*
1980	Carter would develop good relations with other countries	.41*	.36*	.30*

*significant at ≤ .01
All figures are tau-b's.

focused. Such events confront the nation as a whole, are salient to the public, and gain public attention and interest. Mueller also included the inaugural period of a president's term (we dealt with this earlier in the chapter).[43]

The theory behind attributing significance to rally events is that the public will increase its support of the president in times of crisis or during major international events, at least in the short run, because he is the symbol of the country and the primary focus of attention at such times. Moreover, people do not want to hurt the country's chances of success by opposing the president, and the president has an opportunity to look masterful and evoke patriotic reaction among the people.

As we note in Appendix B, those doing time-series analyses of the impact of rally events have generally had to assume that the impact of all

TABLE 6.15 CORRELATIONS BETWEEN PERCEPTIONS OF PERSONAL
CHARACTERISTICS OF THE PRESIDENT AND PRESIDENTIAL APPROVAL

Year	Expectation	Demo-crats	Indepen-dents	Repub-licans
1972	Trust Nixon	.57*	.60*	.29*
1972	Nixon right personality	.47*	.48*	.20*
1976	Trust Ford	.50*	.46*	.31*
1976	Ford right personality	.46*	.34*	.17*
1976	Ford would bring moral and religious standards to government	.43*	.32*	.20*
1978	Trust Carter	.44*	.45*	.49*
1980	Carter moral	.25*	.29*	.15*
1980	Carter dishonest	−.22*	−.26*	−.09
1980	Carter weak	−.30*	−.42*	−.29*
1980	Carter knowledgeable	.35*	.30*	.27*
1980	Carter inspiring	.44*	.35*	.32*
1980	Carter would provide strong leadership	.53*	.49*	.40*

*significant ≤ .01
All figures are tau-b's.

such events was equal, at least initially, and that their impact had a particular duration. Some form of time-series analysis is essential for studying the rally phenomenon because we must compare two points close in time. However, we should not assume that potential rally events create a sudden surge of support for the president. That is a subject for testing, not faith.

How will we know an impact of a rally event if we see one? The theory underlying the rally phenomenon directs us to look for sharp increases in presidential approval. This requires us to compare changes in approval levels from one poll to the next for each partisan group in each of our 450 polls. Adopting any figure as evidence of the impact of a rally event is inevitably somewhat arbitrary, but an increase of 10 percentage points in approval of the president seems reasonable. Since a 6-percentage-point difference for the entire sample could be due to sampling error, a 10-percentage-point difference is really a conservative threshold. The potential error range for the party groups is about 12 percentage points at the .01 confidence level.

Having established a baseline for the impact of a rally event, there are two ways to proceed, and we follow both of them. First, we examine all sudden surges in presidential approval to see if they were preceded by a potential rally event. Second, we examine potential rally events to see if they were followed by a surge in presidential approval.

As Table 6.16 shows, there were 21 occasions from 1953 to 1980 when at least one of the three party groups increased their approval of the president 10 percentage points between two consecutive polls. In one instance these polls were two months apart. On only 7 occasions did more than one of the groups increase approval. The pool of potential rally events is not large, and, of course, all the polls listed do not necessarily reflect the impact of a rally event. Overall, we must be impressed with the basic stability of presidential approval in the short run.

TABLE 6.16   10-PERCENTAGE-POINT INCREASES IN PRESIDENTIAL APPROVAL, 1953–1980

Date of Poll	Party Group	Rally Event Since Preceding Poll
December 11–16, 1953	D	Eisenhower UN "Atoms for Peace" Speech
July 16–21, 1954	D,I	None
December 2–7, 1954	D	None
November 17–22, 1955*	D	None
December 10–15, 1959	D,I	Eisenhower European-Asian "Peace" Trip
July 30–August 4, 1960	I	None
September 28–October 2, 1960	I	None
November 16–21, 1962	D,R	Cuban Missile Crisis
August 15–20, 1963	R	None
October 27–November 1, 1967	D	None
April 4–9, 1968	R	None
July 24–29, 1969	I	Moon Landing
November 12–17, 1969	D,I	Nixon "Vietnamization" Speech
January 15–20, 1970	R	None
January 26–29, 1973	D,I	Vietnam Peace Agreement
May 30–June 2, 1975	D,R	Mayaguez Crisis
January 2–5, 1976	I	None
November 4–7, 1977	R	None
September 15–18, 1978	I	Camp David Accords
November 30–December 3, 1979	D,R,I	Iranian Hostage Crisis
September 12–15, 1980	D	None

*2 months since previous poll
D = Democrat
R = Republican
I = Independent
SOURCE: Gallup Poll.

The last column of the table indicates the rally event, if any, associated with the surge in the president's support. In over half of the cases of surges in presidential approval, no rally event preceded them.[44] The impact of rally events, defined as they are above, is very limited.

There are a number of anomalies in Table 6.16. President Eisenhower's heart attack undoubtedly precipitated the increase in support from Democrats in November 1955, and the death of President Kennedy's son probably produced support from Republicans in the August 1963 poll. Such occurrences do not fall within our definition of rally events.

The "surges" in presidential support in the July–August 1960 and January 1975 polls appear to be the results of inexplicably low support levels among Independents in the immediately preceding polls.

In early December 1975 President Ford traveled to China, but he received no substantial increase in public support in the poll that followed; I did not credit to his trip the rise in approval among Independents a month later. On the other hand, I have listed the Iranian hostage crisis as the rally event responsible for the surge in presidential approval in the November 30–December 3, 1978, poll. Although the hostages were taken on November 4, 1979, public opinion did not change substantially in the November 16–19 poll. Nevertheless, the crisis gained in prominence over time. Thus, I feel confident in attributing public opinion change to the hostage crisis.

The rise in Republican presidential approval in the April 1968 poll is probably due to President Johnson's decision to remove himself from the race for the Democratic presidential nomination, thus diminishing the salience of his party identification, rather than to the partial bombing halt of North Vietnam that he announced at the same time. It is reasonable to expect that the bombing halt would appeal more to Democrats than Republicans.

Finally, the increase in approval of President Carter among Democrats in September 1980 is probably due to his renomination and attempts to unify the party. It is interesting that his approval level did not rise until two polls after his nomination.

One reason for the lack of impact of potential rally events among those identifying with the president's party is the high level of support they are already giving the president. There is not much room for them to increase their support. Only twice during the 16 years of Republican presidents covered in Table 6.16 did Republicans increase their approval of the president by at least 10 percentage points from one poll to the next. Democrats were only slightly more volatile, with 4 instances over 12 years of Democratic presidents. Once again we see the importance of disaggregating public opinion into partisan groupings.

Other research indicates that those who have previously opposed the president (rather than those in the "no opinion" category) provide most of the new support for a president during a rally event,[45] and such persons turn to disapproval of the president's handling of the issue at a higher rate than other citizens.[46] Thus, even when surges of support occur, we should not expect them to be sustained.

Table 6.17 is very revealing regarding the rally phenomenon. It presents a list of events, by no means exhaustive, that fit the general conception of a rally event but that did *not* produce a 10-point or larger percentage increase in any partisan group's approval of the president. The two tables reveal many anomalies. The ending of U.S. involvement in Vietnam substantially increased the president's approval level, but the ending of the Korean War did not; U.S. military actions against the Soviet Union in Cuba and Cambodia (regarding the *Mayaguez*) brought forth surges of support, but military actions against Cuba (Bay of Pigs), Lebanon, the Dominican Republic, North Vietnam, and Cambodia did not; the capture of American hostages by Iranian radicals brought President Carter the single largest increase in presidential approval in the history of the Gallup Poll, but the capture of the *Pueblo* by North Korea had little impact on the president's standing in the public; President Eisenhower's 1959 goodwill trip to Europe and Asia increased his public support, but all future presidential trips abroad had less significance for public approval; and President Eisenhower's "atoms for peace" proposal increased his support while President Kennedy's signing of a nuclear test ban treaty in 1963 made little impact. In other words, most of the events that we might expect to cause the public to rally behind the president do not have that effect.

Although we have found few sudden substantial increases in presidential approval, it does not necessarily follow that potential rally events have not had a significant impact. Other factors or events may have intervened to depress the positive influence of the rally phenomenon. In such a case the rally event would have buttressed the president's approval, perhaps keeping it from rapidly declining, but would not result in a substantial increase in approval. It is not likely, however, that long-term factors would cause presidential support in the public to take a rapid nose dive, and evidence of discrete events that might counteract rally events is lacking. (A more detailed discussion of the problems of before-and-after studies of public opinion is found in Chapter 2.)

It is also possible that the impact of a rally event will not be fully reflected in the polls because it occurred in the middle of an interviewing period, which typically lasts four to six days. In such a case at least part of the sample would be evaluating the president without the potential influence of the rally event. With further checking, however, we find that this does not explain the lack of public response to potential rally events such as those listed in Table 6.17.

In sum, the impact of the rally phenomenon is difficult to isolate,

TABLE 6.17 POTENTIAL RALLY EVENTS NOT FOLLOWED BY A
SUBSTANTIAL INCREASE IN PRESIDENTIAL APPROVAL, 1953–1980

Event	Year
Korean Truce	1953
Sputnik I Launched	1957
U.S. Troops Sent to Lebanon	1958
U-2 Shot Down	1960
Bay of Pigs Invasion	1961
Berlin Crisis	1961
Test Ban Treaty Signed	1963
Dominican Republic Invasion	1965
Pueblo Capture	1968
Tet Offensive	1968
Cambodian Invasion	1970
Mining Haiphong Harbor	1972
Christmas Bombing of North Vietnam	1972
Nixon Trip to China	1972
Fall of Cambodia	1975
Fall of Vietnam	1975
Ford Trip to China	1975
Soviet Invasion of Afghanistan	1979
Summit Meetings with Soviet Leaders	1955, 1959, 1960, 1961, 1967, 1972, 1973, 1974

SOURCE: Gallup Poll.

but the preponderance of evidence indicates that it rarely appears, and
that the events that generate it are highly idiosyncratic and do not seem
to significantly differ from other events that were not followed by significant surges in presidential approval.[47] Moreover, the events that
cause sudden increases in public support are not restricted to international affairs, and most international events that would seem to be potential rally events fail to generate much additional approval of the
president.

RECIPROCAL INFLUENCE

The preceding discussion of causes of presidential approval has been
premised on the view that our independent variables (i.e., the "causes")
are possible influences on presidential approval. One might argue, however, that people's evaluations of the president also influence their responses to more specific questions about him. For example, it is theoretically possible that instead of evaluations of the president's handling of

inflation influencing respondents' overall approval, people might generalize *from* an overall evaluation to an evaluation of the president's performance in this issue area. If reciprocal causation occurs, the coefficients for the relationships we have discussed will be inflated spuriously. Since this and the following section are somewhat technical, some readers may wish to move directly to the conclusion.

Reciprocal causation is inevitably somewhat difficult to investigate, but there are some relevant tests we can employ. If the substantial relationships that we found between evaluations of the president's handling of policy and overall approval of the president are largely artifacts of reciprocal causation, then the public's responses to policy performance evaluation questions should be highly related because they are all due to responses to the overall approval question. Table 6.18 shows the coefficients resulting from crosstabulating evaluations of President Carter's handling of a range of issues in 1980.

The relationships between the three indicators of economic performance—inflation, unemployment, and economic problems—range from moderate to reasonably strong, as we would expect. These issue areas are substantially related, and it is only natural that respondents would see them as such. Still, the coefficients are not so high that we should conclude that respondents do not differentiate between them. It is also worth noting that inflation and unemployment are more strongly related with each other than with overall approval of the president. The same is true,

TABLE 6.18 RELATIONSHIPS BETWEEN EVALUATIONS OF CARTER'S HANDLING OF ISSUES IN 1980

Issue Areas	Demo- crats	Indepen- dents	Repub- licans
Inflation and Unemployment	.53	.53	.53
Inflation and Hostages	.43	.32	.38
Inflation and Afghanistan	.19	.15	.13
Inflation and Energy	.45	.33	.38
Inflation and Economic Problems	.45	.45	.38
Unemployment and Hostages	.38	.26	.40
Unemployment and Afghanistan	.11	.18	.09
Unemployment and Energy	.39	.31	.37
Unemployment and Economic Problems	.35	.32	.33
Hostages and Afghanistan	.22	.25	.16
Hostages and Energy	.36	.31	.33
Hostages and Economic Problems	.32	.30	.26
Afghanistan and Energy	.19	.18	.16
Afghanistan and Economic Problems	.10	.18	.13
Energy and Economic Problems	.35	.25	.37

All figures are tau-b's.

for Republicans, of their relationship with solving economic problems. The coefficients between the economic performance evaluations and the remaining issue areas are of only modest strength.

At the other extreme from the economic performance evaluations are evaluations of the president's handling of the Soviet invasion of Afghanistan. Responses to this latter question do not relate strongly to evaluations of presidential performance in any other issue area. Its strongest coefficients appear for the other foreign policy issue here, the hostage crisis in Iran, and these are only modest in strength. Evaluations of President Carter's handling of the hostage situation and energy policy are only moderately related to evaluations of his performance in other issue areas.

In sum, examining the relationships between evaluations of the president's policy performance on a range of issues does not reveal evidence to support reciprocal influence. This conclusion is supported by research that has shown that the public differentiates among candidates' characteristics and capabilities to deal with various problems.[48] It does not generalize from candidate affect.

A related method of checking for reciprocal causation is to examine *levels* of support for the president overall and in a variety of issue areas. If substantial reciprocal causation occurs, then we would expect the levels of support for the president's handling of specific policy areas to be similar to each other and to the level of the president's overall support.

Table 6.19 contains comparisons between the president's overall handling of his job and his handling of other issues. Because the CBS News/ *The New York Times* polls, from which the issue data are drawn, worded the overall question a bit differently from the issue area questions ("Do you have a favorable opinion about Jimmy Carter?"), I have included the Gallup polls for the relevant months (averaged if there were more than one poll taken within the month). The Gallup question was worded the same as the more specific issue questions, except that it asked about the president's handling of his job as president rather than specific issue areas.

Comparing the president's overall job rating with his rating in handling the economy and foreign policy, we find that there are substantial differences between them, ranging as high as 32 percentage points in February 1980. Moreover, ratings of the president's handling of issue areas never exceeded ratings for his overall job performance. The latter were buttressed by his handling of other issues, especially the Iranian crisis, and personal characteristics.[49] Once again, we fail to find evidence of substantial reciprocal causation.

Reciprocal causation may also take place in respondents' evaluations of candidates' policy positions. Coefficients for issue proximity scores were provided in Tables 6.12 and 6.13. It is theoretically possible that approval of the president may lead respondents to project their own

TABLE 6.19   EVALUATIONS OF PRESIDENTIAL PERFORMANCE IN 1980

Area	% Approve					
	January	February	March	April	June	August
Overall*	57	55	45	39	34	32
Overall†	45	58	48	43	33	33
Foreign Policy†	45	48	34	31	20	18
Economy†	27	26	23	21	18	19

SOURCE: *Gallup Poll.
　　　　†CBS News/*The New York Times* Poll reported in Kathleen A. Frankovic, "Public Opinion Trends," in Marlene Michels Pompers, ed., *The Election of 1980: Reports and Interpretations* (Chatham, N.J.: Chatham House, 1981), pp. 100–01.

policy views onto the president ("projection") or to adopt the president's policy views as their own ("persuasion").[50] The opposite could theoretically occur with presidents of which respondents disapprove. Either type of rationalization would influence the distance respondents perceive between themselves and the president on issues, making the distance smaller or larger, depending on respondents' approval or disapproval of the president. This would increase spuriously the coefficients for the relationships between issue proximity and presidential approval.

Studies have shown that both projection and persuasion effects occur in voters' identifying candidates' issue positions,[51] although these findings have recently been challenged.[52] The impact of these psychological processes on voting itself, however, is less clear, even with the use of nonrecursive equations, but the best evidence seems to be that it is not very important.[53]

We cannot be sure of the impact of projection and persuasion on the relationships between issue proximity scores and overall presidential approval. We can see, however, the substantial variation in coefficients within party groups, including many representing relationships that are modest or weak (especially for Republicans). Both the variation and the level of strength of the coefficients support the argument that reciprocal causation is not a strong influence here. The same response can be made regarding concern that reciprocal causation inflates relationships between presidential approval and evaluations of the president's personal characteristics. The coefficients in Table 6.15 vary greatly within party groups and are often modest in strength.

In sum, we cannot show that reciprocal causation does not exist, and that it does not artificially increase the coefficients upon which our analysis of presidential approval is based. Nevertheless, we have not found evidence that reciprocal causation plays a significant role, and we have considerable reason to doubt its significance.[54]

MULTIVARIATE ANALYSIS

It is useful to employ multivariate analysis to test some of the findings regarding the importance of variables in explaining presidential approval. Once again, however, we face the limitations of secondary analysis of data. Only the 1980 election Center for Political Studies poll provides a range of data broad enough to serve our purposes.

We must emphasize that this analysis is designed to test whether variables have the same general and relative impact on presidential approval as we found in our earlier analysis when they are all placed in the same equation and serve as controls on each other. We must be conservative in our interpretation of the results, because we have data from only one point in time and lack some of the precision we would have under ideal conditions for the measurement of the independent variables.

Where the data are appropriate, we employ additive indexes to represent complex variables. These include measures of the evaluation of foreign policy performance, economic policy performance, issue proximity to the president, the president's personal characteristics, economic conditions, and the respondents' economic circumstances. Indexes provide more comprehensive and more accurate measures of complex concepts while serving as data reduction devices summarizing responses to several questions in a single score.

Potential items for each index come from the questions in the 1980 poll listed in Tables 6.6–6.9, 6.11, and 6.13–6.15. These potential items were evaluated on both substantive and statistical grounds for inclusion in an index. Inter-item correlations were used to determine whether the items were related closely enough to be considered part of the same dimension but not so closely that they were redundant. Only those items meeting all these criteria are included in an index. All items within an index are weighted equally, and when a response for one item is missing, an average of the remaining items in the index serves as the measure for that respondent. All items are coded so that positive evaluations of the president, the economy, or personal circumstances or agreement with the president are in the same direction as approval of the president.

Only one measure of the public's evaluation of presidential domestic policy performance is available for 1980, and that is the question of the president's handling of energy policy. Party identification also enters into the equation as a single variable.

Because our dependent variable, presidential approval, is dichotomous, we employ a probit analysis rather than ordinary least-squares regression analysis. Probit produces maximum likelihood estimates (MLEs), estimates of the change on the cumulative standard normal distribution that result from a change in one unit in an independent variable with the remaining independent variables held constant.[55] In order to compare the impact of independent variables measured on different scales, we then standardize the MLEs.[56] This puts the variables on the same scale. The results of these computations are presented in Table 6.20.

The standardized MLEs are consistent with our earlier analysis. Economic conditions and personal economic circumstances are not significantly related to presidential approval at .01 while the other six independent variables are. The strongest influence, at least in 1980, is the public's evaluation of presidential economic policy performance, followed by evaluation of the president's personal characteristics, party identification, views of issue proximity, and evaluation of presidential foreign policy performance. The president's handling of energy policy, our only indicator of domestic, noneconomic policy performance, is the weakest of the statistically significant variables.

The influence of political party may be surprising at first glance, as we would expect it to be more powerful in relation to other variables. The explanation for its more modest coefficients is straightforward, however, and actually helps us to understand the central role of party even further. The problem is one of multicollinearity. Party is notably related to five of the other independent variables as well as to presidential approval. In a multivariate analysis this causes problems: it artificially reduces the MLE for party.

When multicollinearity exists, the independent variables covary with one another. Further, for each independent variable, part of this covariance overlaps with the covariance between the dependent variable and that particular independent variable. The variable with the strongest

TABLE 6.20 PROBIT ESTIMATES OF PREDICTORS OF PRESIDENTIAL APPROVAL, 1980

Variable	MLE	Standardized MLE
Economic policy performance	.94*	.92
Personal characteristics	.80*	.76
Party	.12*	.48
Issue proximity	.22*	.48
Foreign policy performance	.47*	.48
Handling energy policy	.08*	.32
Economic conditions	.86	.20
Respondents' economic circumstances	.10	.04

$\hat{R}^2 = .61$
% of cases correctly predicted = 82
N = 1278
$x^2 = 699.09$
d.f. = 8
*significant $\leq$ .01

covariance with the dependent variable, in this case presidential economic policy performance, enters the equation first. This variable is then allocated that portion of the variation of the dependent variable that it shares with the other independent variable(s). The MLE for party is lessened as a consequence. When party is placed into the equation alone, its MLE increases almost three times to .29 (standardized to 1.16).

The estimated $\hat{R}^2$ is .61 and 82% of the cases are correctly predicted by the model. This prediction is about a 50% improvement over chance. In sum, the results of the probit analysis provide strong support for the conclusions of our earlier analysis.

CONCLUSION

Presidential approval is the product of many factors. At the base of evaluations of the president is the predisposition of many people to support the president. Political party identification provides the basic underpinning of approval or disapproval and mediates the impact of other factors. The positivity bias and the bandwagon effect buttress approval levels, at least for a while.

Changes in approval levels appear to be due primarily to the public's evaluation of how the president is handling policy areas such as the economy, war, energy, and foreign affairs. Citizens seem to focus on the president's efforts and his stands on issues rather than on his personality or how his policies affect them or even whether his policies are successful in the short run. Job-related personal characteristics of the president also play an important role in influencing presidential approval. Conversely, rally events may provide an occasional increment of support, but in general they do not seem to be very significant.

The public, then, is not necessarily unreasonable in evaluating the president. It appears willing to give him the benefit of the doubt and takes more into consideration than simple short-run success. It does, however, expect the president to handle policy issues well and to possess the proper personal characteristics.

Although we have made substantial progress in identifying the immediate bases for the public's evaluation of the president, we still need to increase our understanding of how people arrive at their perceptions of the president. Policy efforts, issue stands, and personal characteristics are more nebulous than unemployment, the cost of living, and war casualties. They are subject to a wide range of interpretations, few of which will be based on firsthand experience. Thus the manner in which the president presents himself to the public and the way he is portrayed in the press take on increased importance. The potential for style to dominate substance in evaluations of presidential performance appears to be substantial. Public perceptions, then, are an important subject for future research.

APPENDIX A: MEASURES OF PRESIDENTIAL APPROVAL

There are three basic types of measures of presidential approval. The most common is the question asked by the Gallup Poll on whether respondents "approve" or "disapprove" of the president's job performance. A second type of measure asks respondents to evaluate the president's performance on a scale with four or five categories. The Louis Harris organization often asks such a question. The results of a national survey in the fall of 1978 employing these two types of questions is shown in Table 6.21.

Table 6.22 shows comparisons of the two questions. Almost all of those who evaluate the president's performance as "very good" or "good" also "approve" of the way he is handling his job. Similarly, almost all those who evaluate the president's performance as "poor" or "very poor" also "disapprove" of the way he is handling his job. The middle category

TABLE 6.21 ALTERNATIVE PRESIDENTIAL APPROVAL RATINGS, FALL 1978

Question: "How would you rate the job President Carter has been doing over the past two years—would you say that he has been doing a very good job, good, fair, poor, or a very poor job?"

Ratings	%
Very good	7
Good	28
Fair	47
Poor	12
Very poor	4
Other	3

Question: "Do you approve or disapprove of the way Mr. Carter is handling his job as president?"

Ratings	%
Approve	58
Disapprove	30
Other	11

SOURCE: Center for Political Studies, 1978 Election Study.

of performance rating, "fair," is much more evenly divided between approval and disapproval. The bottom portion of the table shows the same relationships in a different way. Fifty-four percent of those who "approve" of the president's handling of his job rate him as "very good" or "good." On the other hand, 45% of those who "disapprove" of his handling of his job rate him as doing "poor" or "very poor." Once again, the "fair" rating is ambiguous, selected by large percentages of both those who "approve" and those who "disapprove" of the president.

There are several reasons why we choose to rely upon the Gallup "approval" question here. The first is quite pragmatic: it allows us to exploit more data. The Gallup presidential approval question is probably the most frequently asked attitude question in the history of survey research. As we noted early in this chapter, we obtained the results of 450 polls in which it was asked of national samples from 1953 through 1980. In addition, the Center for Political Studies at the University of Michigan asked it in its in-depth election studies in 1972, 1974, 1976, 1978, and 1980, studies that we shall analyze in considerable detail.[57] Thus, our data base for analyzing presidential approval using the Gallup question is very extensive.

A second reason for relying on the Gallup question is that it is straightforward and simple. "Approve" and "disapprove" are relatively easy for both respondents (the public) and analysts to understand. Moreover, these are probably the categories that busy policymakers use when they evaluate the president's standing in the public. The Harris-type question, on the other hand, is more difficult to interpret because of the middle, "fair," category. For some respondents this is a positive

TABLE 6.22   COMPARISON OF PRESIDENTIAL APPROVAL MEASURES, FALL 1978

	% Approve	% Disapprove	% Other
Very good	97	2	1
Good	91	3	6
Fair	52	33	15
Poor	9	85	7
Very poor	8	90	2

	% Very Good	% Good	% Fair	% Poor	% Very Poor	% Other
Approve	11	43	42	2	1	2
Disapprove	0	3	51	32	13	1

SOURCE: Center for Political Studies, 1978 Election Survey.

rating of the president while for others it carries a negative connotation.

Of course, not all approval of the president is equally strong and we give up a certain degree of refinement when, in effect, we collapse categories. Nevertheless, the advantages of relying on the Gallup approval question for our study of presidential approval far outweigh any disadvantages.[58]

There is a third measure of presidential approval: the "feeling thermometer." It was used in the 1970, 1972, 1974, 1976, 1978, and 1980 election studies done by the Survey Research Center. In this measure respondents are asked how "favorable and warm" they feel towards the president on a scale of 1 to 100. Table 6.23 shows the average (mean) rating on the feeling thermometer given by those who fall into each of the Gallup and Harris-type presidential evaluation categories. All three of the questions were asked in the 1978 Center for Political Studies election study. As we would expect, the lower the level of support indicated by a Gallup or Harris-type category, the lower the average rating on the feeling thermometer.

The feeling thermometer is appealing because it is measured on an interval level scale, which permits the use of sophisticated measures of association. The independent variables that we will be considering, however, are really not appropriate for regression analysis, so the interval nature of the feeling thermometer loses some of its potential utility.

The measure also has some disadvantages, not the least of which is its availability in only a few polls. Perhaps the most important drawback is its ambiguity. It is very difficult to interpret "feelings." As one leading scholar of public opinion put it, "no one really knows what thermometer scores measure."[59] The thermometer probably taps some of the public's

TABLE 6.23 COMPARISONS WITH THE FEELING THERMOMETER
QUESTION, FALL 1978

	Feeling Thermometer Mean Ratings
Very good	90
Good	79
Fair	62
Poor	39
Very poor	25

	Feeling Thermometer Mean Ratings
Approve	75
Disapprove	45

SOURCE: Center for Political Studies, 1978 Election Survey.

personal affection for the president and some of their views on his performance in office, but we do not really know. We do know that citizens may like presidents such as Gerald Ford and Jimmy Carter without feeling they are performing well as president. For example, in a July 1978 Gallup poll Carter's overall approval rating as president was only 39%. Yet 76% of the public felt he was "a likeable person."[60] "Feeling," then, is not synonymous with "approving."

The Gallup measure, on the other hand, explicitly elicits responses regarding the president's job performance and was designed to avoid answers based on liking or disliking him as a person.[61] The Gallup approval question is also more visible to policymakers than is the thermometer question, and it has been used in most previous studies of presidential approval, facilitating comparisons of findings.

When these advantages of the Gallup question are combined with those mentioned above, our choice to rely primarily on it appears to be a reasonable one. We should keep in mind, however, that all three measures are related. The basic conclusions we reach using the Gallup question should also hold for the other measures of presidential approval. Moreover, analysis in the chapter requires that we use the Harris-type question for the 1968 Center for Political Studies survey and the feeling thermometer for the 1970 survey, because the Gallup question was not asked in these.

APPENDIX B: TIME–SERIES ANALYSIS

Most studies of presidential approval have relied upon time-series analysis.[62] In essence, scholars have compared the rise and fall in presidential approval (treated as a dependent variable) over time with the rise and fall of possible explanatory variables, such as unemployment and inflation. The greater the change in presidential approval that is associated with a change in the independent variable, the greater our ability to explain presidential approval, at least according to this approach.

Time-series studies have made a major contribution by focusing our attention on presidential approval and possible explanations of it, but there are several reasons why I have chosen not to rely heavily upon time-series analysis to try to explain presidential approval. The first reason is technical. In the words of a close student of studies of presidential approval,

> Time-series analysis is a statistical minefield, where a single misstep can cause the entire analysis to blow up in the face of the unwary researcher. Virtually every conceivable statistical problem shows up in its most virulent form in time-series analysis, and the technical fixes not infrequently

surpass the understanding of reader and researcher alike. The complexity of these problems and solutions means that substantive conclusions about presidential popularity are often based on inappropriate statistical procedures and that these conclusions have gained broad currency because readers who are unable to judge for themselves whether a statistical analysis is competent have accepted them at face value.[63]

In time-series analysis "technical" problems include autocorrelation (the correlation of variables with themselves over time, which distorts findings); gaps in data sets (that many researchers either ignore or complete through interpolation without alerting the reader); the selection of time units of months, quarters, or years; and the use of changes in levels or absolute levels of presidential approval as the dependent variables. There is also the problem of the coding of independent variables occurring in some previous month: How long should we assume they have an impact? How fast should we discount their impact over time? Do people blame the president for conditions, such as the state of the economy, that were determined before he took office? Do people compare the present with the past or just consider current conditions as absolutes? Finally, small fluctuations in presidential approval between two points in time may be due to sampling error or other polling limitations.

Despite the confusion and uncertainty that generally pervade time-series analysis of presidential approval, this is not the heart of their limitations. Their biggest drawback is in the area of theory. The implicit theory underlying correlating variables, such as economic conditions, with presidential approval in time-series analyses is that as the environment and circumstances of individuals change, their level of support for the president will also change. If unemployment and presidential approval vary together, for example, then researchers conclude that unemployment levels are part of the explanation for presidential approval.

The careful reader will note that in time-series analysis scholars must use aggregate data (the national Consumer Price Index, for example) because they lack individual-level data. Yet they often make inferences to the individual level. Conclusions as to what group decreases its support of the president—the unemployed, those worried about unemployment more generally, etc.—must be speculative, however. Aggregate data do not allow us to answer such questions.

The best way to test such propositions is to obtain individual-level data and then examine it to see what (if any) circumstances or perceptions of persons are related to differences in presidential approval. In this way we can make reasonable inferences about the impact of various factors on presidential approval and see whether their direct impact on individuals causes approval levels to rise and fall, or whether persons react to other considerations. In other words, we can increase our understanding of *why* people evaluate presidents as they do.

Individual-level data is very useful in another way. In time-series analyses it is often unclear what certain variables measure. "Dummy" variables representing Watergate, international crises, and individual presidents cannot contribute much to our understanding of the causes of presidential approval. They are imprecise, and we have no idea how people perceive them. Moreover, arbitrary judgments must be made on how to weight each factor and how long its impact lasts. Dramatic, sharply focused international crises, for example, often referred to as "rally events," are generally all weighted the same, and the researcher must make a decision as to the duration of their possible impact on public opinion *prior* to testing for any impact.

No more theoretically illuminating are the conclusions based upon variables measuring the public's level of approval of the president in the month prior to the survey or over longer periods. Even if strong correlations result from the use of such variables, we do not know how to interpret them. We do not know what the variables really measure or why they affect the president's standing in the public.

Another problem inherent in time-series analyses is that the meaning we attribute to variables may change over time, although the theories underlying their use hold that their meaning is constant. For example, although reports of the unemployment rate continue to count the percentage of the population that is unemployed, the composition of the unemployed has changed over time and the hardship caused by unemployment has been reduced. Women and youths now compose a larger percentage of the unemployed than in the 1950s. Since many of these people are not the primary wage earners in their families, the correspondence between hardship and unemployment is probably less now than in earlier decades. More liberal eligibility requirements for unemployment insurance and welfare programs and increased payments over time buttress the argument that unemployment has a different impact on people's lives today than in the past. The extent to which this difference translates into impact on presidential approval is, of course, an open question. The point is that a variable may have different meaning over time, further reducing the reliability of findings. Cross-sectional analysis allows us to compare the effect, if any, of a variable at different points in time to see if it has changed and if it is greater when the values of the variable are extreme, such as in the case of high unemployment.

A final difficulty with aggregate social indicators is that they are often poor measures of what they purport to represent. Statistics concerning the Vietnam War are notoriously suspect. Numerous articles appear in scholarly journals on the limitations of economic indicators such as the Consumer Price Index and the unemployment rate. Even to the extent that the latter is an accurate measure at any one time, the figures that are employed in time-series analyses may not reflect the total percentage of the population unemployed in a year. The rate may be stable while newly unemployed people replace those who found employment. Thus many more people may be unemployed in a year than the official rate indicates.[64] Rather than relying on measures that are of doubtful validity and are not congruent with our theorizing, it is preferable to find out how individuals perceive their circumstances and the degree to which their circumstances have changed. This is the approach we follow.

NOTES

1. George C. Edwards III, *Presidential Influence in Congress* (San Francisco: W. H. Freeman, 1980), pp. 86–100. See also Richard E. Neustadt, *Presidential Power: The Politics of Leadership From FDR to Carter* (New York: Wiley, 1980), chap. 5 and p. 238.
2. See, for example, Sidney Kraus and Dennis Davis, *The Effects of Mass Communications on Political Behavior* (University Park, Pa.: Pennsylvania State University Press, 1976); Leon Festinger, *A Theory of Cognitive Dissonance* (Evanston, Ill.: Row, Peterson, 1957); Jack W. Brehm and Arthur C. Cohen, *Explorations in Cognitive Dissonance* (New York: Wiley, 1962); John S. Steinbruner, *The Cybernetic Theory of Decision* (Princeton, N.J.: Princeton University Press, 1974), chap. 4.
3. For a recent overview of this point, see David B. Hill and Norman R. Luttbeg, *Trends in American Electoral Behavior* (Itasca, Ill.: Peacock, 1980), chap. 2.
4. The seminal work on perceptual screening is Bernard R. Berelson, Paul F. Lazarsfeld, and William N. McPhee, *Voting: A Study of Opinion Formation in a Presidential Campaign* (Chicago: University of Chicago Press, 1954). See also Benjamin I. Page, *Choices and Echoes in Presidential Elections: Rational Man and Electoral Democracy* (Chicago: University of Chicago Press, 1978), pp. 184–86.
5. Alan I. Abramowitz, "The Impact of a Presidential Debate on Voter Rationality," *American Journal of Political Science* 22 (August 1978), pp. 680–90; Robert S. Erikson, Norman R. Luttbeg, and Kent L. Tedin, *American Public Opinion: Its Origins, Content, and Impact*, 2nd ed. (New York: Wiley, 1980), pp. 212, 214, 215.
6. See Angus Campbell, Philip E. Converse, Warren E. Miller, and Donald E. Stokes, *The American Voter* (New York: Wiley, 1964), chap. 5, for a discussion of the impact of party identification on candidate evaluation. See also Roberta S. Sigel, "Effect of Partisanship on the Perception of Political Candidates," *Public Opinion Quarterly* 28 (Fall 1964), pp. 483–96.
7. Philip E. Converse and George Dupeux, "De Gaulle and Eisenhower: The Public Image of the Victorious General," in Angus Campbell, Philip E. Converse, Warren E. Miller, and Donald E. Stokes, *Elections and the Political Order* (New York: Wiley, 1966), pp. 324–25.
8. Since these averages are the product of averaging all the relevant Gallup polls

in a year, the precise average for each year is affected by the number of polls taken during any given period of the year. Thus, if more polls are taken during a time when the president is popular than when he is unpopular, for example, the average will be biased on the high side. Normally, however, polls are taken at relatively stable intervals. For our purposes this should not be a serious problem since we are comparing groups in the public that are included in each poll.

9. For an overview of trends concerning Independents, see Hill and Luttbeg, *Trends in American Electoral Behavior*, pp. 33–34.

10. For discussion of positivity, see David O. Sears, "Political Socialization," in *Micropolitical Theory*, Volume 2 of *Handbook of Political Science*, Fred I. Greenstein and Nelson Polsby, eds. (Reading, Mass.: Addison-Wesley, 1975), p. 177; David O. Sears, "Political Behavior," in *Applied Social Psychology*, Volume 5 of *Handbook of Social Psychology*, 2nd ed., Gardney Lindzey and Elliot Aronson, eds. (Reading, Mass.: Addison-Wesley, 1968), pp. 424–31; David O. Sears and Richard E. Whitney, "Political Persuasion," in *Handbook of Communication*, Ithiel de Sola Pool and Wilber Schramm, et al., eds. (Chicago: Rand McNally, 1976), pp. 271–76; and sources cited therein.

11. Positivity bias does not seem to be an artifact of the survey instrument employed, however. See Richard R. Lau, David O. Sears, and Richard Centers, "The 'Positivity Bias' in Evaluations of Public Figures: Evidence Against Instrument Artifacts," *Public Opinion Quarterly*, 43 (Fall 1979), pp. 347–58.

12. Sears and Whitney, "Political Persuasion," p. 275.

13. I. H. Paul, "Impressions of Personality: Authoritarianism and the *fait accompli* Effect," *Journal of Abnormal and Social Psychology* 53 (November 1956), pp. 338–44; George Stricker, "The Operation of Cognitive Dissonance in Pre- and Postelection Attitudes," *Journal of Social Psychology* 63 (June 1964), pp. 111–19; Bertram H. Raven and Philip S. Gallo, "The Effects of Nominating Conventions, Elections, and Reference Group Identification Upon the Perception of Political Figures," *Human Relations* 18 (August 1965), pp. 217–29; Lynn R. Anderson and Alan R. Bass, "Some Effects of Victory or Defeat Upon Perception of Political Candidates," *Journal of Social Psychology* 73 (October 1967), pp. 227–40; Larry R. Baas and Ian B. Thomas, "The Impact of the Election and the Inauguration on Identification with the President," *Presidential Studies Quarterly* 10 (Fall 1980), pp. 544–49. For exceptions to these findings, see Dan Nimmo and Robert L. Savage, *Candidates and Their Images: Concepts, Methods, and Findings* (Pacific Palisades, Calif.: Goodyear, 1976), pp. 168–81, including their summary of a paper by Allan J. Cigler and Russell Getter, "After the Election: Individual Responses to a Collective Decision" (paper presented at the Annual Meeting of the Southwestern Political Science Association, Dallas, March 1974).

14. John E. Mueller, *War, Presidents and Public Opinion* (New York: Wiley, 1970), pp. 205–6.

15. "Remarks of the President at a Meeting with Non-Washington Editors and Broadcasters," Office of the White House Press Secretary, September 21, 1979, pp. 11–12.

16. *CBS News/The New York Times Poll, Part I*, January 1982, Table 34.

17. "Institutions: Confidence Even in Difficult Times," *Public Opinion*, June-July 1981, p. 33.

18. See, for example, Fred I. Greenstein and Robert Wright, "Reagan . . . Another Ike?" *Public Opinion*, December–January 1981, p. 51.

19. Campbell, et al., *American Voter*, p. 25.

20. Harvey G. Zeidenstein, "Presidential Popularity and Presidential Support in Congress: Eisenhower and Carter," *Presidential Studies Quarterly* 10 (Spring 1980), p. 228.

21. Converse and Dupeux, "De Gaulle and Eisenhower," p. 326.

22. Neustadt, *Presidential Power*, pp. 69–73.

23. *Ibid.*, p. 70; Bert A. Rockman, "Constants, Cycles, Trends, and Persona in Presidential Governance: Carter's Troubles Reviewed" (paper presented at the Annual Meeting of the American Political Science Association, Washington, D.C., August–September 1979), pp. 42–43.

24. "Reagan: A Likeable Guy," *Public Opinion*, December–January 1981, p. 24.

25. For some interesting comments by President Carter regarding this, see Richard E. Meyer, "Carter Parcels Out Blame for Popularity Fall," *New Orleans Times-Picayune*, September 9, 1977, section 1, p. 3; "For Whom the Polls Toll," *Newsweek*, July 17, 1978, p. 26.

26. Richard A. Brody and Benjamin I. Page, "The Impact of Events on Presidential Popularity: The Johnson and Nixon Administrations," in *Perspectives on the Presidency*, Aaron Wildavsky, ed. (Boston: Little, Brown, 1975), pp. 136–48; Philip Stone and Richard Brody, "Modeling Opinion Responsiveness to Daily News: The Public and Lyndon Johnson, 1965–1968," *Social Science Information* 9 (February 1970), pp. 95–122; Timothy Haight and Richard A. Brody, "The Mass Media and Presidential Popularity: Presidential Broadcasting and the News in the Nixon Administration," *Communication Research* 4 (January 1977), pp. 41–60.

27. Herbert F. Weisberg, "Models of Statistical Relationship," *American Political Science Review* 68 (December 1974), especially p. 1654.

28. Jere Bruner, "What's the Question to That Answer? Measures and Marginals in Crosstabulation," *American Journal of Political Science* 20 (November 1976), pp. 781–804.

29. Edwards, *Presidential Influence in Congress*, pp. 86–100.

30. Neustadt, *Presidential Power*, p. 73.

31. Jack Valenti, *A Very Human President* (New York: Norton, 1975), p. 151.

32. Donald R. Kinder and Roderick Kiewiet, "Sociotropic Politics: The American Case," *British Journal of Political Science* 11 (April 1981), p. 131. See pages 129–31 for a review of the conventional wisdom.

33. Donald R. Kinder, "Presidents, Prosperity, and Public Opinion," *Public Opinion Quarterly* 45 (Spring 1981), pp. 1–21; Richard Lau and David O. Sears, "Cognitive Links Between Economic Grievances and Political Responses," *Political Behavior* 3 (No. 4, 1981), pp. 279–302.

34. See, for example, David O. Sears, Richard R. Lau, Tom R. Tyler, and Harris M. Allen, Jr., "Self-Interest vs. Symbolic Politics in Policy Attitudes and Presidential Voting," *American Political Science Review* 74 (September 1980), pp. 670–84; David O. Sears, Carl P. Hensler, and Leslie K. Speer, "Whites' Opposition to 'Busing': Self-Interest or Symbolic Politics?" *American Political Science*

Review 73 (June 1979), pp. 369–84; David O. Sears, Tom R. Tyler, Jack Citrin, and Donald R. Kinder, "Political System Support and Public Response to the Energy Crisis," *American Journal of Political Science* 22 (February 1978), pp. 56–82; Douglas S. Gatlin, Michael Giles, and Everett F. Cataldo, "Policy Support Within a Target Group: The Case of School Desegregation," *American Political Science Review* 72 (September 1978), pp. 985–95; Richard R. Lau, Thad A. Brown, and David O. Sears, "Self-Interest and Civilians' Attitudes Toward the War in Vietnam," *Public Opinion Quarterly* 42 (Winter 1978), pp. 464–83; John B. McConahay, "Self-Interest versus Racial Attitudes as Correlates of Anti-Busing Attitudes in Louisville: Is It the Buses or the Blacks?" *Journal of Politics* 44 (August 1982), pp. 692–720; and sources cited therein.

35. The evidence on voting is decidedly mixed. Some aggregate studies have found a relationship between economic conditions and congressional voting. See Gerald H. Kramer, "Short-Term Fluctuations in U.S. Voting Behavior, 1896–1964," *American Political Science Review* 65 (March 1971), pp. 131–43; Edward R. Tufte, "Determinants of the Outcomes of Midterm Congressional Elections," *American Political Science Review* 69 (September 1975), pp. 812–26. Others have found a relationship with voting for president. See Edward R. Tufte, *Political Control of the Economy* (Princeton, N.J.: Princeton University Press, 1978), pp. 120–23; Allan H. Meltzer and Mark Vellrath, "The Effects of Economic Policies on Votes for the Presidency: Some Evidence from Recent Elections," *Journal of Law and Economics* 18 (December 1975), pp. 781–98; Ray C. Fair, "The Effects of Economic Events on Votes for President," *Review of Economics and Statistics* 60 (May 1978), pp. 159–73.

Yet other aggregate studies have found relationships only in bad economic times [Howard S. Bloom and H. Douglas Price, "Voter Response to Short-Run Economic Conditions: The Asymmetric Effect of Prosperity and Recession," *American Political Science Review* 69 (December 1975), pp. 1240–54] or only for in-party incumbents, especially senior incumbents [John R. Hibbing and John R. Alford, "The Electoral Impact of Economic Conditions: Who Is Held Responsible?" *American Journal of Political Science* 25 (August 1981), pp. 423–39]. Some studies have found no relationships at all. See, for example, Francisco Arcelus and Allan H. Meltzer, "The Effect of Aggregate Economic Variables on Congressional Elections," *American Political Science Review* 69 (December 1975), pp. 1232–39; George J. Stigler, "General Economic Conditions and National Elections," *American Economic Review Proceedings* 64 (May 1973), pp. 160–67.

Individual-level studies, in which researchers can determine the characteristics of persons voting for a particular candidate, have also produced mixed results. They have found relationships between individuals' economic conditions and their presidential voting [Jeffrey W. Wides, "Self-perceived Economic Change and Political Orientations: A Preliminary Exploration," *American Politics Quarterly* 4 (October 1976), pp. 395–411]; relationships for presidential voting but not for congressional voting [Morris P. Fiorina, "Economic Retrospective Voting in American National Elections: A Micro-Analysis," *American Journal of Political Science* 22 (May 1978), pp. 426–43; Stanley Feldman, "Economic Self-Interest and Political Behavior," *American Journal of Political Science* 26 (August 1982), pp. 453–55]; no relationship for congressional voting [Donald R. Kinder and D. Roderick Kiewiet, "Economic Discontent and Political Behavior: The Role of Personal Grievances and Collective Economic Judgments in Congressional Voting," *American Journal of Political Science* 23 (August 1979), pp. 495–527; Kinder and Kiewiet, "Sociotropic Politics: The American Case," pp. 129–161]; and generally weak or no relationships with presidential voting [Lee Sigelman and Yung-mei Tsai, "Personal Finances and Voting Behavior: A Reanalysis," *American Politics Quarterly* 9 (October 1981), pp. 371–400; Kinder and Kiewiet, "Sociotropic Politics"; Jeffrey W. Wides, "Perceived Economic Competency and the Ford/Carter Election," *Public Opinion Quarterly* 43 (Winter 1979), pp. 535–43].

Other individual-level studies have had less clear-cut results. They have found relationships between individuals' economic circumstances and voting for in-party incumbents [Hibbing and Alford, "The Electoral Impact of Economic Conditions"]; for working-class voters hurt by recession [M. Stephen Weatherford, "Economic Conditions and Electoral Outcomes: Class Differences in the Political Response to Recession," *American Journal of Political Science* 22 (November 1978), pp. 917–38]; different results for different offices and for different election years [Ricardo Klorman, "Trend in Personal Finances and the Vote," *Public Opinion Quarterly* 42 (Spring 1978), pp. 31–38]; for future expectations of voters but not for past economic experiences and only for the Senate, not the House [James H. Kuklinski and Darrell M. West, "Economic Expectations and Voting Behavior in United States House and Senate Elections," *American Political Science Review* 75 (June 1981), pp. 436–47]; and effects for unemployment but not inflation, especially in pre-1970 elections [D. Roderick Kiewiet, "Policy-Oriented Voting in Response to Economic Issues," *American Political Science Review* 75 (June 1981), pp. 448–59].

36. Richard A. Brody and Paul Sniderman, "From Life Space to Polling Place," *British Journal of Political Science* 7 (July 1977), pp. 337–60; Paul Sniderman and Richard A. Brody, "Coping: The Ethic of Self-Reliance," *American Journal of Political Science* 21 (August 1977), pp. 501–22. See also Feldman, "Economic Self-Interest and Political Behavior," pp. 449–52.

37. Kay L. Schlozman and Sidney Verba, *Injury to Insult: Unemployment, Class and Political Response* (Cambridge, Mass.: Harvard University Press, 1979).

38. *Public Opinion*, June–July 1981, p. 36.

39. Sigelman and Tsai, "Personal Finances and Voting Behavior," pp. 391–93. See also Feldman, "Economic Self-Interest and Political Behavior," pp. 452–53.

40. Kuklinski and West, "Economic Expectations and Voting Behavior in United States House and Senate Elections," pp. 436–47.

41. Kinder and Kiewiet, "Sociotropic Politics: The American Case," pp. 148–52.

42. There were also questions dealing only with the respondent's experience in the armed forces, but there were too few respondents with recent military experience for us to analyze their responses. The number of respondents who answered affirmatively about family members was larger, but still small enough for us to add a note of caution to the interpretation of our findings.

43. Mueller, *War, Presidents and Public Opinion*, pp. 208–13.

44. Tables in *ibid.*, p. 211; Jong R. Lee, "Rallying Around the Flag: Foreign Policy Events and Presidential Popularity," *Presidential Studies Quarterly* 7 (Fall 1977),

pp. 254–55; and yearly volumes of *Facts on File* were useful in identifying potential rally events.

45. John Wanat, "The Dynamics of Presidential Popularity Shifts: Estimating the Degree of Opinion Shift from Aggregate Data," *American Politics Quarterly* 10 (April 1982), pp. 181–96. See also Mueller, *War, Presidents and Public Opinion*, p. 250.

46. Lee Sigelman and Pamela Johnston Conover, "The Dynamics of Presidential Support During International Conflict Situations: The Iranian Hostage Crisis," *Political Behavior* 3 (No. 4, 1981), pp. 303–18.

47. For compatible findings regarding the relative lack of significance of rally events, see R. Darcy and Sarah Slavin Schramm, "Comment on Kernell," *American Political Science Review* 73 (June 1979), pp. 544–45.

48. See Arthur H. Miller and Martin P. Wattenberg, "Policy Performance Voting in the 1980 Election" (paper presented at the Annual Meeting of the American Political Science Association, New York, September 1981) and sources cited therein.

49. For similar findings, see William Schneider, "The November 4 Vote for President: What Did It Mean?" in Austin Ranney, ed. *The American Elections of 1980* (Washington, D.C.: American Enterprise Institute, 1981), pp. 228–29; Miller and Wattenberg, "Policy Performance Voting in the 1980 Election," p. 4 and fn. 4.

50. See, for example, Richard A. Brody and Benjamin I. Page, "Comment: The Assessment of Policy Voting," *American Political Science Review* 66 (June 1972), pp. 457–58.

51. See, for example, Berelson, Lazarsfeld, and McPhee, *Voting*, pp. 220–22; Benjamin I. Page and Richard A. Brody, "Policy Voting and the Electoral Process: The Vietnam War Issue," *American Political Science Review* 66 (September 1972), pp. 986–87; Arthur H. Miller, Warren E. Miller, Alden S. Raine, and Thad A. Brown, "A Majority Party in Disarray: Policy Polarization in the 1972 Election," *American Political Science Review* 70 (September 1976), pp. 764–66; Gregory B. Markus and Philip E. Converse, "A Dynamic Simultaneous Equation Model of Electoral Choice," *American Political Science Review* 73 (December 1979), pp. 1061–64; Benjamin I. Page and Calvin C. Jones, "Reciprocal Effects of Policy Preferences, Party Loyalties and the Vote," *American Political Science Review* 73 (December 1979), pp. 1083–84; Samuel A. Kirkpatrick, "Political Attitude Structure and Component Change," *Public Opinion Quarterly* 34 (Fall 1970), pp. 403–8; Drury R. Sherrod, "Selective Perception of Political Candidates," *Public Opinion Quarterly* 35 (Winter 1971–72), pp. 554–62; Michael King, "Assimilation and Contrast of Presidential Candidates' Issue Positions," *Public Opinion Quarterly* 41 (Winter 1977–78), pp. 515–22; Page, *Choices and Echoes in Presidential Elections*, pp. 184–86; Donald R. Kinder, "Political Person Perception: The Asymmetrical Influence of Sentiment and Choice on Perceptions of Presidential Candidates," *Journal of Personality and Social Psychology* 36 (August 1978), pp. 859–71; Donald Granberg and Edward E. Brent, Jr., "Dove–Hawk Placement in the 1968 Election: Application of Social Judgment and Balance Theories," *Journal of Personality and Social Psychology* 29 (May 1974), pp. 687–95.

52. Pamela Johnston Conover and Stanley Feldman, "Projection and Perception

of Candidates' Issue Positions," *Western Political Quarterly* 35 (June 1982), pp. 228–44.

53. Contrast Markus and Converse, "A Dynamic Simultaneous Equation Model of Electoral Choice," p. 1068, with Page and Jones, "Reciprocal Effects of Policy Preferences, Party Loyalties, and the Vote," pp. 1083–84.

54. See also Kinder, "Presidents, Prosperity, and Public Opinion," pp. 12–13, who found that presidential approval was not significantly related to sociotropic judgments.

55. For discussions and illustrations of the use of probit analysis, see Carol B. Cassel and David B. Hill, "Explanations of Turnout Decline: A Multivariate Test," *American Politics Quarterly* 9 (April 1981), pp. 181–95; J. C. Blydenburgh, "Probit Analysis: A Method of Coping with Dichotomous Dependent Variables," *Social Science Quarterly*, 51 (March 1971), pp. 889–99; John Aldrich and Charles Cnudde, "Probing the Bounds of Conventional Wisdom: A Comparison of Regression, Probit, and Discriminant Analysis," *American Journal of Political Science* 19 (August 1975), pp. 571–608; Orley Ashenfelter and Stanley Kelly, Jr., "Determinants of Participation in Presidential Elections," *The Journal of Law and Economics* 18 (December 1975), pp. 695–733; Morris P. Fiorina, *Retrospective Voting in American National Elections* (New Haven: Yale University Press, 1981), Appendix A; Raymond E. Wolfinger and Steven J. Rosenstone, *Who Votes?* (New Haven: Yale University Press, 1980), Appendix C; and Richard D. McKelvey and William Zavoina, "A Statistical Model for the Analysis of Ordinal Level Dependent Variables," *Journal of Mathematical Sociology* 4 (No. 1, 1975), pp. 103–20.

56. The standardization of the MLE's was accomplished through the usual procedure, i.e., multiplying the MLE by the ratio of the standard deviation of the independent variable to the standard deviation of the dependent variable. See McKelvey and Zavoina, "A Statistical Model," pp. 115–16.

57. The Harris-type question was asked only in 1968 and 1978.

58. An interesting exchange occurs between R. Darcy and Sarah Slavin Schramm on the one hand and Samuel Kernell on the other in the *American Political Science Review* 73 (June 1979), pp. 543–46, over the issue of the contamination of responses due to the position of the question on presidential approval within the survey questionnaire. At present, there is no evidence of serious contamination. See also Lee Sigelman, "Question Order Effects on Presidential Popularity," *Public Opinion Quarterly* 45 (Summer 1981), pp. 199–207.

59. Fiorina, *Retrospective Voting in American National Elections*, p. 154.

60. *Gallup Opinion Index*, November 1978, pp. 8–9.

61. Irving Crespi, "The Case of Presidential Popularity," in Albert H. Cantril, ed. *Polling on the Issues* (Cabin John, Md.: Seven Locks Press, 1980), fn. 14, p. 45.

62. See, for example, Kristen R. Monroe, "Presidential Popularity: An Almon Distributed Lag Model," *Political Methodology* 7 (No. 1, 1981), pp. 43–70; Samuel Kernell, "Explaining Presidential Popularity," *American Political Science Review* 72 (June 1978), pp. 506–22; Mueller, *War, Presidents and Public Opinion*, chaps. 9–10; Douglas A. Hibbs, Jr., "The Dynamics of Political Support for American Presidents Among Occupational and Partisan Groups," *American Journal of Political Science* 26 (May 1982), pp. 312–32; and sources cited therein.

For a recent exception see Kinder, "Presidents, Prosperity, and Public Opinion."

63. Lee Sigelman, "Presidential Popularity: Some Unresolved Issues," Presidency Research Group *Newsletter* 3 (April 1981), p. 9.

64. See, for example, United States Department of Labor, *News*, July 20, 1982, pp. 1–2.

EPILOGUE

We have come full circle. We began our exploration of the public presidency by examining the president's ability to understand and lead public opinion, and then moved to a discussion of the press's portrayal of the president and his efforts to influence it. Now that in Chapters 5 and 6 we have increased our understanding of the basis of public evaluations of the president, we can more fully appreciate the interrelationships of the various aspects of the public presidency.

The public appears to award or withhold its support of the president largely on job-performance grounds, yet its perceptions of issues and the president's actions are hazy. This would seem to offer ample opportunity for the president, directly and through the press, to influence public perceptions of his skills and character, his stands on issues, and his performance in meeting expectations and handling issues. At the same time, the public is often not responsive to leadership, and the press may be neither sympathetic to the White House nor amenable to its blandishments.

Ronald Reagan's tenure as president has shown little change in these parameters. A national poll in May 1982 found that only 27% of those polled knew the inflation rate had been decreasing. Thirty-four percent thought it had been increasing.[1] A national poll two months earlier found that most respondents did not know which side the U.S. supported in the civil war in El Salvador.[2] These results, on issues of high priority to the Reagan administration, must have been very frustrating to the president, who is often referred to in the press as the "Great Communicator."

The press provided its normal level of frustration as well. In August 1982 President Reagan was so upset at coverage of his decision to limit arms sales to Taiwan that he telephoned anchorman and managing editor Dan Rather during the "CBS Evening News" to complain. At about the same time, Rather wrote in the *Wall Street Journal* that "when it comes to real and serious and important reportage we're not glutted. We're starved."[3]

Thus, the public presidency continues to revolve around a central paradox: the necessity as well as the frustration of the president's seeking public support. If he is to play an effective leadership role in American politics, the president must have the support of the public. There are no guarantees that he will receive approval, yet he has no choice but to seek it.

NOTES

1. *CBS News/The New York Times Poll,* May 27, 1982, p. 3 and Table 30a.
2. *CBS News/The New York Times Poll,* March 20, 1982, p. 1 and Table 16.
3. Dan Rather, "An Anchorman's Views of the News on Television," *Wall Street Journal,* August 5, 1982, p. 16.

INDEX